# SUN SIGNS
## FOR KIDS

# Sun Signs
## for Kids

## AN ASTROLOGICAL GUIDE
## FOR PARENTS

# Lynne Burmyn
# and
# Christina Baldwin

ST. MARTIN'S PRESS     NEW YORK

Editor: Toni Lopopolo
Editorial Assistant: Andrew Charron
Production Editor: Amelie Littell
Copy Editor: Carol Anderson
Agent: Connie Clausen

Design by Kingsley Parker

Library of Congress Cataloging in Publication Data

Burmyn, Lynne.
    Sun signs for kids.
    1. Astrology and child rearing. I. Baldwin,
Christina. II. Title. III. Title: Astrological guide
for parents.
BF1729.C45B87   1985      133.5      84-22257
ISBN 0-312-77562-8 (pbk.)

First Edition

10  9  8  7  6  5  4  3  2  1

This book was written for Thena C.
It is dedicated to Thena and Jase,
with love from Lynne.


To the children in my life:
Tavish and Jamelah MacLean,
Kyle, Bryn & Colleen Dougherty,
Nathan Garcia and
Upcoming Baby,
with love from Nonnie/Auntie Christina.

# CONTENTS

# CONTENTS

# ACKNOWLEDGMENTS

Primary thanks need to go to our agent, Connie Clausen, for believing in this project, for taking it on and taking it back and generally guiding us toward publication. Next we want to thank Kenneth W. Green, legal and friendly counsel to many area writers, whose words of encouragement and occasional prodding have been much appreciated. Through our private practices, as astrologer and psychotherapist, we have dealt with the continuing importance and influence of childhood on adults' lives. We need to thank, therefore, the many clients who have shared their experiences with us, contributed to our growth and urged us to find a way to communicate some of these insights directly to the parents of children. As friends read individual chapters, their comments on their own childhoods and child-rearing experiences kept us moving excitedly from sign to sign.

In the production of the book itself, we need to thank Gail Holcomb for her early encouragements and precise editing and Barbara Messick, typist extraordinaire, for hours of work on the manuscript itself. Thank you also to Urscia Mahring, Carol Walker, and Margaret Kloster, and, especially, to Jean Eckerly and Joy Hoenig for professional and personal support throughout.

We two authors have been friends for a long time. We had fun writing this book together and we are still friends: this is no small achievement. So we wanted to acknowledge each other for providing the wholeness to this project that neither one of us could have accomplished alone.

LYNNE BURMYN
CHRISTINA BALDWIN
Minneapolis, St. Paul
Summer 1984

# INTRODUCTION
## ASTROLOGY AND HUMAN BEHAVIOR

Astrology, as presented in daily newspaper columns, sometimes seems to be a system for giving up our personal determination and letting the stars take care of life for us. Psychology, as presented in dozens of self-help books, sometimes seems to be a system for making changes without regard to our individuality.

In reality, both astrology and psychology are systems that explain and adapt human behavior by taking personal choice and individuality into account. Both systems, for looking at ourselves and how we relate to the world, are effective and ethical teaching tools when they are in the hands of effective and ethical people. This book contains large quantities of astrological and psychological information to make the nurture, growth and appreciation of the children in our lives easier and more rewarding for all.

Astrology is the study of the precise positions of the sun, moon and planets with the assumption that these heavenly bodies have some discernible correlation to human behavior. Astrology simply supposes there is an attraction, a sort of magnetic sympathy, created between the sun, moon and planets, and the newborn baby emerging from the womb into the earth's atmosphere. Individuals reflect this magnetic sympathy, but this does not mean we are pawns to our horoscopes. Planets do not make things happen; placement of planets merely reflects certain tendencies. Astrologers believe we all have certain inborn traits, but whether, when and how we develop these traits is a combination of personal drive and environmental factors. Thoughtful astrologers encourage people to assume personal responsibility for their lives by presenting a nearly limitless catalogue of choices and possibilities within which we all choose the directions in which we grow. The astrological information in this book is presented to parents to help them encourage their children's growth and to increase a parent's understanding of the context in which each child is making his or her personal choices.

Astrologers use horoscopes, charts of the symbolic positions of the sun, moon and planets at the exact moment and place of an individual's birth. Since the sun is often considered the strongest planetary influence in the sky, it is usually considered the major determining feature of the horoscope and describes those characteristics most obvious in people. The placement of the sun is called the sun sign; and when people ask "What sign are you?" they are asking, "What sign was the sun in on the day you were born?" The sun stays in one sign (approximately in front of one constellation) for about thirty days, changing signs around the twenty-first of each month. Although the dates vary slightly from year to year, the usual dates of change are listed at the top of each chapter of this book and in the Contents.

There are two other major determining factors in a person's horoscope, the moon sign and the rising sign. Both require knowledge of time of birth, and the rising sign requires knowledge of the location of birth as well, the longitude and latitude. Two children born at exactly the same time, but one born in Alaska and one born in Florida, will have the same sun and moon signs, but will probably have different rising signs.

These three major factors of the horoscope describe three major aspects of our personalities. It is helpful to know about these factors when reading this book and thinking about the personalities of our children and ourselves.

The *sun sign* represents our essential personality, who we feel ourselves to be and those characteristics we are proud of.

The *moon sign* represents how we feel, what we need to feel safe, how we nurture and respond to nurturing and behaviors that may be less than conscious.

The *rising sign* represents how we adapt to our environment, how we tend to present ourselves socially, how we come across to other people and what traits and skills we feel comfortable showing others.

Combining these three major factors gives the most accurate, brief representation of personality. For more information on how to receive a complete horoscope interpretation for a particular child (or adult), write to Lynne Burmyn, c/o ACS, P.O. Box 16430, San Diego, CA 92116.

# HOW TO USE THIS BOOK

Each chapter is a sun sign. Find the sign that contains the birthday of the person you want to read about. The chapter is divided into categories; each chapter has the same categories.

*General Characteristics:* Examines the behavior, attitudes, ways of seeing life, themselves and other people that will be evident, to some degree, in all children of a particular sign. Included in this section are many helpful tips for parenting and helping each child use the particularities of his/her sign to the best advantage.

*Needs:* Lists the emotional emphasis of this sign as explained more fully in the *General Characteristics* section.

*Common Assumptions:* Presents a few common adages or sayings that are typical of how this sun sign thinks about life.

*Sensitivities:* This section discusses in more detail areas that might be sources of misunderstanding between people of different signs and how parents can respond to these areas in ways helpful to themselves and their children.

*Relationships:* Briefly explains the ways this child is likely to view Mom, Dad, siblings, friends and relationships in general.

*Mind/Information/School:* Describes how the child thinks about, perceives and absorbs information. It describes behavior and attitude toward school and higher education and helps parents support the individuality of each child's learning process.

*Responsibility/Work/Rewards:* Explains each sun sign's approach to work, in whatever definition suits the age of the child (school, chores, projects, part-time jobs, etc.) and lists acceptable rewards.

*Home:* Describes the child's attitudes toward his living space and any special needs or tastes, including favorite colors and decorating tips for his room.

*Health:* Discusses the function of illness in each child's life, the attitude of this sign toward health and any areas in which this certain sign might have special susceptibility.

*Childhood Ages:* Childhood is divided into age brackets to help parents tailor their response to their children both by age and by sun sign. Several paragraphs detail the most notable qualities of the child at this age, followed by a specific list of needs and fears.

# WHAT ALL CHILDREN NEED

All children, no matter what their signs and birthdates, have some common basic needs. The intensity of their need for specific things may differ and approaches to meeting their needs may vary, but the list of children's human rights is the same.

- All children need to know they are loved, wanted and cherished.
- All children deserve protection and nurturing.
- All children need support and encouragement.
- All children have the right and need to be unique.
- Children are not here to fulfill adults' needs.
- Children have a right to have their needs met by caring adults.
- Children need permission to have their feelings and need to be taught skills for using their feelings effectively in solving problems.
- Children have the right to be competent and smart.
- Children have the right to have their bodies respected.
- Children never deserve to be hurt.

# THE SUN KIDS

# ARIES CHILDREN

**MARCH 21 – APRIL 19**

## GENERAL CHARACTERISTICS

*(Note: While many characteristics described below will be accurate for most Aries, other, sometimes contradictory, traits may also be evident in an individual child.)*

Parents of newborn Aries will be enchanted with her clear and alert expression. Almost from birth, little Aries will steadily meet the eyes of those nearby. She exhibits great curiosity about her environment and is observant and alert to her surroundings. She is intrigued by all that is happening around her. Baby Aries is quick to make her needs known and equally quick to express her appreciation. Her sunny smile and willingness to interact with those nearby make her an endearing infant, though she may be somewhat disconcerting to adults who do not expect such frank interaction from a baby. Baby Aries is a child who is hard to resist.

There is no ignoring the Aries child. She is insistent and demanding when uncomfortable and expects her needs to be met quickly and efficiently. What she wants, she wants *now*. Often the howl of tiny Aries in distress can be heard some distance away. She does not like delayed gratification but is as quick to forgive and forget as she is to demand. She expresses her needs with intense urgency, but these needs are usually minor and easily satisfied. Conscientious parents will have little trouble giving their child what she wants and thereby earning that dazzling smile of gratitude and love.

The Aries infant is a miniature person who arrives complete with her own identity. Parents who harbor fantasies of molding a newborn child to preconceived ideas of the perfect baby will have to reevaluate their expectations. Tiny Aries is quite her own person, with very specific ideas of who she is and what she wants and needs.

1

Though she is charming, cute and precocious, she is adamant at being seen as a person in her own right. She becomes quite irritable when she senses she is being asked to conform to someone else's mold and will often respond to such expectations by becoming more distinctly herself. Parents who want a close and trusting relationship with their Aries child need to notice and validate those parts of herself she claims as especially her own.

The Aries child is social and friendly, and she often reaches out easily to those she loves. Right from birth she needs a great deal of interaction with those around her. She responds with delight to gentle stimulation in her environment: music, touch and colorful mobiles are all exciting to this alert baby. Aries loves being talked to and especially loves being played with, given attention and noticed.

The Aries baby loves the knowledge and idea that she can make things outside of herself respond to her. She needs and likes to see the consequences of her actions. For example: a wet and hungry Aries baby may howl in discomfort to see what happens in her environment when she cries. Appropriately, a parent responds to the cry, changes baby's diaper, feeds her, cuddles and reassures her. More than children of other sun signs, infant Aries seems to comprehend cause and effect and to test actively the ways in which she can make her environment respond. Loving response will not spoil her! Loving response will increase her sense of trust in the world as a friendly place and provide a calm center for her energetic growth.

Though her need for interaction and stimulation is stronger than that of children of most other sun signs (except Leo), the Aries child also needs quiet, private periods. She will usually let parents know exactly what she needs and what she is ready for. As soon as she can crawl or walk, she will seek quiet places for retreat. Since Aries is very socially adaptable, parents need to preserve alone time with and for their Aries baby. Parents may be so delighted in their child's ability to get along with other people that they allow everyone to care for her, thereby sacrificing the development of proper bonding. Despite her independence and sociability, the Aries infant, like any other baby, feels much safer knowing exactly whom she belongs to and who will be her primary care-givers and recipients of her love.

Aries children seem independent almost from the beginning of their lives. They dislike restraint of any kind and will chafe to see what's on the other side of the mountain—or at least what's behind the sofa, down the stairs, around the corner, etc. They are comfortable being alone and will often contentedly choose solitary pursuits. They do not like being swooped up and cuddled, or otherwise disturbed while quietly amusing themselves, and are generally quite happy to be on their own with minimal interference from adults. Interaction with Aries children is more often a matter of quality rather than quantity. Since both response and privacy are important to little Aries, parents need to exercise extra sensitivity in noting which mood she's in so they can respond appropriately.

The Aries child usually has *big* energy. Parents who try to keep up with their little dynamo will fight a losing battle. Most of the time, the best option for parents is to relax, keep enough watch to assure safety or offer help and let the child go. If young Aries experiences approval of her energy and encouragement for her explorations, she will grow up to appreciate both her body and her mind. She will often celebrate her capabilities in sports, dance and a variety of creative activities. If young Aries experiences disapproval, she may grow up ashamed of her energy and expend a great deal of effort trying to hide it. In this case, she may appear depressed or lethargic.

Delight in her body as the source of energy is a tremendously strong Aries characteristic. If this delight is thwarted, the child may turn enjoyment into concern, become fearful about health and bodily functions and worry unnecessarily about, or completely ignore, physical risks. However, thwarting Aries's energy is not an easy thing to do. Parents need not be overly concerned about safeguarding little Aries's concept of body and self; she will do that herself.

There is an amazing, though often nonverbal, sense of physical confidence in the Aries child. One six-year-old Aries, learning wheelies on his banana-seat bicycle, fell and broke his two front baby teeth. The next day he was out practicing again, assuming he could continue breaking teeth and they would continue to grow back. His mother had to sit down and explain that people have only two sets of teeth in their mouths, not an inexhaustible supply.

Thwarted Aries's energy may become an intense and sometimes intrusive interest in the well-being of others. The bossiness sometimes associated with Aries is often the result of not being allowed to feel in charge of their own lives and trying to discharge the energy by taking charge of other people's lives.

Usually, however, little Aries focuses inward to deal with her restlessness and need for activity. She is enthusiastic and intense and needs outlets for bursts of physical and/or mental energy. She loves variety. The Aries child is excited by the world and its possibilities, and she seeks adventure like none other. To Aries, activity is essential. It is her source of fun. When she stops enjoying something, or feels she has mastered a task adequately, she will move on. She thinks, "I've done that, now what else can I do?" Other people who join Aries in her activities are frequently astonished to find that she's already gone and may interpret this momentum as a lack of commitment or loyalty. In reality, Aries has simply done what she does best; she's begun something, created something from nothing, made an idea a reality.

Aries children love initiating. They love beginnings and usually hate endings. Since they are impatient and have difficulty waiting for others to catch up, tolerating delays or trusting others to do the job right, Aries children often believe they can and should do any task alone. Indeed, they usually work best separately or in positions of leadership. They are better at completing tasks when they can claim responsibility for the task or project themselves. "See, I made this for you, all by myself" and "I cleaned my room all by myself" are favorite Aries announcements.

Aries's thinking style is rapid, full of ideas. As she grows older, she will need to have guidance in learning to finish things and to take enjoyment from completion. Sometimes, on the other hand, little Aries will feel tremendous inner pressure to finish things and may not permit herself to relax until she's completed an arduous task.

Aries children usually meet the world head on with eagerness. They are optimistic and resourceful, eternally seeking the positive aspects in any situation. They are playful and generous. The enthusiasm of little Aries is often contagious, and they are among the best motivators in the zodiac. They are spontaneous and endearing and will often offer solutions to problems that have eluded even the nearby adults. They can be so resolutely cheerful that problems seem workable and people become less discouraged.

The fast pace of young Aries children can lead to frustration, injury and exhaustion. They may become reckless or careless. Though they typically recover easily and quickly from exhaustion, Aries children need permission to relax and need to be taught how to relax. They play well but may have trouble slowing down for pleasure. For example, after arranging a family expedition out for ice-cream sundaes, young Aries may be licking her bowl while the rest of the family is still munching the maraschino cherry.

Though they are oddly self-disciplined in ways that may not be readily apparent to others, Aries children often fear they will lose some kind of control if they let down their guard. Most frequently, they fear that if they truly relax they won't know how to get started again. They are afraid of mysteriously losing their energy, which is seen as an essential part of themselves. An Aries child, told to lie down and rest in the afternoon, may easily obey but take with her a book, a favorite toy, crayons and paper in case she should get bored. The Aries child may feel most alive when she is most busy.

The Aries child likes to be trusted. In all of us, Aries is the sign that rules integrity, and the Aries child takes her honesty and integrity quite seriously. If she says she will do something, she likes to think she will do it. Often she finds herself staying up late to fulfill these promises or feeling frantic as she tries to keep up with all of her commitments. She fears being seen as irresponsible if she's too tired to do something or doesn't perform well. Parents watching their frazzled little child attempting to fulfill a multitude of real or imagined obligations need to teach her how to prioritize activities, how to refuse requests and how to pace herself.

Honesty is very important to the young Aries. She gives honest and complete answers when asked and expects the same from others. Small Aries will answer questions with great sincerity and accuracy and seems to elicit sincere responses from other people. The Aries child can get away with asking questions no one else would dare to ask, and she does it with such guilelessness that others aren't offended. "Uncle Jack, is that really a wig?" "How does it stay on in the wind?" "Why don't you like being bald?"

In her efforts to be truthful at all times, the young Aries may seem blunt or tactless, but her friends often value her honesty, insight and reliability. Aries quickly says all she has to say and may seem curt when she changes the subject and moves on to something else. There are very few topics a young Aries won't discuss. Adults who ask for her insights should be prepared to hear unadorned truths and observations that may or may not be particularly flattering, though they will be honest.

Aries is usually impatient with people who complain and won't solve problems. She has instant ideas for problem solving and will often offer suggestions before the other person has even finished describing the situation. Because her mind is so busy offering options for her next activity, it takes a long time for Aries to realize that not everyone thinks in the same rapid pattern she does. She would rather listen to the problems of twenty friends once than listen to the problems of one friend twenty times. She will listen sympathetically to her brother complain about his position on the hockey team but becomes impatient if he doesn't seem to be doing something about it. She doesn't care what he does, as long as he makes an effort. As long as Aries sees evidence of motion or change in any situation, she is happy, but when people or situations look unchangeable, she is unhappy.

The young Aries's cheerfulness can sometimes become flippant, and she may appear not to take herself seriously. She loves jokes and is sometimes a practical joker. Especially as an older child or adolescent, when she is aware of other people's attraction to her wit, sociability and energy, Aries may use humor as a way of communicating without showing deeper feelings. Aries children are often known for precocious one-liners that become part of the family repertoire. They spend time easily with adults and enjoy telling jokes and stories with grown-ups. They are not afraid to tell stories about themselves that make people laugh and are confident enough not to get their feelings hurt when adults laugh appreciatively at their antics.

Sometimes it's hard for the energetic Aries child to slow down long enough to know what she's feeling. For example, her humor may take on a sarcastic tone before she's aware of being angry. Parents should feel free to pick up such signals and ask straightforward, probing questions to help little Aries slow down and feel. Since the Aries child is so good at asking probing questions herself, and since she fervently believes in honesty and fairness, she is unlikely to resent being asked pointed questions herself. Questions like: "You hurt Billy's feelings, are you mad at him about something?" or "You're acting so busy today, but your eyes look sad. Are you feeling unhappy?" will help greatly. The Aries child will answer specific questions honestly and gratefully express her previously hidden feelings.

Once she expresses these feelings, Aries may need reassurance of their acceptance. She may need to be told that it's okay for her to stop being charming, resourceful and busy for a while; it's okay for her to retreat, to stay quiet and not become involved in all of the family's activities. She may be afraid that if she stops she won't be able to get started again; so after a pause, an invitation from a family member to rejoin group activity will help ease the young Aries back into her active routine.

The Aries concept of integrity has several aspects. Integrity means truthfulness, trustworthiness and maintaining the self as distinct and separate. Integrity also means unity, wholeness and contributing the self to group endeavors. Both aspects of integrity are related to the Aries confidence in her body and her belief in the physical source of energy. This concern with her body as the source of integrity may lead to unexpected fear of sudden physical changes, like the first haircut, fingernail clippings, the sudden onset of puberty. One four-year-old Aries whose hair was cut from braids to a pixie spent the rest of the weekend in her room and needed lots of reassurance that she was still herself—even with short hair.

The Aries child is constantly interested in how the individual fits into larger units while maintaining his or her own integrity. She will experiment with herself in groups from an early age; how to be "one of the kids" and still get attention and recognition as an individual. She may move in and out of groups throughout the school years as part of this experiment. One ten-year-old Aries summed up her dilemma by saying, "I want to be a Brownie, but I don't want to be just another Brownie." For the young Aries, the individual is always more important than the group.

The young Aries often sees groups as one body consisting of its own interrelated parts. When a unit or group breaks up, Aries identifies with the separation as though one body were breaking apart. This concept applies to stamp collections, the peas rolling into her mashed potatoes, or more seriously, to groups of people. It may be hard for Aries to let go of temporary groups: saying goodbye at the end of camp or the school year or parting from cousins after the family reunion. Aries likes to keep together things that belong together. It may be easier for her to give away her whole shell collection than to part with just one shell. When it becomes clear to her that division is necessary, however, the Aries child is adjustable and will learn to think about such divisions in her ongoing explorations of integrity.

Independence is equally as important to the Aries child as unity. She seeks to be different, noticeable, unique. She is reassured by her own distinctiveness. She loves being "the only" or "the first." Little Aries loves doing the impossible and will always seek a challenge or take any dare that does not conflict with her integrity. She delights in individual differences and can often name differences before she can identify similarities.

The Aries child sees herself as a pilgrim on a journey at once individual and universal. This awareness starts quite early, and even the preschool Aries may refer to herself in ways that seem mystical or eerie to adults. At the same time, the young Aries needs to feel that she is part of a great continuity. She recognizes and will validate the "pilgrim" aspects in other people, sometimes to their astonishment, and does not want to slow down. Consequently, even though others often have difficulty understanding this, the Aries child often offers love and affection without strings. She is, in essence, saying to others, "I recognize you. I don't want you to change yourself for me, to stop being who you are or doing what you need to do." Of course, this is exactly the kind of love Aries wants most to receive in return. She mixes love and integrity into one emotion.

Years before an Aries child can articulate such a complex spiritual concept, this mixture of love and integrity shows up in her ways of interacting with others. Parents and other adults who recognize and honor it will have the Aries's undying loyalty. The young Aries whose love has been misunderstood or who has experienced more conditional love, however, may indeed attempt to alter others' behavior and attitudes so they are more like hers.

Aries not only values her own individuality but will fight for other people's right to be different as well. She can often be found defending the underdog or the outcast. Unlike the Aquarius child, who defends ideas and principles, Aries identifies with the personal, human side of issues. It's not a matter of whether buildings should be accessible to the handicapped, but how does little Aries get the school to accommodate her friend Suzy who needs a wheelchair.

Frequently, the young Aries has a strong and inexplicable spiritual connection with an identified minority group and secretly wishes she belonged to it. One teenage Aries so deeply identified with Anne Frank's diary (and with the integrity of that young Jewish writer) that she wanted to be Jewish as well. She read everything she could find on Jewish culture and religion, then moved on to become fascinated by Scottish clans and her own ethnic background.

Parents who are concerned with other people's opinions may find they have their hands full with their Aries child who, most of the time, doesn't much care what others think of her behavior. Aries relies mostly on her own integrity to guide her thoughts and actions. This lack of attention to the values of others may lead ultimately to a feeling of isolation for little Aries, to a false sense of superiority or to unintentionally inappropriate behavior. When disapproved of, the young Aries may respond as she would to any challenge: outdoing those who criticize her, working to "prove" her way is better or defensively asserting her right to continue her behavior despite outside opinion. Such confrontations will most likely peak in adolescence, when Aries is experimenting with her integrity in adult ways. When she's aware of the disparity between what she wants to do and what she ought to do, Aries may find herself in deep internal conflict or high rebellion. Through adult discussion, parents can help instill consideration for societal norms, but they are not likely to be able to force their adolescent Aries to conform. Fortunately, Aries is willing to consistently update her sense of integrity and make compromises that allow her to meet expectations *and* keep her freedom.

Though the young Aries has all the attributes of a natural leader, she frequently rejects roles of formal leadership. If all of her friends are learning to play the piano, Aries will decide to take trumpet lessons instead. Then she'll have such fun with it and make it look so exciting that her friends will abandon their keyboards for shiny brass horns. In this indirect fashion, Aries often acts as an inadvertent leader in her peer group, but she doesn't want to take responsibility for other people's willingness to follow. About the time the rest of the class is getting good at trumpet solos, little Aries is just as likely to quit and take drum lessons as she is to remain with one instrument.

Small Aries tends to generalize from herself to others. This means that she will assume what is true about herself or her experience is also true about other people and their experience. If she is trustworthy, she expects others to be trustworthy. Oftentimes her expectations are so sincere they are well met, but this is a haphazard way to judge character. As she grows older and more thoughtful, some of this naiveté may disappear, but in the meantime she has to learn over and over that she cannot assume that what is true about herself is true about others. Her best friend may be gossiping behind her back while little Aries sincerely insists such a thing could not happen. Though painful, this is not a dangerous lesson between children, but the Aries child needs special safeguarding from unscrupulous adults.

To an Aries child, trust is a gift she gives willingly, as one would ask a friend to hold a cherished object. Parents need to help Aries base her trust on experience and reliability, to bestow it more slowly and to think about it in relation to a person's behavior. If her best friend is behaving nastily, little Aries may need help in reevaluating the friendship, removing the bestowed trust and grieving her loss.

Especially when very young, the Aries child cannot understand what she has not experienced directly. This leads to a tremendous drive for a variety of experience. The Aries baby wants to taste-touch-smell-see everything in her environment. She is especially sight and movement oriented and will remain so. She tends to learn best with firsthand experience and often gains new information the hard way, through trial and error. If you tell her the stove is hot and she is not to touch it, she will touch it—but only once. Especially in the first ten years of childhood, Aries is a first-class explorer who wants to process all of life through her senses and body. She may understand and remember only events and experiences that seem personally relevant or she may take personally things that have nothing to do with her.

The Aries child angers easily. When tired, under stress or restrained, she can become irritable and petulant. She tends to hide hurt feelings under angry behavior. She may appear hostile or arrogant as she tries to bend circumstances to her will. Sometimes she seems to behave as though her impatience can make things happen if only she is impatient enough. "Aren't we there yet? You said it would only take an hour to drive, and we've been in the car an hour and twenty minutes. How much farther do we have to go?!"

Though Aries can be assertive and insistent, she quickly learns to sweeten her demands with tact and humor. She often gets her way— with no harm done—as people tend to cooperate with her and enjoy being around her. Little Aries is as quick to forgive and forget as she is to flare. To her, bearing grudges is an astonishing waste of time, though she won't forget people who have disregarded her integrity or betrayed her trust. She will be hurt and confused if she is punished long after an event or if old misbehaviors are brought up after they've been dealt with.

The Aries child loves as easily as she angers. She is sensitive and intuitive, sweet and considerate once her attention is captured. She sees herself as a solitary wanderer, a chaser of rainbows. Life to little Aries is often perceived as a great game that she is determined to play well. She welcomes and protects the new and different. She thrives on ideas, activity and challenge.

The Aries child is deeply spiritual, often in an unorthodox way, and usually has a special connection with nature and with people others have cast aside. Aries has a nearly unshakable faith in the essential goodness of all living things and often looks toward the future with delight and anticipation. Little Aries's buoyancy, resilience, generosity, willingness to help and her deep sense of humor and delight make her an irresistible member of almost any family.

## NEEDS (Aries's emotional emphasis)

Response.
Recognition.
Responsibility.
Affection.
Reciprocal trust.
Autonomy.
Respect.
Compassion and humor from nearby adults.
Stimulation.
Experiences: to understand events, connections.
Alone time with each parent (or significant adult).
Honest answers.
Explanations.
Physical activity.
Reasonable limits.
Quiet relaxation time.
Realistic expectations about finishing things.
Strong support.

Knowledge of consequences.
Help enjoying the present.
Permission to ask for help.
Guidance in pacing herself.
Guidance in assessing dangers.
Information on uses of anger.
Variety.

## COMMON ASSUMPTIONS (How Aries views the world around her)

The best defense is a good offense.
Needs not met immediately will forever be ignored.
Live and let live.
It's easier to ask forgiveness than to get permission.

## SENSITIVITIES (Potential sources of misunderstanding)

*Selfishness:* The ability of an Aries child to focus intensely on a single goal, her need to understand all things subjectively and her tendency to act first and think later may lead to behavior that appears selfish or thoughtless. In reality, her behavior is often extremely respectful. She expects others to take care of themselves in the same way she is tending to herself. She assumes she doesn't have to spend needless time worrying about the adults around her. With children younger or weaker than herself, little Aries is often gentle and considerate; she assumes older, stronger children can fend for themselves. If she is reminded that she has overlooked something or inadvertently hurt someone's feelings, the young Aries is often quite chagrined and eager to make amends.

*Playfulness:* Aries children like to treat people of all ages as equals. They also invite people of all ages to play with them and often become quite competitive in the spirit of the game. They like to win. If someone else wins through his or her best effort, that's okay; but the Aries child will seldom decide to let a little brother win at checkers and doesn't want to feel older people let her win. She likes to win fair and square.

Adults are sometimes so delighted to rediscover their own dormant playfulness around an Aries child that they may forget to stay in a position of responsibility. Sometimes even adults get their feelings hurt when the Aries child isn't taking care of them during playtimes. Grown-ups need to remain responsible in order to supervise and set appropriate limits during playtimes. They should not expect the child to take over this function.

Adults who are self-conscious about the playful aspects in themselves may perceive Aries's joy, play and single-mindedness as threatening. They may want to frighten or shame their sometimes boisterous child into more docile behavior. While this does make the Aries child more manageable, it has the same effect in the family as extinguishing a brightly burning light.

*Spontaneity:* Young Aries children are renowned for their spontaneity. This is a delightful aspect for people who share Aries's love for change, challenge and excitement; however, spontaneous little Aries is less endearing to more conservative folks. The Aries child needs to learn that not everyone appreciates surprises and some people feel more secure and happy carrying out preplanned activities.

Aries's spontaneity is a combination of the joy and speed inherent in the sign. Aries children are quick to make decisions and have the energy to carry them out. If the Aries child has not learned to consider consequences, at least some of the time, or if she is too young, responsible adults may become quite tense at the necessity of monitoring and second-guessing their tiny Aries's next move. The Aries child needs to be encouraged to think before she acts or speaks, as much as is appropriate for her age.

*Independence:* Aries's need for freedom of thought and physical motion is so strong that nearly any sort of guidance may be felt as restrictive. This is a child who can, and should, be parented with a velvet glove. Loving parents need to keep their interference to a minimum. As all children do, the Aries child needs guidance and protection, but the young Aries needs to be parented in the gentlest ways possible. Questions and choices, presenting hypothetical situations for little Aries to resolve and reminders to be considerate of other people's needs work best in parenting the Aries child. Being told outright what to do and what not to do works the worst. Brief, to-the-point reasons appeal to the active mind of the Aries child and invite her to join with her parents in problem solving instead of competing with them. The Aries child needs to feel free to pursue her own interests, even when they vary from family interests and concerns. She will resent (and may rebel against) any attempts to control her psyche.

Parents who feel that this minimizes their control of this highly active child need to remember the sense of inborn integrity that is guiding their youngster underneath her daily expenditure of energy. The young Aries needs the freedom to experience and learn on her own and to sometimes fail. Parents who are arbitrary and authoritarian in their enforcement of rules will find a formidable opponent in their Aries child. When challenged and constrained, little Aries becomes fiercely determined to have her own way and, if she cannot get it by direct action, she will attempt to wear a parent down with persistence or simply go ahead and disobey. However, she is open to compromise and willing to hear and consider differences of opinion.

Parents who expend a little extra effort to see that their young Aries gets at least part of what she wants will find child-raising infinitely more relaxed. "I can't buy you a new bicycle right now, but I'll buy you a mirror and streamers and help you fix up the one you have," works to everyone's benefit. Aries children who have been taught negotiation skills with parents will have fewer problems compromising with friends and siblings.

*Spirit:* Spirit is a key word for the Aries child. She is spirited and spiritual. Her energy radiates like a Fourth of July sparkler. This energy is such an integral part of Aries that she is often quite unselfconscious and eagerly shares her delight in the family. Aries children are naturally joyous adventurers. There is no such thing as a healthy, *docile* Aries. A healthy Aries is an energetic Aries: curious, determined, exploratory, unafraid.

Unfortunately, some adults consider that much spark inappropriate in a child and attempt to instill their own standards of behavior, disregarding the difference in age and temperament. Aries children unlucky enough to have been quelled into submission become as afraid of their energy and spirit as their parents were and are determined to control it in themselves and others. Parenting techniques designed to break a child's will are most often used on Aries children, who are obvious and exuberant targets.

One Aries woman who grew up in a home in which her energy was treated as threatening recalls her childhood: "As early as five or six,

I remember being aware of a hidden part of myself that my parents could not affect. I behaved docilely in the family, but I knew they were never going to be able to break my spirit." This is not an uncommon Aries insight, for it is nearly impossible to completely sever the Aries from her true self and, if successful, parents will not want to live with the person who results.

*Dependence:* Infancy is potentially the most uncomfortable time for Aries, who doesn't like being dependent. If she later feels her baby needs were cumbersome, inconvenient or burdensome to caretaking adults, she may despise the needs in herself that must be met by others. She may become angry when she has needs and push others away just when she wants them to come close enough to help her. If she is successful in keeping people at a distance with her anger, she gains more space, privacy and freedom, but she loses nurture, help and support. The young Aries must be reminded that she can have both support and independence. She may perceive her needs as weaknesses and feel contempt for herself, though she is quite willing to help others with identical needs (and often gives others precisely what she herself wants). If this behavior is allowed to continue, little Aries may ultimately come to believe that no one else can or will meet her needs and that she must meet them herself or do without. This "I can (and must) do it myself" attitude may lead to a strong sense of isolation in later years or to the denial of any needs at all.

The young Aries can also fear dependence on things and, if she feels she's becoming too attached to a possession, person or behavior, she may challenge herself to give it up or pretend it isn't important. The Aries child is capable of remarkable feats of self-discipline or self-denial and will sometimes see these as a form of play. "How long can I hold my breath in the bathtub?" "How long can I go without Popsicles?" "How far (or how fast) can I run?" are all internal games of chance and challenge Aries plays with her confidence in body and self. Parents need to keep sufficient track of these challenges to make sure their child doesn't hurt herself.

Little Aries is uncomfortable with other people's dependence. She may carefully consider whether or not to help a friend, fearing the friend will come to rely on her or feel obligated. Whatever she offers, she wants it to be taken freely, without expectations or strings. She wants validation but not a big fuss or interference. The

SUN SIGNS FOR KIDS

Aries child offers help by problem solving and may find it difficult simply to be present when someone else suffers without trying to fix things or feeling like she wants to run away.

The Aries child assumes real nurturing is both spontaneous and quiet. Because she considers the consequences before offering help and nurtures through words, the young Aries may not regard herself as particularly giving. She may even decide she is selfish. Little Aries needs to be taught that there are many valid kinds of nurturing and hers is as valuable as any other way of showing care.

*Identity:* More than any other sun sign, young Aries needs to be recognized and valued for her real self. She wants to have even the "bad" parts of herself acknowledged and will choose negative attention over no attention at all. She is acutely aware and proud of her differences. She does not stand above the crowd but apart from it. The young Aries is a reluctant joiner and dislikes labels and fads. The current popularity of any trend is nearly guaranteed to keep her away. One eight-year-old Aries proclaimed, "One of my goals is to *never* own a single Smurf."

The young Aries will experiment with many roles and identities in her childhood, but there will be common threads throughout: fairness, enthusiasm, focus and devotion. She needs the freedom to experience her life in her own way, and only through her own errors and achievements will she really learn.

*Future:* The Aries child is a dreamer and planner who tends to spend substantial time in the future. If she is not planning, she may be worrying. Since the future is not predictable, it often represents an intriguing, if scary, challenge for little Aries. She may get more excited about the prospects for a positive or negative future than she is about the present.

The young Aries can make anything into an adventure, a trait that is alternately endearing and troublesome. Imagining the intensity of an upcoming challenge or potential crisis may be her way of coping with a dull present. Such fantasies feel quite real to the Aries child. She may become animated, angry or fearful, just in contemplation of what might happen next. Sometimes this chronic sense of urgency and impatience is the little Aries's way of scaring herself, of maintaining excitement and guarding against missing something. The Aries child needs to be taught to enjoy life without constant excitement or stimulation (internal or external) and to participate in the pleasures of the present without always creating challenges. She needs to be reminded that uncheerful, low-key children are also acceptable, and reassured that quiet, low energy is neither a permanent nor an addictive position.

## RELATIONSHIPS

Little Aries prefers relationships that are deep and intimate, though she does not seem to need to spend lots of time with any one person. She wants her connections to be productive and meaningful when they occur and is content with long periods between meetings. She usually has a few very good friends and many acquaintances. She seldom lacks companionship; her more urgent need is often for solitude. If she cannot get intimacy through conversation, she may try to get it through anger or arguing.

*Mom:* Young Aries expects Mom to be a typical, stereotyped, nurturing mother. Mothers of Aries, however, are often preoccupied with someting else and may have neither the desire nor the ability to give their young Aries the exclusive attention she occasionally needs.

Instead of trying to be a perfect mom to suit little Aries's vision, Mom need only be certain that she gives her Aries child her undivided attention periodically, especially when Aries asks for it. The young Aries also needs Mom's unquestioned and unconditional support. With periodic attention and unstinting support, the Aries child will usually overlook the differences between her real mom and her fantasy mother.

*Dad:* The young Aries also expects Dad to be traditional. He should go to work and go fishing, love baseball and provide his child with a sense of security and rules.

Dads who vary from this conventional mold will be forgiven by their Aries child if they continue to offer protection and security regardless of circumstances. In fact, the young Aries is more likely to accept thoughtful restriction from her father than from anyone else.

Little Aries is likely to feel most off balance if Mom and Dad don't live together, if they do not at least appear to have a "normal" family. While she is resourceful, adaptable and brave, the young Aries may suffer most at the breakup of a family, hope longest for reconciliation and be most (sweetly) resentful of a stepparent. Sometimes Aries may also find these circumstances fertile grounds for getting her needs met by playing one parent against the other. Although it may seem easier for separated parents to give in to little Aries, it is also dangerous: the Aries child must believe the adults around her are stronger, smarter and wiser than she is.

*Siblings:* If little Aries is an oldest child or the oldest of her sex, she may assume responsibility for younger siblings and take being a role model for them quite seriously. If she's not the eldest, she can be quite free with siblings, seeing them as equals and friends. In either case, she is usually comfortable letting siblings be themselves and relates to them with periodic advice-giving and problem-solving conversations.

*Friends:* The young Aries has a few intense friendships, many acquaintances and long periods between visits. While Aries children have the ability to connect with others intensely, they are often too restless to maintain intimacy for long periods of time. Instead, they come back and check in occasionally. The Aries child treats friends and siblings in much the same manner. She prefers to do most things alone and chooses friends rather than requiring them. Often popular, respected and well liked, the young Aries fears other people's dependence on her and usually maintains careful limits to prevent restriction from others and maintain time for solitude. Though the Aries child offers and expects a lot of freedom, she tends to insist that her way is best and that things be done her way or not at all. Little Aries does not like jealous playmates.

The energetic glow that often surrounds the Aries child is appealing to other children and adults alike. Little Aries may seem to have people lined up wanting to be friends with her. She is often popular. As a motivator, she is often elected to positions of responsibility she may not want. Non-Aries parents who felt unpopular as children may be astonished at their child's apparent disinterest in popularity; non-Aries parents who were popular when young may not understand the young Aries's rejection of its obvious benefits.

## MIND/INFORMATION/SCHOOL

The young Aries's reaction to information is perhaps the most idiosyncratic of all the signs and, therefore, the most difficult to describe. Aries children are usually precocious, quick, bright, eager to solve problems and share their knowledge. They love ideas and patterns, and they are curious and full of questions. They love games, and if learning is presented to the young Aries as a great and delightful game, she will often approach school with eagerness and delight. She may, however, become bored and have trouble concentrating in a formal classroom situation, especially in classes that are rigidly structured, or she may find life outside of school infinitely more interesting, rewarding or challenging.

Since Aries children learn best by experience, they need as much direct contact with subject matter as possible. They are often mechanically and technically skilled. They learn well through trial and error and experimentation, and hate repetition. The young Aries becomes impatient to use information once she's learned it and may remember only that which is useful, unique or funny. She may study for a test today, get an A and forget it all by tomorrow. She learns well through both reading and conversation and often rehearses what she knows or says.

Since most Aries children don't particularly seek the approval of adults, they are seldom motivated by intimidation or threats. Like all children, little Aries do like praise, and they work best in positive, supportive atmospheres that allow them to set their own pace and, as much as possible, to follow their own interests. Aries children are quite capable of doing more than one thing at a time; simultaneous activities need not be perceived as lack of attention.

The young Aries often believes that if she knows something, she must act on it. She also needs a great deal of information in order to feel safe. Thus, to avoid feeling enormous pressure to do something about everything she knows, the young Aries may deny her knowledge. Concerned adults should reassure little Aries that it's perfectly okay to know something and choose not to do anything about it.

*Higher Education:* The Aries child often seeks to expand her education in unorthodox ways: through extended travel, independent investigation of particular areas (especially religion, philosophy or the arts), or intensive study with a specific person or group of people. If she does seek formal additional education, it is often in order to be able to travel or study in her own areas of interest later on. The Aries's range of interests is so varied that she's likely to investigate many subjects before she settles on one, and she is often as surprised as everyone else at her final decision. Aries will spend her lifetime seeking information, regardless of formal circumstances.

## RESPONSIBILITY/WORK/REWARDS

*Responsibility and Work:* Aries children take responsibility seriously and will usually try to do what they've said they will do. Strong and autonomous, they tend to assume more than their share of responsibility and to feel guilty or to assume blame even in situations that do not concern them. Though the young Aries may not complete a task on time, adults can be fairly certain it will get done. Aries children often need more reminding than other children and resent it less.

Aries children do nearly everything fast, but not always on time. Other more intriguing activities may temporarily capture their interest and waylay them, resulting in late starts and late finishes regardless of the speed of the activity or the intention. These side trips are often little Aries's primary source of pleasure, however, and need not be discouraged as much as managed.

*Rewards:* Time and freedom are primary rewards for the Aries child: "If you finish this now, I won't bother you for the rest of the day." Related to this are the feelings of security little Aries gets from a job completed well and the release from internal pressure and guilt: getting it over with now is wonderfully freeing for small Aries. Playtime and play equipment are certainly acceptable rewards for the Aries child, as are, of course, praise and money.

## HOME

Small Aries children see their homes as havens of nurturing and safety. They may never feel that the place they live in as children is really theirs; it's more a gracious and hospitable place they occupy for a while. The space of the Aries child often looks temporary. It is functional and comfortable but is perhaps seen more as a place to come home to than as a place in which to live.

Aries children need lots of space, preferably private and quiet. They frequently exercise in their living area and need lots of room to move around. They prefer reds, ivories and bright colors, and easy to care for, often portable or easily rearranged furniture. They are most likely to decorate with books, posters and objects from nature—including living animals (cage birds, hamsters, etc.).

## HEALTH

Though she may not use the information she has, the young Aries is usually quite knowledgeable concerning health matters. The illness of the young Aries is usually connected somehow to fatigue: exhaustion from pushing herself too hard or from stifling her energy, or cuts and bruises from carelessness. The Aries child may, in fact, use illness as a way of permitting herself to slow down and relax or to gain much-needed solitude and privacy. When sick, little Aries therefore wants and needs just minimal care; mostly she needs to rest and be left alone.

Traditionally, Aries rules the head and skull. The young Aries who has health difficulties may experience fevers, bumps on the head, headaches, nosebleeds, itching (especially from insect bites), and, later, acne.

## CHILDHOOD AGES

*(Note: The fears detailed in this section are* never *to be used as punishment. They are presented as avenues for reassurance and caring.)*

### BIRTH–6 MONTHS

The Aries infant is vocal, alert, active and, some would say, bold. Visually attentive to her surroundings right from the beginning, she enjoys direct eye contact with people and is seldom shy. She loves and needs interaction with her environment; she very much needs to know that she can make things happen and that people will respond to her appropriately. Games like Patticake were undoubtedly invented by an Aries. The Aries infant is delighted when her toothless grin elicits an answering smile and when her howl brings speedy help. She does not respond well to schedules.

*Needs*

Human interaction.

Swift response.

Alone, private time with each parent.

Freedom from restriction (including restrictive clothes).

Affection.

Supervision.

*Fears*

Restriction.

Being ignored.

Being left alone.

Being dependent.

### 6 MONTHS–18 MONTHS

The Aries baby seems to be all over the place. Though she finds that learning is fun and is endlessly curious, little Aries may become quite frustrated with her own inability to do things as quickly or as well as she wants to. Her evolving mobility is a delight for her, but she may find the relative slowness of crawling a source of distress or she may try to run ten minutes after she's taken her first step. The Aries baby can become quite angry when she can't do what she wants to do.

In spite of her already apparent haste, the Aries child fears hurting herself and needs close supervision when in motion and around fire. This little Aries needs to make her own mistakes in safe areas and learns best by actually doing. She welcomes new experiences and people and is a charming, if noisy, companion.

*Needs*

Help and supervision.

Permission to explore.

To learn through experience.

Mild restriction.

Interaction with her environment.

*Fears*

Restraint.

Hurting herself.

Enforced isolation.

Being ignored or left behind.

18 MONTHS–3 YEARS

The Aries toddler is inquisitive and resourceful. She is friendly and charming most of the time, and her questions may seem endless. She is quite busy figuring things out, evaluating and testing her environment, and may sometimes appear stubborn, argumentative or contrary as she begins to establish an identity entirely separate from those around her. As she experiments with values and decisions different from those of her family, she often seems quite rebellious, defying those nearby and pushing limits she has previously accepted. The frustrated Aries toddler continues to attempt feats beyond her physical capacities. At this age, Aries begins the subjective generalizing that will characterize her thinking later on.

*Toilet Training:* The Aries toddler will complete toilet training exactly, and only, when she is ready. Parents noting little Aries's precocity in other areas may expect greater physiological control than their child actually has or may take her achievement for granted. Little Aries may initially express anger when this task is begun but usually responds to the challenge of being the first one of her friends to do it or to the promise of increased mobility once she is toilet trained. The Aries toddler is more likely to respond to Dad's attention in this area.

> *Needs*
> Permission to explore.
> Permission to be different.
> Permission to argue, hassle, question.
> Direct experience.
> Patience with herself.
> Patience from nearby adults.
> Firm limits.
> Help and support.
>
> *Fears*
> Humiliation: being laughed at.
> Being ignored.
> Being condescended to.
> Lack of boundaries and limits.
> Lack of protection and help.

SUN SIGNS FOR KIDS

The preschool Aries is volatile. She may act angry and threatening and challenge everything one moment, then suddenly be very little, loving, tender and compassionate the next. She is extremely subjective and may overreact, taking even the most innocuous remark personally as a criticism or a veiled hint. She needs to be first and suffers if she must wait or be second. On the other hand, the preschool Aries is usually busy testing her newly forming adult skills. She may appear overresponsible—a pleasant, if illusory, relief to adults who are weary of watching their little bundle of energy. Preschool responsibility of this sort is premature, and little Aries needs to be reassured that she doesn't have to act grown-up yet. This child is also quite involved with her emerging comparison skills and is eager to know who or what is first, best, biggest, most, etc.

*Needs*
Honest reactions to role experiments.
Information.
Protection.
Explanations, not lectures.
Reassurance.
Reasonable development of patience.
Humor and compassion from adults.

*Fears*
Being labeled.
Being rejected.
Being bullied.
Being humiliated.
Restriction.
Boredom.
Waiting.
Having to function on an adult level.
Not being able to function at an adult level.

6 YEARS–12 YEARS

The school-age Aries usually continues those patterns begun by the toddler Aries. She is still energetic and possibly acting angry. She

*Needs*

Trust in her integrity.

Information about sexuality.

Accountability: to be held responsible for her actions.

Defined consequences.

Permission to challenge authority and rules.

Answers to questions.

Nonsexual friendships with members of the opposite sex.

Honesty and honest reactions.

*Hates*

Humiliation, being made fun of.

Having her justifiable anger met with others' automatic anger.

Being punished for telling the truth.

Secrets.

Being forced to finish.

Hand-me-downs.

Intimidation.

Restriction.

Advice.

Slowness, waiting.

People who "ego-trip."

Boredom.

Dependence.

Being told to slow down.

Being told, "What will other people think?"

Being told, "But it's always done that way . . ."

Being told, "When I was a kid . . ."

# TAURUS CHILDREN

**APRIL 20—MAY 20**

## GENERAL CHARACTERISTICS

*(Note: While many characteristics described below will be accurate for most Taureans, other, sometimes contradictory, traits may also be evident in an individual child.)*

The placid and affectionate Taurus infant will captivate even the most jaded of hearts as soon as he enters the world. This loving baby is easy to care for and grateful for all attention and ministrations. While his sweet smile is ample reward for attention given, parents are likely to find themselves learning about relaxation and affection while interacting with their tiny Taurus and perhaps giving themselves extra time to enjoy this serene baby.

One of the first noticeable traits of a Taurus baby is his love of physical touch: touching and being touched, whether it be a mirror, a toy, Dad's beard, etc. It is through his tactile sense that little Taurus learns best, and parents will notice how consistently he uses it to teach himself about the world. A crying Taurus baby in the crib may not settle down as soon as he sees Mom approaching but will settle down as soon as he and Mom touch.

This tactile sense continues to develop and often determines the physical relationship of the Taurean to the world around him. Taurus children need to be shown things in concrete, physical terms. Whenever it is safe to do so, they should be allowed to experiment and do things themselves. They learn quickest by doing and often don't believe something exists or that they can achieve a feat until they have actually experienced it directly. "Let me do it!" is a typical Taurean demand, and Taurus children permitted "hands-on" experience with their world are fast and adept learners. Taureans are the apprentices of the zodiac.

Since sensory experience is so important to the young Taurus, he benefits from all sorts of stimulation in his environment. Parents can take much pleasure introducing new stimuli to their Taurus child and watching his delight—almost rapture—at having something new to touch, explore, snuggle up to, stick his fingers into and so on. He likes comfort and is known as the little sensualist. Pleasant sensory experiences are perfectly suited to his needs: soft, furry, fuzzy, fluffy, rounded objects and people are his favorites. He likes both physical and emotional warmth. He likes to be happy.

From a very early age Taurus will reach out to embrace those things he especially likes and will react with negative fervor to stimulation and experiences he finds uncomfortable or painful. Unlike Scorpio, who is often fascinated by things that repulse others, little Taurus will nearly always gravitate toward appealing things. He may want to eat his Jell-O with his fingers, but parents seldom find him playing in the kitty litter box.

The young Taurus's need for direct experience is so great that in his early years he may appear quite literal and confused by the symbolic. A three-year-old Taurus whose family was expecting another sibling was read several books about a little boy and a baby sister. Because the baby in the story was female, he thoroughly assumed his family's baby would be a girl too and had a hard time adjusting to the arrival of a little brother. Taurus may also apply examples in a literal sense. One school-age Taurus believed for years that the illustrations on dress pattern envelopes dictated the kind and color of cloth to be used and would not allow her mother to buy any pattern whose illustration she didn't like. It was quite a shock to her to realize that she could select the material herself.

The young Taurus can be just as literal in the application of rules, following stated rules to the letter but refusing to generalize from them. For example, the little Taurus told not to eat cookies before dinner may assume it's perfectly acceptable for him to eat crackers instead. Parents need to be sure little Taurus understands the principles behind their requests or rules as well as the example given. "No, you can't have a cookie, or anything else, because supper will be on the table in fifteen minutes." As part of the teaching process, parents can ask the young Taurus to use his imagination to provide other examples: "I don't want you to have a cookie. What else do you think I don't want you to eat right now? Why do you think I don't want you to snack?"

The humor of the Taurus child provides another example of his literal mind. He loves slapstick, body jokes and physical pranks, but if the punch line is abstract or ironic, he may need to have the joke explained. He especially loves body humor: the quick (but gentle) poke, easy tickling, unexpected kisses on the cheek and the like. Even as an infant, Taurus often enjoys unexpected hugs, pats and kisses and will usually offer the same in return.

The Taurus child is deeply aware of his body and filters all feelings and learning through his physical being. If he is upset, he may physically react by needing more food or by rejecting food. If he is happy, he may react with bounding, gleeful energy. He finds great comfort in touch and will often stroke Mom's arm or scratch behind the dog's ear for his own or their comfort. When in distress himself, a light acknowledging touch or warm hug is more important than words. A small Taurus will usually consent to being held and cuddled for as long as someone safe and comfortable cares to provide this service. Maintaining physical contact during times of stress is often quite comforting to little Taurus. The comfort works both ways; adults often find themselves equally soothed by the Taurus child's physical presence and touch when they need support.

The kinds of touch, and Taurus's comfort with touching, discussed so far assume a pleasure-based interaction between adult and child. The young Taurus is very sensitive to intrusion and to touch that is not meant to give pleasure. Loving parents will need to exercise extra care when they touch their Taurus child in order to help him safeguard this precious, tactile bonding with the world around him. A tiny Taurus who has learned it is not safe to touch or that it is painful to be touched is an extremely saddened child. Unlike the air signs who can usually detach themselves from physical sensations at will, earthy little Taurus is irrevocably aware of his body and experiences a heightened physical reaction during times of pain or pleasure. He will squawk sooner when hurt and smile sooner when delighted. Parents need to take Taurean body sensations seriously and resist denying the importance of physical feeling. The Taurus child, like all children, needs to be touched with respect, on his own terms and in his own way. He needs to have his wishes regarded, to be let go and put down when he has had enough cuddling.

Physical punishment of a Taurus child needs to be moderate and direct. A gentle spanking is sufficient reprimand. Being deprived of touch, handled roughly or not allowed to eat are all cruel and misunderstood forms of punishment when applied to a naughty Taurus. Anger should be explained in direct terms, and there needs to be a cause and effect relationship between the misbehavior and the discipline.

Because he is so bodily based, comfort is especially important to the Taurus child. He is not usually able to simply ignore discomfort; he must do something about it or suffer. This is not a child who will survive well on a rainy night in a tent. He will want some recourse for being able to "fix" his discomfort and may display the famous Taurean stubbornness until the whole family packs up and goes home, or he, at least, is allowed to sleep in the relative comfort of the car.

Comfortable clothing is imperative for the Taurus child. Both girls and boys often value comfort, practicality and durability over stylishness. They may not care much for fashion or follow its trends and will simply not wear articles of clothing that are itchy, scratchy, too tight or binding. "Ohh, that looks comfortable," is a common Taurus compliment.

Taureans are concerned about other people's comfort as well as their own. Older children and adult Tauruses make wonderful hosts and are considerate of people's comfort in any social setting as well as sensitive to both their emotional and physical ease. The seeds of this consideration are sown in childhood when small Taurus often vows: "I will never be this uncomfortable again—and neither will anyone around me!" This concern is often preventive in nature: Young Taurus would rather coax Dad away from a drafty window before he gets chilled than have to care for him once he's caught cold. Sometimes little Taurus sounds like a little "mother hen," warning others to take an umbrella or button up their sweaters on a blustery day.

Hand in hand with comfort, security is essential to small Taurus. He likes things to be predictable and resists changes for which he is not prepared. He dislikes the unexpected, though he welcomes happy surprises. He loves and seeks the familiar and finds safety in routine. He often associates security and safety with particular things that have special happy meaning for him: a security blanket, a smoothed stone from the seashore or even a certain series of words that he perceives to be lucky or protective. Some Taurus children create this sort of security for themselves by having their own money or by collecting things or wearing and being surrounded by beautiful and expensive decorations. Tauruses born from 1975 through 1981 may show particular ambivalence in creating security through things, first collecting things in order to feel secure and then giving it all away (or selling it) and starting over again.

The young Taurus does feel safer having his own money in his pocket, even just his allowance. He likes to have enough money to feel secure and generous, to be able to treat his friends without having to deny himself something that he wants, too. When a Taurus believes he cannot have what he wants he may become quite frightened; and his first priority becomes finding some way to feel safe and secure again. During this time, little Taurus may suddenly look selfish to outsiders, but as soon as he has reestablished his security base he reverts to his sweet generous nature. A little Taurus who looks grabby and worried over getting his fair share may need some help dealing with his fear and learning how to maintain his security in times of change or real external scarcity.

If the Taurus child is a member of a large family, he frequently doubts that anyone else will take care of his needs and resolves to watch out for himself. If Mom brings home a chocolate cake when small Taurus isn't around, he doesn't believe anyone will stand up for him and say, "Hey, save a piece for little Taurie!" Parents who wish to reassure their Taurus child obviously need to save him a portion of the goodies, whether he is present or not and regardless of his recent behavior. Recently, a nine-year-old Taurus was in "isolation" in her room for half an hour when the rest of the family happened to make popcorn. Her parents saved her a bowlful and gave it to her after her discipline time. This is a fine example of appropriate parenting and reassurance, and may have a profound comforting effect on the child long after other family members have forgotten the kindness.

Though the Taurus child is generous and caring, he needs to know that part of the turf belongs to him. He likes to know what the boundaries are, what belongs to whom and to have others respect boundaries and possessions as conscientiously as he does. He does not generally like sharing. For example, the young Taurus usually hates to have someone pick food off his plate—though he is more than willing to clean up someone else's. The issue for him concerns territory. He'll cheerfully get up and get the whole family another serving but needs to know that his place will be protected. The Taurus child needs to have certain chores, or parts of chores, that are his exclusive responsibility. If it's his job to water the plants, his feelings will be hurt if he finds Dad watering them too, and he may be especially hurt to find someone testing the soil and "checking up" on him. If it's his job, he'll do it; and he needs the family to trust him to do it. Seeing someone else assume responsibility in his territory confuses him, and he may immobilize, become angry and grabby or give up.

Little Taurus is often quite willing to do whatever work is necessary to assure his security. He likes to be paid for doing his chores, in things or money, and sometimes with hugs and recognition. It may be difficult to convince a Taurus child to work without reward, but he is so easy to reward that this doesn't really present a problem. Taurus believes there should be some purpose to his effort in the form of a tangible product or reward at the end. While little Taurus is comfortable with delayed gratification and can wait a long time for his reward—like working toward a new bicycle—he needs evidence that the reward is really coming. One adolescent Taurus, saving her money to buy a horse, kept her savings in a large mason jar so she could actually see it, count it and touch it whenever she needed reassurance that she would attain her goal.

Sometimes the Taurus's need for purpose sounds selfish to others. He openly wants to know "What's in it for me?" The Taurus child is simply being more honest about his motivations than children (or adults) of other signs. He is more willing to state outright the conditions under which he is willing to cooperate. "I'll vacuum the dining room as long as I don't have to do it during my favorite TV show times and if you'll help me keep Bobby out of my rock collection." Parents who don't fly off the handle will notice that the child has pretty good negotiating skills, and once they make contracts with their Taurus child, they don't have to worry about their fulfillment.

Taurus is the sign that rules pleasure and relaxation. Taurus children have much to teach harried adults about stopping to smell the daisies, about rewarding oneself for effort and taking care of oneself with little pleasures. Taurus children are usually quite conscious of why they are doing something, and they don't lose sight of their end goal—which often includes a pleasant reward. One mother of a five-year-old Taurus watched her son slip luxuriantly into a bubble bath at the end of the day enough times to decide that she too deserved such a treat. Tauruses tend to work in order to play and become furious when their playtime is denied or withdrawn. Adults who have trouble watching a little Taurus savoring the fruits of his labors sometimes see the child as self-indulgent or lazy, especially if these adults were taught in their own childhoods that such pleasure-taking was wrong. Instead of trying to thwart little Taurus in his enjoyment, maybe they need to learn from him and reevaluate their own sense of pleasure-taking. Taurus children need to be encouraged to continue their pleasure-seeking behaviors. It does no one any harm and ensures that all around them will get their share of enjoyment as well. Tauruses understand that in order to care about others one needs to replenish oneself.

Even very young Tauruses are excellent at setting priorities and evaluating things and events around them, and this is another way to look at their life attitude. They are quite able to determine what is more important than what else, and they frequently find it easy to overlook or neglect tasks they have deemed insignificant. They are likely to place a high priority on pleasure and remind the rest of us to consider doing the same. Taurus children are often surprised to discover that their priority setting is a talent not everyone has and that everyone doesn't share their value of comfort and pleasure.

The young Taurus tends to believe that everyone is like him and is frequently surprised at other people's differences in a variety of areas. If he likes to be hugged when unhappy, he may assume his sister wants to be hugged when she's unhappy. When friends come to him for help in decision making, he may think they already know what to do and are just flattering him. If he is kind, he expects others to be kind. If he has just done something sneaky, he may believe the people around him are being sneaky, too. Teaching little Taurus to separate his own experience from his assumptions of what's happening around him is an ongoing task for both parents and child.

Though the bull is the symbol for the sign of Taurus, the Taurean child has difficulty protecting himself. Seldom a raging bull, he is more like Ferdinand, the flower-loving, gentle and gullible bull. The typical Taurus personality contains a ton of power and protective skills, combined with an inability or unwillingness to use his power to protect himself. The most frequently called upon defense is simply to wait things through, to procrastinate in decision making or do nothing. Young Taurus may believe he is so powerful that he can't unleash his strength without hurting someone or losing control. He may feel guilty or ashamed of needing to protect himself in the first place, as though he should have been able to prevent the situation from occurring. For example, playing with his father, he may not tell Dad the tickling is making him sick because he doesn't want to hurt Dad's feelings. He may not tell Mom he wants to be alone now because he's afraid she'll feel rejected.

Similarly, the young Taurus may battle with what appears to be an unduly strict sense of conscience. He may report every minor transgression because he's sure he will be caught anyhow and because if he protected himself by not telling, he fears others will be angry with him. Parents may want to overprotect this gentle, conscientious child but need instead to give him the skills and permission to take care of himself. Instead of proclaiming, "Why didn't you let me handle that?" parents need to offer praise, encouragement and reassurance that little Taurus's autonomous and protective behavior is not devastating.

A Taurus child who is not permitted to develop ways to take care of himself or who is not taught how to defend himself directly will invent indirect ways. He may appear to comply with other people's wishes and then proceed to do his own thing. He may "ignore" what is going on around him or people's requests of him. He may simply not do what he said he would do and appear lethargic and slow. These behaviors are the source of Taurus's renowned stubbornness but are not necessarily stubborn in origin. Often young Taurus's sense of timing *is* different—slower—than that of others around him. He is often more willing to let things take care of themselves than more worry-oriented signs. Concerned parents will take the time to discover the source of their child's recalcitrance and modify their expectations to accommodate Taurus's timing. Consistent teaching of skills for self-protection and assertiveness are also helpful when Taurus looks passive.

The same Taurean characteristics that are so frustrating to parents in a hurry can be quite valuable in helping the family cope with stress. When warned ahead of time about approaching changes, the young Taurus can be quite mellow and adaptable and serve to help the rest of the family through transitions. He is resourceful in finding ways to make unpleasant things enjoyable, and his patience, endurance and stamina are particularly appealing in times of stress. The Taurus child is a little tower of stability and centeredness who will seek to maximize comfort for all concerned, even in the most chaotic situations. His behavior is predictable and reliable, and he can be counted on to work very hard at tasks he believes in. He is able to take a wait-and-see stance without needing to control outcomes, and he usually expects and encourages others to do their own thing and to find their own paths.

The young Taurus does not like ambiguity, however, and may step in to do something when situations remain ambiguous beyond his tolerance. For example, if no one else in the family can decide which restaurant to go to, little Taurus may develop a firm and directive opinion simply to get the question settled. Taurus likes to see things as clear-cut and obvious; the Taurus child does not handle subtleties well. He will make any decision rather than no decision and may push other people to also make decisions. If little Susy takes too long to decide between orange juice or milk, the young Taurus may arbitrarily pour the juice. If he has to decide between football or trumpet lessons, he may flip a coin just to get the decision over with. Little Taurus would be comfortable living in an either/or world, and it is the parents' task to teach this child how to cope when things aren't simple.

Though little Taurus likes to have his mind made up, he may experience changes of heart. If something feels right to him, he will do it, or he may change his decision based on strong, intuitive feeling. He is loyal and prefers to maintain the status quo but will alter his behavior or attitude if change feels more comfortable than not changing or when his heart overrules his mind. Reasoning with a small Taurus is a matter of appealing to his sense of expedience and comfort; though he may not respond well to hard logic, he will respond quickly to practicalities and sentiment.

Little Taurus looks basically conservative and is content to remain with what he knows rather than experiment with new and untried areas. Within that larger framework, he is creative and artistic, especially in areas that are potentially useful. He has a deep love of nature, especially forests, and loves and respects woods in particular.

This is a pragmatic child with the heart of a romantic. He can offer the most practical applications for the most idealistic schemes. Having a Taurus child around is like sitting by a warm fire in winter; he is comforting, practical, unassuming, requires a minimum of feeding and attention, and gives an enormous amount of enjoyment in return. Families often find themselves relying on Taurus's predictability, warmth and sensitivity to discomfort, and learn to value their own pleasure and relaxation more in his presence.


NEEDS (Taurus's emotional emphasis)

Affection.
Comfortable clothing and environment.
Safety and security.
Sensory stimulation.
Explanations with examples.
Being allowed to do things for himself.
Preparation for change.
Permission to go at own speed.
Permission to protect himself.
Permission to have things that represent security.
Relaxation and pleasure time.
Direct experience.
Control over his own money and possessions.
A sense of territory all his own.
Help in evaluating decisions.


COMMON ASSUMPTIONS (How Taurus views the world around him)

What exists now will exist forever.
If I don't watch out for myself, nobody else will.
If I can't see it or touch it, it may not be real.

SENSITIVITIES (Potential sources of misunderstanding)

*Selfishness and Laziness:* What appears to be selfish behavior in a Taurus is almost always behavior designed to make the child feel safe enough to resume his usual mellow behaviors. If the Taurus child believes he is going to be forgotten or deprived in some way, he is most likely to defend himself by taking what is available. Even though he may take more than he needs (in order to have enough, as a squirrel stores nuts for the winter) and though he may seem very demanding until his needs are met, Taurus is the most easily pleased and satisfied child of the zodiac. When offered assurances that he is not going to be overlooked, that there is enough to go around and that he will not be asked to share unnecessarily, the young Taurus often relaxes and begins to believe he can get taken care of by others. While Taurus does not like to share his possessions, he willingly sees to it that others get what they need. And most of the time, his generosity stems from a true sense of abundance and not from sharing because he "should."

Sometimes little Taurus's apparently selfish behavior occurs when he has assumed that others want exactly what he wants. He may therefore hesitate to say what he really wants because he believes if he values it, others will, too. He may then provide others with what *he* wants without thinking to check out the assumption. For example, he may reason, "I want to play this record; they want to hear this record, too. I will please them by playing this record." When reminded of the need to check out his assumptions, the young Taurus is often quite willing to do so, and his "selfishness" looks considerate again. Little Taurus may also believe that something he wants or owns is even more valuable if someone else wants it, too.

Taurus likes expediency. He usually prefers exerting minimum effort for maximum return. He may take shortcuts, not do things he believes are unnecessary or work intensely for brief periods of time and then need to rest. He may appear to "do nothing" while he makes decisions about the most expedient approach to problem solving, but during these times he is busily thinking, certainly a worthwhile activity.

While all of these behaviors may appear "lazy" to parents who want tasks done more quickly or thoroughly, the "laziness" is really a difference in approach and can be negotiated between parent and child with mutual respect. The physics law of inertia—"An object in motion tends to remain in motion; an object at rests tends to remain at rest"—is typical of Taurus. Once he gets going, it's hard to stop him; once stopped, it may be hard to get him going again.

*Security:* Security is more important to the young Taurus than almost anything else, and his drive to maintain security is often misunderstood. The Taurus child's resistance to change may look stubborn or rigid; his need for comfort and love of pleasure may look self-indulgent; his need to know what's going to happen next may look controlling. Early in life his need for a security blanket may look immature; later in life his need for money, territory or possessions may look simply materialistic. All of these behaviors are designed to protect and maintain security.

This child will attempt to organize his environment so that he feels more secure and less scared. Even in the midst of great change, the Taurus child needs something to stay the same. Allowing the young Taurus to hang on to those items and routines that mean security to him, symbolically or literally, is the kindest and best way to encourage this child to explore and eventually meet his own needs for safety without having to change the world around him. Of course, in order for this strategy to work, little Taurus must not be shamed or teased for seeing security as important or for trying to protect himself through external means. The Taurean drive for security is mutually beneficial. He will see to it that the people around him feel good too, and the young Taurus is often well liked by people in all age groups because he is so careful and nonthreatening.

*Protection:* The Taurus child needs permission to protect himself without guilt. Teaching small Taurus how to assess situations and then how to defend his position through negotiation, thoughtful argument or withdrawal, are ways in which parents can extend behavior options for their child and still permit him to grow. Once again, it is more helpful to teach little Taurus to fend for himself than to step in and do it for him.

## RELATIONSHIPS

The Taurus child is usually rather relaxed about the idea of relationships. He is loyal and expects similar loyalty from people he relates to, but he seldom has many additional expectations. He is easy to be with and often attracts people whose lives seem more interesting or difficult. He is frequently the stable, enduring, apparently more caring person in a relationship, and he can be counted on to "be there" whenever necessary. Often he's more comfortable when people seek him out; he likes people to come visit him. Although it takes a great deal of abuse to alienate a Taurus child, once antagonized he is not likely to forget. Only an extraordinary amount of effort by the offending person can win back small Taurus's affection and trust.

*Mom:* The young Taurus fully expects Mom to be the boss and usually feels safe and secure when she takes charge. He expects Mom to be predictable, warm, firm, consistent and benevolent. As he grows older, the Taurus child may treat Mom more as a friend, which usually delights her and allows both of them wider options for interaction.

Mom may tend to want to overprotect her young Taurus and may push, think for, hurry or criticize him. For the sake of expedience, she may make decisions for little Taurus or carry out tasks when the child is procrastinating.

Mothers who don't want to nag their Taurus child may need to adjust their sense of timing about when chores get done and develop more lenient expectations about how Taurus goes about his daily routine. This does not necessarily mean mothers need to lower their standards, but they will need to work out mutually satisfying ways to meet goals.

*Dad:* The Taurus child may see Dad as a friend before he is willing to view Mom in that way. He often feels more sure that Dad accepts him just as he is and seeks support for his experiments in growing up primarily from his father. He expects his dad to teach him the ways of the world. Occasionally the Taurus child may feel that instead of it being safe and acceptable for him to become like his father, he is supposed to become somehow different or opposite. During any such time of confusion, a Taurus's father needs to be particularly clear and concise regarding expectations of his child's behavior and choices.

Sometimes the young Taurus sees Dad as "the good parent" because he seems to accept so much of the child's behavior. Mom may then become, in contrast, "the bad parent," since she provides more of the criticism and guidance. Concerned parents will make the effort to equalize the situation by giving Dad a more guiding role and allowing Mom to assume more of the general support. This often works better in any case, since young Taurus seems not to get as defensive when criticism comes from Dad.

*Siblings:* The Taurus child expects tight bonds with siblings. He will often care for them, see that they are comfortable and get what they need in the family. He expects, or hopes, to be nurtured and regarded kindly by them in return. He likes to feel comfortable around them and will return favors and concern with generosity.

*Friends:* The Taurus child generally adopts a laissez-faire attitude toward friends and friendships. His friends tend to be artistic and not consistently available, but after the loyalty prerequisite has been met, the demands of the young Taurus are minimal. Often Taurus ends up taking care of his friends and expending more energy on them than they expend on him. This pattern may be obvious from toddler age on. If Taurus gets angry enough about the imbalance, he may refuse to do anything more until the score is evened up. Little Taurus may idealize his friends, even when they are taking advantage of him, and may take a long time to see them realistically.

## MIND/INFORMATION/SCHOOL

The young Taurus has a literal, retentive, orderly mind that responds well to routine. He learns like a sponge, soaking up what he sees around him rather than what he is told. He has the mind of an apprentice and learns best through imitation. Awareness of the practical application of what he is learning helps him retain information, and he loves to produce a product for his efforts. He is cautious and conservative in his methods of learning, and once the Taurus child has learned something or come to a decision, he is likely to retain the information or maintain the stance for a very long time. Because much of his knowledge is intuitive, he may not be able to verbally defend what he knows. The young Taurus is likely to believe that others, especially those who are more articulate, are smarter than he is and to acquiesce to their demands and information.

The young Taurus has a literal, pragmatic approach to things and responds best to concrete examples. Especially when very young, he tends to believe what people tell him without question and will usually follow standard rules and procedures. He most likes involvement in learning activities but prefers those that do not require a great deal of physical effort. And, as mentioned earlier, he enjoys getting frequent rewards along the way.

The Taurus child is frequently exceptionally talented in at least one area. His creativity is often of the pragmatic sort. He can be resourceful and innovative when it comes to "making do," and he expects his artistic efforts also to have practical application. Taurus's manual dexterity and often exceptional voice may combine to lead to talent in areas such as puppetry or certain areas of music.

*Higher Education:* In spite of his desire for the security of credentials, Taurus's pursuit of higher education is often delayed or interrupted. Young Taurus may find making that sort of long-term commitment difficult, or he may rebel if he feels forced to continue his schooling. When he does decide, however, he often chooses a field that has immediate practical application and financial and/or security rewards. Once again, he prefers training that permits internship or apprenticeship and allows hands-on learning. The young Taurus usually likes to be taught and responds better to motivation from others; he is seldom self-motivated in an educational setting and needs the promise of reward or the threat of disaster to spur him on.

## RESPONSIBILITY/WORK/REWARDS

*Responsibility and Work:* The young Taurus takes his responsibilities very seriously. As a result, if he believes he cannot do an adequate job, he may postpone his endeavor. This can lead to behavior that appears procrastinating. The Taurus child does have some difficulty beginning projects and help starting things is a great boost for this little child who sometimes just can't seem to get going. Once on his way, Taurus is a conscientious worker if he likes what he is doing. He likes to see the results of his efforts, and as stated previously, he loves both the internal and external rewards that occur when a goal is achieved. If he does not like the work he's doing, the Taurus child may be less thorough and do only that which he perceives is absolutely necessary. Once again, he likes routine and doing things *his* way and, unlike Capricorn, who tends to do things the hard way, the Taurus child usually manages to get the most done with the least effort.

Once involved in a task, little Taurus is likely to see it through to completion. He has an enormous amount of stamina and endurance and can be persistent and relentless when trying to achieve something. If it doesn't work the first time, he will do it again. The Taurus child's patience in the face of resistance is a powerful lesson for all the non-Tauruses around. He may complain the entire time; he may rant and yell a little; but the Taurus child *will* have his way in the end.

The young Taurus prefers tasks that have a routine procedure and a definite end—a point at which he can sit back, breathe a sigh of relief and announce, "Well, that's done." He needs to be in charge of his portion of a task and to receive appropriate recognition exclusively for his part.

*Rewards:* Tauruses of all ages dislike being in debt emotionally or financially. A primary reward for the young Taurus is release of an obligation, debt or commitment. Other appropriate rewards include verbal recognition, hugs, money and lovely things. The Taurus child often responds to food as a reward, but such gifts should be used sparingly if parents do not want an overweight child.

## HOME

The young Taurus's home is indeed his castle. He often prefers to have people visit him rather than go to their homes. His area is not necessarily neat, but it is usually clean and is a wonderful, comfortable place for entertaining. The Taurus child uses his space as an area to house his collections and other belongings. While the general environment may change periodically as he grows or upgrades his possessions, it usually remains pretty much the same throughout childhood.

The Taurus child puts more value on comfort and durability than on style, and his surroundings often reflect that priority. His furniture will be usable and comfortable, and he may have many things that simply feel good lying around. The young Taurus prefers saturated earth-tone colors.

## HEALTH

When Taurus gets sick, he needs pleasant surroundings and welcomes attention and conversation. He doesn't like to worry about his care and wants to believe someone else is concerned and in charge. He likes to have a fuss made over him and to be catered to while ill. He also needs to be extremely comfortable during illness and is grateful for clean sheets, many pillows, good food and soft pajamas.

Little Taurus may not realize he's sick until he feels uncomfortable, or he may be so afraid of discomfort that he worries over any symptom. He is especially prone to illness if he feels too pressured by responsibilities or when overtired. Catering to little Taurus periodically *before* he gets sick may be one way to forestall illness.

Traditionally, Taurus rules the throat and ears. Little Taureans experiencing health problems may contract ear or throat infections, laryngitis, tonsillitis or thyroid problems. They may appear lethargic or sluggish, and they may gain weight or feel numbness in parts of their bodies. Early symptoms of pending illness include teeth grinding or other dental problems and stiffness or tension in the upper neck or shoulder regions.

## CHILDHOOD AGES

*(Note: The fears detailed in this section are* never *to be used as punishment. They are presented as avenues for reassurance and caring.)*

### BIRTH–6 MONTHS

The Taurus infant is usually placid and easy to please. He loves cuddling and touching and warmly welcomes most demonstrations of affection. He responds quickly to touch of all sorts and can usually be calmed with an affectionate gesture or by being held. He loves to be rocked and often to be swaddled as well. He is extremely sensitive to physical discomfort, however, and his often vociferous squalling may not be stilled until the source of his discomfort is located and eliminated. Generally, tiny Taurus likes his food and finds closeness with the person feeding him most rewarding and satisfying.

> *Needs*
> Physical attention, affection and comfort.
> Comfortable clothes and environment.

Adequate food supply (on demand, if possible).
Advance warning of and preparation for changes.
Strong physical support.

*Fears*
Insufficient food.
Being dropped.
Being neglected, forgotten, overlooked.
Being too needy.

6 MONTHS–18 MONTHS

In order to learn about his environment, the Taurus baby needs to touch and feel things and, often, to taste them as well. He begins to like taking things apart long before he enjoys putting them back together. He still loves to be cuddled and physically attended to, and if he does not feel he's getting adequate physical attention, he will find some way to make up the deficit himself, often through eating, sometimes by connecting very strongly with nature. At this early age, Taurus discovers his love and connection with nature, an interaction felt mostly through his senses. His need for security and safety also begins at this time, and he may be a cautious baby, checking in with Mom a lot to make sure she is still there and still cares. Grown-ups have a tendency to overprotect this cautious but curious little baby, and some parents may begin to resent the ways in which he is different from them. Provisions can be made that will allow tiny Taurus to discover his own capabilities and differences without jeopardizing either his safety or his parents' self-confidence.

Tauruses of this age already prefer that things be brought to them and people visit them rather than having to seek out interaction. They fear physical discomfort and physical threats and are already beginning to learn to avoid both. Toward the end of this period, Taurus children begin to be able to make decisions of their own. They need to be taught how to make choices; young Tauruses especially need two yeses for every no. ("No, you can't play with the scissors. Do you want the wooden spoon or a teddy bear?")

Baby Taureans may appear "slow" to parents who are eager to see their little child keep up with peers. Taurus is a late bloomer; what appears to be "slowness" at this age is simply the baby's determination to enjoy the pleasures of this period and to make the best use of his time.

### Needs
Reassurances of safety, supply and love.
A home base.
Physical comfort; absence of physical threat.
Routine, predictability.
Beginning permission to make his own choices.
Permission to be different.
Loving touch.
Permission to learn through his senses.

### Fears
Being coerced into making choices.
Being hungry or otherwise deprived.
Threats.
Being hurried.
Being uncomfortable.
Feeling unsafe, insecure.
Being overprotected, feeling undermined.

## 18 MONTHS–3 YEARS

While the Taurus toddler retains his charm and cuddliness, he begins to acquire some of the stubbornness that will become stamina and endurance later in his life. "No!" may appear to be his favorite response to everything, and even the most serene parent may be tempted into power struggles with this contrary little child. Especially if he is angry, the Taurus toddler may be resistant at the most inconvenient times. He can become quietly immobile and passively resistant or throw tantrums and noisily rebel. His sensuality continues, and he is still most easily calmed and comforted by loving touch.

Taurus toddlers especially tend to have literal little minds and need to have concepts explained with several examples and in great detail. During this period, young Taurus begins his lifelong love of collections.

*Toilet Training:* Toilet training a Taurus toddler can be quite an undertaking. If he is at all angry (and most two-year-olds are), young Taurus will quickly figure out that refusal to toilet train is a way to upset his parents. Taurus resents being hurried, and small Taurus may apply the same resistance to pressure around toilet training that he applies to pressure to finish tasks. He may want others to do it for him, or he may not want to exert effort when he's not in the mood. The best way to little Taurus's heart is through rewards: developing a system of positive reinforcement for a job well done and ignoring accidents is the approach most likely to succeed.

*Needs*

Hands-on experience.
Explanations with examples.
Advance preparation and explanation for change.
Beginning lessons in compromise.
Beginning lessons in assertiveness.
Permission to protect himself in ways that still allow him to get what he wants.
Physical comfort and attention.
Rewards.

*Fears*

Being coerced, hurried.
Being laughed at, shamed, humiliated.
Being threatened.
Lack of attention or not having enough of anything.
Being neglected.

## 3 YEARS–6 YEARS

The preschool Taurus is an odd mixture of old and new behaviors. He continues to be affectionate, caring and loving but may become less easy to please, complaining and whining at things he had previously overlooked. He may take personally things that have little to do with him, and he may ask or try to trick other people into thinking for him, making his decisions and choices and, in general, guiding his life. He is more active than before and may begin instigating activity but is also be more competitive and more sulky if he feels he has "lost" what he was competing for. He can appear more selfish and worry more, and he may be more concerned about getting his "fair" share. Fairness is very important to the preschool Taurus, and he watches for it closely. Though still reliably calm, little Taurus sometimes experiences moody or melancholy periods, and he may act dramatic instead of even tempered. Affection, gentle humor, attention and rewards for responsible behavior will do wonders for temporarily unhappy little Taurus's spirits.

*Needs*

Reassurance of love, worth—ample supply.
Information.
Compassion.
Permission to change his mind and behavior.
Permission to experiment with different roles.
Affection, warmth and gentle humor.
Permission to be private.
Encouragement to be competent and think for himself.
Attention and affection even when he isn't placid.
Physical comfort.

*Fears*

Being isolated or stuck in a particular role; being labeled.
Being told to hurry.
Being told that his anger or needs will get out of hand.
Being told that he is unlovable when he is not cheerful.
Being told that there isn't enough to go around.

## 6 YEARS–12 YEARS

The school-age Taurus continues the pattern set in preschool years. He is simultaneously charming, caring, affectionate stubborn, resistant and rebellious. As he seeks ways to become his own person and to be different from others, he tries on a number of different roles and he may appear contrary and defiant while establishing his own identity. Ironically, he may appear inflexible and rigid as he experiments with a variety of different behaviors, and he may act as if each step in growth or each change is final and permanent. Parents need to support his reality without patronizing their child and to emphasize the positive aspects of each role while resisting the temptation to label each new set of behaviors "just a stage."

The school-age Taurus may feel stuck much of the time. He may feel he is not proceeding fast enough or that his progress is inferior when compared with that of his friends. He can seem sullen or sulky, and he may want to maintain the safety of the status quo in order to regain his earlier sense of security. He can appear exceptionally cautious and may make choices that represent the greatest comfort. He may insist that things be done his way or not at all; he may become defensive, possessive and quite materialistic or status-conscious. He may resist authority almost completely, often by refusing to listen. School-age Taurus continues to be competitive and may decide that if he can't be the best, he will be the worst.

On the other hand, the school-age Taurus is often quite helpful, thorough and conscientious when motivated. His love of nature intensifies, and he continues to count and collect things. His abilities to set priorities and evaluate become obvious now, and any talents that have been latent will often bloom at this age. He is extremely generous—both with things and in spirit—with people he loves and is often intensely interested in what is going on around him. While the young Taurus's need for physical affection continues, he may become self-conscious about having this need met. Loving parents will initiate times of cuddling and intimate contact during this period even if their child does not.

*Needs*
Explanations and preparation for change ahead of time.
Information and experiences.
Reassurance of security and supply.
Appreciation.
Encouragement, support, affection, rewards.
Permission to count, collect, arrange.
Lessons in negotiation and compromise.
Verbal and experiential reminders of self-worth.
Permission to passionately believe in what is occurring at the moment.
Reassurances that what is occurring now is not forever.

*Fears*
Being pushed, pressured, hurried.
Being out of control.

**49**

Being taken advantage of; obligations.
Belittlement of his values.
Being called selfish or lazy.
Lack of routine, predictability; chaos.
Being last.
Being rejected or ignored when not cheerful.

## 12 YEARS–18 YEARS

The adolescent Taurus continues the patterns established by school-age Taurus. Unlike teenagers of most other signs, he is more likely to have his social act together at this time and less subject to the mood swings of the previous period. More of his life is internal, and he needs more privacy. Adults are likely to know less about what's going on inside the mind of their adolescent Taurus than they did before.

The teenage Taurus may find security in art or crafts activities or in hoarding and/or counting those things that are important to him. He may appear bossy as he tries to arrange people and events to fit his preconceived ideas of what is right, safe or productive.

The youthful Taurus may seek security and predictability in close relationships with peers. He is intensely aware of his body during this period and may cover his self-consciousness by eating, which can lead to a temporary weight gain and add to his self-consciousness. Taurus may experience a variety of disturbances in his eating patterns during adolescence, and parents should be particularly alert for signs of anorexia nervosa. He may rebel against family expectations of proper appearance, and he or his parents may think he looks funny during some part of his adolescence. The young Taurus tries to compensate for those areas in which he feels self-conscious by increasing the decorations he wears, usually through a change in clothing. He can appear unusually conventional and seem a temporary "slave" to the values of the peer group. Loving parents will emphasize their unconditional love, support and acceptance regardless of how their child looks and not tease or humiliate their uncomfortable budding adult.

The adolescent Taurus still needs affection and often far prefers touching and cuddling to being sexual. In some circumstances, he may be willing to trade sexual behavior for affection, but he can be taught well in advance that affection is his birthright as a human, and he does not have to "pay" for it. Respectful and unselfconscious discussions of sexuality and sensuality, and of the moral and ethical implications of sexual behavior, will help the teenage Taurus to establish his own values in this area and perhaps assure that he gets exactly what he wants.

*Needs*
> Information about sexuality, body changes, nutrition.
> Information about appearance (i.e., makeup, modeling school, weight training, etc.)
> Loving support and encouragement.
> Privacy.
> Affection.
> Adequate spending money.
> Reassurance that he isn't forgotten even when he's not around.
> Reminders of his self-worth, areas that are particularly valuable and lovable.
> Comfort, predictability.
> Permission to slow down and relax.
> Permission to enjoy himself.
> Permission to decorate himself as he pleases.

*Hates*
> Being teased or humiliated, especially about his appearance.
> Being forced, pushed or manipulated.
> Being hurried.
> Being compared with other people.
> Not having enough money.
> Feeling insecure, unsafe.
> Chaos.
> Being called lazy, selfish, slow, possessive, materialistic.
> Being told, "Opportunity only knocks once . . ."
> Being told, "You'll never know until you try . . ."

# GEMINI CHILDREN

**MAY 21 – June 20**

## GENERAL CHARACTERISTICS

*(Note: While many characteristics described below will be accurate for most Geminis, other, sometimes contradictory, traits may also be evident in any individual child.)*

Parents will be immediately drawn to, and possibly surprised at, newborn Gemini's solemnity and alertness. In contrast to verbal, older Geminis, baby Gemini is often quiet and reserved. Tiny Gemini uses her eyes almost immediately as her main connection to the world around her and seems from the beginning to be recording occurrences in her environment. She invites interaction, especially through eye contact, and loves to be talked to. Little Gemini will attempt to respond verbally right away with cooing and other baby-noise copies of speech. She loves laughter and funny sounds. Left alone with a mirror, infant Gemini will practice both her eye contact and cooing at the image of herself. Parents of a tiny Gemini will most likely be delighted at such interactions and enjoy giving their infant the response she needs and seeks.

Communication, interaction and visual orientation are key concepts for the Gemini child. As an infant, baby Gemini loves hand, toe and finger games. As she gets older, she will be dexterous, rhythmic and adept. Baby Gemini will charm with her eyes first, then with words. The older Gemini baby and toddler loves to exchange chatter, coo and copy sounds. Geminis often grow into talkative, charming and witty adults. They usually speak precociously early and are often quite capable of holding their own in adult company. They seem to know innately how to elicit smiles from grown-ups and will most likely continue this charm throughout their lives.

Events, experiences and knowledge don't quite feel real to a Gemini child until she has had the chance to tell someone about them. Learning happens most effectively when she can verbalize her data for someone else. "I don't know what I think until I hear myself say it," is a common Gemini phrase. In a young child, this behavior will be obvious long before she can verbalize the reason behind it. Before she goes to bed at night, the typical Gemini child needs time with a parent, or other friendly, older listener, to tell of her day and get feedback on events and lessons learned. The time, interest and patience to listen may be an important gift a parent can give the Gemini child.

Because it is so important to Gemini to be articulate and understood, she frequently comprehends and uses a great number of words, though she may belittle her ability to communicate or underestimate the power of her vocabulary. It was a great shock to a six-year-old Gemini to read on her first-grade report card that her teacher thought she had "a sixth-grade vocabulary." Sometimes Gemini has difficulty deciding the relative importance of data and details, and tends to give all information equal weight. This can be frustrating to parents who are waiting for the point of a story or to find out what happened after the kitten climbed the apple tree and before their little Gemini daughter showed up at home with mud all over her face. While the child is still young, parents may have to listen carefully to determine what is really important to little Gemini and what is merely of passing interest. Later they can help their child learn to make distinctions between details by telling her, "There, that's what I've been waiting to hear . . ." or "Get back to the part about the kitten because I have to finish cooking dinner, and I want to know how you got the kitten out of the tree."

Watching and being watched is also important to the Gemini child and relates to the importance she places on seeing. When she needs to know how things work, she is most likely to learn through observing or actually taking a thing apart. Gemini memorizes visually. She will know how to bake a batch of cookies after watching Mom do it only a couple of times. The excited, demanding cry, "Watch me, watch me, Mom!" is a Gemini cry. Just as she needs to tell something to make sure it's real, she sometimes needs to be seen doing something to make sure she can do it. Little Gemini knows for sure she can ride her bicycle without the training wheels because

Daddy saw her do it and celebrated the accomplishment with her. She may also have a hard time believing that something just happened if she didn't get a chance to see it herself. If her brother says he saw a deer just disappear into the woods and Gemini didn't see it, she won't know if he's teasing or telling the truth.

While she may have trouble believing others who say they saw something she didn't see, little Gemini believes solidly in what she sees or thinks she sees. This visual child may perceive the shape of a horse in the shadows of the yard and, trusting her senses, insist the horse was there. Due to this reliance on vision and her senses for information, Gemini may appear gullible, suggestible or cynical if she cannot verify what others tell her is true.

Gemini often treasures photographs as records or proof that something really happened. A gift parents can provide her is a photographic record of her childhood accomplishments so that she can look through an album and say, "Here I am getting on the bus the first day of school. Here I am after the mud fight with Billy Larsen. Here I am riding my bike all by myself."

This intrigue with seeing may lead Gemini to a fascination with sleight-of-hand magic and optical illusions. Verbally, this same fascination shows up around words with double meanings and puns. While quite young, Gemini may have a spiritual vision and believe it absolutely to be true. One Gemini child whose pet had recently been run over by a car and killed woke one night to "see" the dog standing by her bed. She announced to her family the next morning, "Nicki's all right. I saw him last night, and he looks just fine. Now I don't have to be so sad anymore." While such a revelation may shock or surprise parents, it would be hard to convince their Gemini daughter that what she'd seen was not so or to shake her belief in the dog's well-being. Since such a vision provides deep insight for a Gemini child, it is best if parents are willing to simply accept her sense of reality about the vision and let it be.

In spite of her need to be watched, young Gemini has an equally powerful need for privacy. A general rule of thumb for parents is to watch their child only when she asks to be watched and to leave her alone the rest of the time. Of course, Gemini babies and toddlers have the same need for safe supervision as any other child.

Little Gemini seeks to understand concepts and is usually more interested in theory than in application. For example, watching her mother plant a garden, she may want to know all about seeds and how they grow without having any intention of eating the vegetables. In order to retain information, Gemini needs a context in which to put it. She needs to know that vegetables are a food group, what that food group offers and the varieties of vegetables available. Once she has such a context for learning, she is creative and quick.

The young Gemini loves categories and labels. She seeks descriptions that progress from the general to the specific. For example, first she wants to know the species of an animal, say CAT/feline; then the kind of cat: Siamese, chocolate-point; then the particulars: female, named Eartha Kitt, age five, the pet of the lady next door.

Little Gemini is eager to please and seeks approval from others. She is also intuitive and perceptive and likely to see both sides of any issue. In her efforts to gain approval, she may decide to tell people what she intuitively knows they want to hear rather than what is true for her, or she may reveal only that portion of the truth she thinks they will approve of. This tendency toward partial information may be seen by adults as lack of trustworthiness. In reality, small Gemini needs permission to express the whole truth or tell all her information without fear of being shamed, ridiculed or discounted. Gemini children who have not had a chance to resolve this problem sometimes appear scattered or elusive, passively waiting to see how others respond before going on with what they have to say. Gemini children who have had opportunities to resolve this issue and support for telling all that they know are usually exceptionally bright, creative and spontaneous in sharing their thoughts, to the delight of all those around them.

Sometimes Geminis appear exceedingly rational and orderly, assuming that everything can be explained. This attitude usually occurs in families that are uncomfortable with the open expression of feelings or when Gemini has decided, for whatever reasons, not to be open in showing her feelings. Gemini therefore attempts to explain her emotions rather than simply feeling or showing them. She may use words as a barrier between herself and others rather than the usual Gemini tendency to use words to connect herself with others. She may explain her behavior to prove she wasn't wrong rather than to exchange information. If parents who are accustomed to the charm in Gemini's stories and to feeling invited to be close to her suddenly feel the reverse sensation—that they are being pushed away—they need to use this response as a warning signal. Some extra end-of-the-day listening and encouragement to feel feelings rather than simply discuss them will help restore Gemini's sense of comfort with herself.

Gemini may offer excuses, explanations and rationalizatons for her behavior instead of attempting to solve a problem or resolve a difference. She may spend a great deal of time and energy explaining why she is not to blame for something. Or Gemini may simply be evasive and become adept at giving answers that really don't provide information. A Gemini child who is reminded that she forgot to feed the dog may tell a long, involved, often true story of all the things that happened to her today that distracted her and "made" her forget. Or she will deny forgetting or blame someone else for not reminding her earlier. All this instead of simply taking the reminder and going ahead and feeding the dog.

Gemini needs help separating the concept of responsibility from blame. Responsibility is simply following through on what one says one is going to do. Blame is being made to feel bad for not doing it and trying to alleviate the bad feelings by pushing them onto something or someone else. This is a common confusion in families and, with a Gemini child in the house, parents need to teach responsibility clearly and not add a burden of bad feelings to a reminder or reprimand to follow through on any given task. Gemini likes to feel connected to other people and to please them; she doesn't need coercion in order to accept doing her part in family chores.

Sometimes a young Gemini's explanations and excuses are deliberately funny, and a crisis is averted through laughter. It's safe for amused parents to relax their standards a little around Gemini. She is grateful to have the rules bent on her behalf and will respond with attempts to be worthy of her parents' trust. On the other hand, small Gemini's need to perceive order around her is very important, and parents need to make sure they don't bend the rules so far that this sense of order is disturbed. For example, permission to stay up on Thursday evenings until 9:00 P.M. to watch a special television show is a gratefully accepted bend in the rules; not knowing her usual bedtime is a disturbance in Gemini's sense of order. Since young Gemini loves and needs explanations, thoughtful parents will explain both their firmness and lenience in language their child can understand. These explanations will both reassure small Gemini that order exists where it is important and help her understand how one decides what is important and what is not. She will learn to evaluate information and events.

The Gemini child often initially reacts to stress with humor. When tensions mount, she will want to relieve the awkwardness through some anecdote or quick retort and is often very successful at doing this. The family may come to count on her moments of impasse to help dispel the crisis through some remark or antic that makes everyone laugh and see the situation in a less threatening light. Her second choice of action is to withdraw in order to protect herself. Withdrawal in a young Gemini does not look the same as it does in an older child. The Gemini child may continue to be pleasant and conversational but is simultaneously remote and unresponsive. The sensation is one of the words still sounding appropriate, but there's "no one home." Gemini has removed herself psychically from threat. Sarcasm is an equally effective method of removing herself. In either case, when young Gemini cannot relieve external tension, she may reduce the tension internally through some form of withdrawal.

Occasionally a Gemini child being questioned will respond with words that make no sense or with statements that are blatantly untrue. This behavior generally occurs when the child is extremely frightened and needs to be seen as a moment of crisis for her rather than as willful disobedience or lying. Parents who find small Gemini distorting the truth for purposes other than entertainment need to respond with kindness and corrective measures rather than punishment or shaming.

Because of her ability to disengage from uncomfortable situations, the Gemini child may appear dreamy and unfocused. In school especially, she may be distracted by the intensity of the activities around her or she may initiate the activity that distracts everyone else. When she is in need of privacy or comfort, the Gemini child can simply ignore her environment even in the most crowded situations. This detachment permits the young Gemini to maintain perspective and retain her objectivity within noisy, chaotic or emotionally charged situations. As a result, she is quite resilient and may move unscathed through events in which other children suffer hurt feelings. Gemini makes a good "middle child," a good member of a large family and may emerge from unhappy situations with less harm than children of other sun signs. This is not, however, an indication that she needs any less love and care than other children, only that she has an innate ability to tend to herself when necessary.

The Gemini's ability to detach herself from situations may interfere with signals from her body. She may be able to endure more pain than her companions, or hike long distances without complaining of tiredness or being aware that her feet have blistered. She may ignore symptoms of physical distress until they are unbearable or until there is something she can "see" is wrong. She is the type who won't cry until she bleeds, who may not stop until she stumbles. Gemini may also have difficulty enjoying her body and experiencing pleasure. In both cases, she needs help from watchful adults to help her tune into physical sensation. Sometimes Geminis have trouble understanding or empathizing with people who suffer physically or emotionally.

Gemini is the sign of the twin, and her sense of duality is a legendary trait. The Gemini child is keenly aware of opposites and polarities. She may have difficulty making decisions or sticking to the ones she has made. She may appear to change her mind a lot, or she may seem nearly immobilized in her effort to make a single, permanent, responsible choice or commitment. To ask a Gemini child "Would you rather take tap dancing or ballet lessons?" can start up a chain reaction of indecision rather than provide the expected simple choice. She may spend a lot of time trying to figure out how to have both sides of any choice, not necessarily because she wants to do both but because it's less work than having to choose only one thing. This behavior may seem greedy to others, but it's really based on indecision, not greed. Parents will need to spend some time helping a young Gemini choose, giving her permission to make choices and mistakes and not worry about pleasing others.

Despite the difficulties of indecision, Gemini, more than any other sign, loves choice. The young Gemini is delighted when offered options and feels very much her own person when making decisions. She often welcomes and arranges situations that involve choice and seems to want literally to practice the whole process of decision making. Discussions about her choices and what she is thinking through in the process of making these choices are ways in which she shares herself with others and feels close in conversations. This delight in choices may seem in direct contradiction with her indecisiveness, but both are true: it is one of the polarities of the sign.

While the young Gemini loves choices, she detests repetition. She resists activities that require long periods of repetitive movement. And though she excels at manual dexterity, she may protest against small, repetitive hand motions unless they serve a productive purpose (this child is not one likely to grow up to be a factory worker). For example, she may enjoy knitting but detest sorting pins and needles or putting buttons into small boxes. In fact, small Gemini's restlessness precludes her contentment with sitting still for very long. She generally has a fairly short attention span and likes to move on when her curiosity is satisfied. Often she returns later to finish tasks, and she may have several things going at once in different parts of the house. She needs to be able to take frequent breaks and to move about freely. Young Gemini is quite capable of doing more than one thing at a time and often needs this simultaneous variety in order to deal with her restlessness. A young Gemini can talk on the phone while doing dishes, have one eye on the television, supervise a younger sibling and know exactly what is happening in each activity. Obviously, Gemini children do not handle boredom well.

Another way Gemini's twinness, or ability to duplicate, shows up in her personality is through her ability to mimic. She is remarkable at accurately picking up accents, inflection and body language, and will do so quite unconsciously. She might be encouraged toward the art of mime, or her ear for dialogue could make her an excellent playwright. The Gemini child tries out many roles and often performs each of them with convincing appeal and finesse. This is a child who will tend to like dressing up, making believe and may develop an intricate fantasy or language with another sibling. One Gemini and her brother used to play a game based on a Donald Duck accent. They developed their own dialect, jokes and code words, and sustained the game for many years until the brother left for college.

Interest in duplication also leads the Gemini child to rehearse events, both before and after their occurrence. She will ask herself,

"What shall I say?" and "What should I have said?" She will rehearse her behavior and anticipate the behavior and response of others. Because of this internal rehearsal, she thinks she already knows what someone else will do or say and becomes impatient for others to do as she planned. At her most intense, the young Gemini can have an entire argument in her head with someone who's not present: "I'll say . . . then he'll say . . . then I'll say . . ." and so on. When the other person in this internal dialogue arrives, she may react to him on the basis of how the argument turned out, leaving the other person with a sense that he doesn't know what is going on. Though this advance preparation is reassuring and natural to the young Gemini, she needs permission not to rehearse and to learn to trust herself to handle interactions as they occur.

Her innate mimicking behavior can lead young Gemini to activities simply because all her friends are participating. If the girl next door gets a kitten, Gemini may suddenly want a kitten too out of her impulse to mimic or copy others. Gemini's need for independence is equally strong, however, and she will not mimic others for very long unless she really has an interest in the activity. She needs a lot of time, privacy and permission to try on different ideas and activities while thinking things through. She does not like to be told what to do or think or say and may become quite stubborn if she feels forced to perform in certain ways or to give up activities while she's still sorting their importance to her.

Another way little Gemini guarantees her independence is by spreading out her needs, loyalties and requests for information among a number of people. She likes to have a group of people to rely on rather than just one or two. Her relationships may therefore look superficial to onlookers, and little Gemini herself may occasionally feel that no single person knows her deeply. Though she is entertaining and often popular in a group, no one in that group may feel particularly close to Gemini, and she may not be included in the group's more intimate activities. For example, she may be liked by nearly everyone in her school class but not get chosen to play jacks or share in a secret the other girls know. Sorting out how she can be independent and close, how she can make choices and commitments is a lifelong goal for Gemini. Parents can help simply by giving their Gemini child the skill to articulate this duality when she is old enough to think about it.

Still another way duality affects a Gemini's life occurs when she finds herself caught between disagreeing factions. Not wanting to "take sides" until she has gathered all the information, little Gemini may appear to support both sides. If each party chooses to believe little Gemini supports only their side, this approval-seeking child is often content to let them continue in this assumption while she merrily continues to collect data. Gemini children often protect and understand the dualities in a family (Mom-Dad, Mom-me, Dad-me, Mom-sibling, Dad-sibling, etc.) and need not to have this understanding taken advantage of during times of stress when any one of these dyads is in conflict.

The Gemini child thinks a great deal more than she acts, and a substantial part of her childhood may occur in her head. Sometimes she postpones action out of a fear that what is in her mind cannot be translated into reality. She may get as much satisfaction from imagining herself doing something as in actually doing it, and the experience will feel real to her either way. If she has already reviewed something to conclusion mentally, she may find no reason to bother doing it externally. Her search for alternatives and choices leads the young Gemini through a wide range of experiences. She will often try a variety of experiences for a short time and makes an exceptional resource person. Her energy level is erratic, with a need for long periods of rest between spurts of activity. She can work hard and play hard for several days in a row but may need to spend the following day catching up on sleep and following a very quiet routine.

The Gemini child is a charming and entertaining addition to any family. Clever and observant, she is able to sum up a situation at a glance or with a catchy phrase. She tends to treat herself lightly, but even in her more capricious moods her intelligence shines through. The young Gemini seems to be everywhere at once and often moves with lightning grace and quickness. Many parents especially enjoy Gemini's skills as a delightful conversationalist, and many a tense or dreary moment has been eased or enlivened with Gemini's energy and wit.

NEEDS (Gemini's emotional emphasis)

Information.
Freedom.

Being listened to and heard.
Support to start and finish things.
Help evaluating situations and making decisions.
Being taken seriously.
Permission to take sides, to have an opinion.
Not to be punished for being competent.
Not to be ignored.
Not to be ridiculed, teased, tickled, coerced.
Permission to explore a variety of areas and roles.
Permission to change her mind.
Permission to take her time (to go slowly).
Help and encouragement in expressing emotions and feelings.
Being taught not to rationalize.
Explanations of rules, lenience in rules, clear rules.
An established sense of order.
Permission to have duplicates, to want two of something.
Permission and encouragement to relax.

## COMMON ASSUMPTIONS (How Gemini views the world around her)

A rolling stone gathers no moss.
You can't hit a moving target.
Out of sight, out of mind.
Anything can be figured out or explained.

## SENSITIVITIES (Potential sources of misunderstanding)

*Detachment:* The young Gemini may seem impersonal or unresponsive to onlookers as she processes information and feelings first through her intellect. Gemini needs to think about things before she has feelings about them or is willing to act. She may experiment internally or externally with a variety of behaviors and reactions before she finds one that "feels right" to her. During such experimentation she may appear fickle, unpredictable or uncommitted, and certainly other people often find Gemini's initial reactions unreliable or contradictory. In reality, the Gemini child is fiercely loyal and will usually follow through in a consistent fashion once she has settled on the focus, action or response that is right for her.

The Gemini child also often prefers to figure things out rather than to feel about them. She may place a high value on what is logical and objective and reject that which she perceives as emotional and subjective. She may appear cold or feelingless and, in fact, she may attempt to avoid feelings all together by explaining or describing events instead of having feelings about them. Patient parents will remind small Gemini that emotions are important too, reassure her that feelings are acceptable and discourage overly rational explanations.

*Reality:* In the process of thinking and figuring things out, the Gemini child may construct her own version of reality, creating her own explanations to account for events and behavior she would otherwise find bewildering. She may also embellish stories in order to be more entertaining, to increase her acceptance as a knowledgeable person or to get attention in the way she knows best. If she feels prematurely pressed for explanations of her behavior, little Gemini may offer anything that comes to mind. It is extremely important that parents and other adults take time to really listen to what little Gemini is saying, to confirm or adjust the reality she presents and teach her to evaluate what is worth saying and how.

*Coercion:* Small Gemini is keenly sensitive to any form of coercion and will react especially negatively to teasing, threats, sarcasm and other forms of verbal manipulation. The Gemini child subjected to sarcasm quickly learns to be sarcastic herself, and uncomfortable parents may discover too late the misuses of their child's articulateness. Gemini children need to hear the straightforward truth, to have jokes labeled as jokes, to have their questions answered briefly and directly and to be protected from forms of teasing they do not understand. They also need to know they will be taken seriously and that the people they care about are really listening and hearing what they say.

*Restlessness:* Small Geminis are extremely curious and seem to want to know the reasons for nearly everything. This intellectual inquisitiveness allows little Gemini to sort data into categories that will later make her a phenomenal resource person. While her questioning is often a way of ascertaining order in her environment, it may also help the Gemini child engage the attention of other people. A little Gemini wants to converse long before she is able to, and she quickly learns that asking questions and getting people to answer her helps to satisfy this need.

The young Gemini may also occasionally be very physically restless. During these periods, she seems constantly in motion. Sometimes this is simply an abundance of energy, but it is more often a sign of boredom or tension. If the problem is boredom, often the Gemini child will find something to do and calm down. If the problem is tension, little Gemini may be trying to distract the adults around her from their problem solving so that she can have the attention and reassurance she wants. The higher the level of adult tension, the higher the level of little Gemini's restlessness. Parents need to notice this restlessness and act quickly for the sake of the child. Parents can assure little Gemini that her sense of order is not disturbed by parental problems or tension and that they remain in charge of solving grown-up issues.

## RELATIONSHIPS

Gemini children need equality and perceive nearly every relationship as a peer relationship, regardless of the actual circumstances. This attitude may be disconcerting to adults who expect to be treated with deference, but it is a sign of respect and acceptance from the Gemini child. Young Geminis often feel they are everyone's sibling and may despair of ever finding a best friend or special person of their very own. These charming and clever children are usually attractive to those around them and find themselves surrounded by admirers. Even in adolescence they are generally playful and eager to share their excitement and information with others. Sometimes, however, young Geminis feel isolated and somehow detached from their friendly peer group. It may be that they are everyone's buddy, but no one's best friend. This detachment may initially feel safe to them, but they may also be saddened by the sense that no one person seems to know them well. Geminis need to be taught that showing emotions is how people make the deepest connections to each other. While words are entertaining and enlightening, expression of feeling is necessary to cement a bond.

*Mom:* The young Gemini may perceive Mom as efficient and somehow intimidating in her efficiency. She may feel that Mom is silently critical of her or that Mom's perfectionist expectations cannot possibly be met.

A mom who doesn't want this sort of image needs to explain to little Gemini the reasons for her behavior and seek Gemini's advice on alternative ways to achieve mutually agreed upon goals. It's all right for mothers to relax their standards a little around their Gemini child. On the other hand, mothers of Geminis can often teach their child how to pursue a task to conclusion and how to enjoy the results. Regardless of external complaints, the Gemini child often finds great comfort and security being near Mom and can adapt rather easily to her mother's eccentricities.

*Dad:* Frequently, the young Gemini does not pay much attention to her dad, or she may feel he doesn't pay much attention to her. She may experience him as emotionally distant or not physically available. Small Gemini may perceive her father as too emotional or sentimental; Dad may perceive his Gemini child as aloof or hard to reach.

In fact, dads of Geminis may be romantic dreamers or visionaries and may consciously need to pay attention to the specific requests for attention by their children, especially to the listening demands of the Gemini child. Sharing his ideals with Gemini is one way to connect, and listening to Gemini's own dreams and visions is certainly another. The Gemini child may idealize Dad or feel sorry for him. In either case, she needs to be reminded to see him realistically, with all his accompanying talents and foibles, and to alter her expectations in order to increase her chances of getting what she wants from him.

*Siblings:* The young Gemini tends to see everyone as a sibling and usually makes no special space for blood sisters and brothers. She may be particularly proud of, or involved with, one sibling and will often take turns nurturing and being nurtured by this particular favorite. Small animals are treated as siblings in the heart of the Gemini child.

*Friends:* The Gemini child may find that friends seem to come and go. She is often attracted to rather flashy, volatile people who seem to be on their way somewhere and who move into and out of gullible little Gemini's life with some rapidity. Since she is not an especially astute judge of character, parents may be tempted to try and shield her among her friends, but such protection seldom works and can trigger Gemini's rebellion. Parents can, however, teach young Gemini how to determine whom to trust and then how to be close to trustworthy people. Given this information, the Gemini child may avoid the feelings of isolation she experiences when her relationships remain entertaining and superficial.

## MIND/INFORMATION/SCHOOL

The Gemini child needs more information than most other children and wants to believe the world is a logical and rational place in which to live. She will therefore spend a great deal of time trying to figure things out and explain them. Thoughtful parents can teach their young Gemini about the richness of emotions and the wealth of life's nonrational surprises and help their child find something in which to believe beyond the realm of physical senses and reason.

The young Gemini is quick, bright and articulate. She sometimes repeats herself. She may be impatient with her own or other people's learning process and, if things cannot be figured out right away, may refuse to think about them at all. She may half learn a particular subject, gleaning the information she has immediate need of and think she knows it all, or she may jump to "logical conclusions" based on incomplete information. She may have difficulty concentrating for long periods of time or think about several things at once. She is full of questions that seem disconnected and in conversation may seem to jump from subject to subject.

There is a logical thread of connection in Gemini's mind, and she can usually report how she got from one subject to the next. Talk of dogs may remind her of the last time she saw a dog, in the school yard, and, since the school is on France Avenue, she thought of French fries and began discussing what she thought about dinner last night. Since the young Gemini loves to be a resource person and to be recognized for what she knows, she constantly seeks these sorts of connections and is often able to see relationships and connections before others do. She may therefore appear to worry, and the things she worries about are often real, even though others may not yet have recognized the impending problem.

The Gemini child can become easily bored and may need to be entertained as well as taught. While she often learns best from repetition, she may find that technique particularly tiresome unless it's made into a sort of game with rewards at the end. Similarly, she may appear to daydream when she should be learning, or her attention may seem sporadic and selective. Certainly if she is interested in the subject, she will learn faster. The challenge to concerned grown-ups is to make even tedious subjects interesting enough to motivate young Gemini to learn. Providing a context for information and making connections to other pieces of information already learned are the easiest ways for teachers to assure that young Gemini understands what is being taught.

Adults who want to teach small Gemini and retain her attention also need to offer many different explanations, approaches and sensory experiences. If there are opposing or contradictory facts, the Gemini child needs to know these too, or she will invent them (remember her love of duality). Giving little Gemini permission to move around and assigning tasks that involve or invite physical motion will also engage this restless, curious child. Asking small Gemini to explain or report on something she has learned allows adults to monitor and correct misinformation and will also cement the information in the child's mind. Asking her to help teach someone else is a wonderful treat. If given adequate freedom and if provisions are made for her learning style, school can be among the happiest and most rewarding experiences for small Gemini.

The young Gemini is often an avid reader and may also enjoy writing. She loves categories and labels and consumes information in large quantity. She is visually oriented and likes to see what she is learning about. She may attempt the most difficult task in a series first as a shortcut to achievement. She loves the idea of a series of things and of discovering shortcuts in her learning process.

*Higher Education:* Many teenage Geminis seek alternative forms of higher education or pursue unusual careers, often relating to communication. They may rebel against the idea of credentials and further training or bemoan the fact that personal experience is not enough to get the position they want. Geminis usually want to interact with as many people as possible and will often seek a career and training that allows this to happen or, since Geminis often excel at tasks that require manual dexterity, they may seek careers that make the most of this talent. Geminis may change their minds several times before deciding on an academic major or career.

## RESPONSIBILITY/WORK/REWARDS

*Responsibility and Work:* Young Geminis are most likely to express their duality around work and responsibility: they either love it or hate it, will work to perfection or not work at all. If they are working hard at their chores, they need rest times and reminders that all their products and projects do not need to be perfect. Without this reminder and periods of rest, they may become immobilized by the enormity of what they expect of themselves. Parents can help their Gemini children plan a strategy of working by breaking large assignments into smaller, more manageable tasks and by rewarding their children each time a portion is completed well.

When young Geminis become immobilized, their behavior can look irresponsible or sloppy: leaving tasks before they are completed or promising to do something and then "forgetting." Gemini children generally "forget" things when to remember would be uncomfortable or when the information they are supposed to remember contradicts something they already know. For example, a Gemini child who's been told to always lock the door when her parents are gone may "forget" to leave the back door open so her brother can get in after football practice.

*Rewards:* Most young Geminis enjoy release from responsibility as a reward for work well done. Such a promise reassures them that they will not be stuck forever doing a chore and can look forward to relaxation. They also like signs of appreciation, especially praise, hugs, money and food, and they enjoy thoughtful little signs that someone is thinking of them while they work. Doing a special chore for Dad so he has extra time to spend talking with little Gemini is a favorite pastime. Young Geminis also feel quite self-satisfied when they've done something well, and while this self-satisfaction is often enough, public acknowledgment is an additional treat.


## HOME

The Gemini child's space is often unexpectedly organized, though the manner of organization is as unique as her mind's ability to make unusual connections. This is not a Virgo's tidiness; the young Gemini's horse books may be stored next to the doll collection because both remind her of Aunt Susan. Gemini likes to surround herself with informational things: stacks of papers and books, calculators, a telephone, radio and other gadgets that help her know and sort data. She often decorates her walls with paper objects: posters, letters, clippings, etc. Her space is usually functional and frequently, if she has the opportunity to choose furniture, it will be utilitarian, shiny and have corners. The colors favored by the Gemini child are often light or pastel: grays, light blues or light yellows.

The young Gemini perceives her home as a place in which to store things and come back to for regrouping and recovery. She may not be there frequently, but when she is, she uses the place well. She thrives on the familiarity of home and likes the space to reflect her own uniqueness and personality.

## HEALTH

The young Gemini can be both disgusted and fascinated by the concept of illness. She may not know quite how to cope with it and fears illness in herself and others. In characteristic fashion, she will try to figure out why something went wrong and therefore may know a great deal about certain parts or functions of the body. Since the Gemini child is frequently out of touch with physical sensation (this is an air sign and tends to be heady), she may be quite sick or in a great deal of pain before she notices and calls it to the attention of an adult. This may cause her to worry about her health and, oddly, the young Gemini often worries about getting old.

When she is sick, a Gemini child likes to have someone else take charge of her care so she can be left alone and retreat into her own little world. In fact, small Gemini may get sick precisely to avoid a decision that seems intolerable or to permit herself to take time off from her usually busy schedule.

Traditionally, Gemini rules eyes, hands and the nervous and respiratory systems. Little Geminis experiencing health problems are likely to feel exhausted and tense and may exhibit these feelings through restlessness or agitated behavior such as tics, hiccups, fingernail biting, stammering or through changes in sleeping habits— either difficulty sleeping or sleeping more than usual. Geminis may catch colds easily or have allergies that affect their breathing, or they may have asthma. As very young infants, Geminis need to be placed in positions that make breathing easy, propped in a baby seat, or put to bed with their heads turned carefully to the side with no pillows, blankets or stuffed toys to crowd their breathing space.

## CHILDHOOD AGES

*(Note: The fears detailed in this section are never to be used as punishment. They are presented as avenues for reassurance and caring).*

### BIRTH–6 MONTHS

The Gemini infant is interested and interesting. She watches everything closely and with great seriousness, and responds quickly when something familiar is out of place or changed. She wants to talk almost immediately and may be quite frustrated by the age of six months that she can't make herself more easily understood. Parents will be enchanted by this gurgling, cooing conversationalist and will probably offer her what she needs most: verbal response, conversation, words and other types of feedback. Tiny Gemini loves laughter and will participate with enthusiasm. She also loves finger and toe games, rhymes and rhythms, and is reassured by softly repetitive motion such as rocking and by rhythmic noises, music, chants and lullabies. Even the murmurs of conversation in the background are reassuring for this tiny child who likes to know that people are nearby.

Small Gemini is very attuned to her senses and responds quickly to sensory stimulation: whispers, touching, mobiles over the crib and the like. She may dramatically dislike certain smells, tastes or noises, and startle easily, appearing high strung or finicky when she makes her dislikes known. She hates restriction of any sort, will struggle mightily with those who try to restrain her and may be particularly restless, both asleep and awake. The Gemini infant is prone to respiratory difficulties, and parents need to be sure that she is kept away from drafts and exposure to other children with colds.

> *Needs*
> Minimal physical restraint.
> Words, rhythms, verbal and physical response from those nearby, including being rocked and sung to.
> Sensory stimulation.
> Space to move around in.
> Mobility: to be taken places.

*Fears*
> Restriction.
> Lack of stimulation.
> Smothering.
> Being left entirely alone.

## 6 MONTHS–18 MONTHS

The Gemini baby is very curious and verbal, and moves around a great deal. She loves being able to talk and may still experience some frustration at not being able to make herself clearly understood. She seeks labels, categories and definitions for everything, and though her attention span is shorter than that of most babies, she ultimately learns a great deal through repetition and "conversation." Any differences in learning styles will surface during this period: parents may want to begin thinking about enrolling their child in a preschool program with an approach specifically geared to their child's style. For example, many small Geminis learn best by actually doing, and parents should select a preschool in which participation is stressed.

This child finds the world exciting and challenging. Even teething may be a somewhat pleasant experience for little Gemini, who likes all signs of increased competence, and walking is positively exhilarating. This little Gemini already exhibits some of the humor and charm that will be so evident later on. She needs a great deal of space and stimulation, followed by equal amounts of quiet and rest time. She may go through periods where she needs a lot of sleep and then very little. Parents will find their baby Gemini hard to predict and interesting and challenging as a result. One does not get bored with a Gemini child.

*Needs*
> Space.
> Answers, conversation, feedback, labels, definitions, laughter.
> Individual attention.
> Permission to change her mind and habits.
> Quiet, relaxed time.
> A variety of environments and contacts.

*Fears*
> Restriction.
> Isolation.
> Having to fit a predetermined mold.
> Big noise, chaos.

## 18 MONTHS–3 YEARS

The Gemini toddler is very busy trying on different roles, locomoting and defining the world. She seldom sits still and loves interacting with both people and objects in the environment. Testing her new verbal skills, tiny Gemini may seem to ask endless questions; testing her new walking skills, she may seem to be everywhere at once. She is hard to pin down and may be doing several things at any given time. She tries on and discards many different roles. Parents will certainly see their own behavior accurately reflected by this tiny mimic and may respond with humor and change as this little dynamo reflects the bad as well as the good.

This child is quite sensitive to hypocrisy and seeks honesty, truth and fairness at all times. Though usually adaptable, she may be quite stubborn as she tests her new skills and quite literal with the information she is currently collecting. She tries to figure everything out and may have explanations for the most unlikely events. This is the time for parents to be certain they interact with each other and with their child honestly and respectfully and that they begin to teach their little Gemini to do the same. Little Gemini may appear quite rebellious as she insists on figuring out her own reality and her own way of doing things. Patient parents will teach their child new skills as she asks for them (she will ask) and will keep their interference to a minimum.

*Toilet Training:* Small Gemini may be erratic in her attempts to become toilet trained. Parents who think they've got it may be disappointed and frustrated when their child relapses once again. Making the training period a social, conversational time will relieve some of the pressure on the child, who will respond to reason but whose attention span may be too short to master this task until later. An orderly routine also helps here: same time, same place, same people (as much as possible) are comforting to the Gemini child.

*Needs*

    Feedback, response, conversation.

    Limits, order, lenient rules.

    Quiet time and activities.

    Permission to disagree.

    Support for thinking and feeling.

    Support for finishing things.

    Answers, information, labels, definitions.

*Fears*

    Restraint.

    Force.

    Invasion.

    Not being listened to.

    Having to do something over and over until it's right.

    Hypocrisy, ridicule, tickling.

3 YEARS–6 YEARS

The preschool Gemini continues the patterns established as a toddler. She is changeable, restless and curious, and she becomes even more involved with testing different roles and with limitations and defining truth. She wants to see if her parents mean what they say. She needs to know there is constancy and order in her life. Her abilities to mimic, entertain, and converse become sharper and, as part of her role trials, she becomes more helpful for brief periods of time. Her experiences with different roles may take the form of copying (little Gemini is sometimes quite literal), and members of the family may be disconcerted to find that they have a little echo around.

Little Gemini is winsome and charming and continues to love choices. She loves to count, categorize and label things but may rebel at being labeled personally. She does not like to be told that she is "the rebel" or "the funny one" or "the creative one" in the family. She also loves expanding and using her vocabulary, and may become temporarily quite nasty as she tries out that sort of behavior along with other roles.

Young Gemini may also go through periods of daydreaming and forgetfulness. She may experience an odd sort of reassurance from being "nagged," or she may believe she simply does not have room in her mind to remember all she thinks she should remember. Gemini may believe that if she behaves too competently, she will get stuck with a chore and left alone, never to be helped again. Her way of handling this concern may be to neglect things periodically, to do a poor or incomplete job and thereby to gain her parents' attention.

The Gemini of this age is intrigued by the process of negotiation and is just learning to debate, hassle and disagree. She may try—especially by means of teasing, smirking, making faces or picking fights—to get her siblings in trouble to see what the resolution will be, even though she herself has trouble finishing things and may leave an argument before a resolution is reached. If she is bored, Gemini may seek change for the sake of change. If she feels lied to or is feeling emotions she cannot cope with, she may behave in ways that seem particularly irresponsible or unpredictable in order to get attention, stir things up or to distract others from the real problem. Gemini is usually a very gentle and appealing sign. Parents who see their little Gemini acting in a peculiar manner need to investigate the cause of the behavior and to change the situation that pushes their child to this uncharacteristic behavior.

### Needs

Honest reactions, information.
Help in dealing with her emotions.
Compassion.
Encouragement to have fantasies (not to be so logical).
Conversation and other interaction.
Uncondescending humor.
Choices.

### Fears

Restraint.
Personal labels.
Coercion.
Condescension.
Being abandoned (other people's withdrawal instead of engagement).
Being lied to.
Being left behind.
Too much responsibility.

## 6 YEARS–12 YEARS

The school-age Gemini again continues the behaviors of the previous age. By this time, she has usually learned to be extremely responsible, though she may do things in unexpected order or ways. She likes doing two things at a time and doesn't want to miss anything; she is inclusive and experimental, and has learned to use her words to connect with others and charm people. She is learning to use words as a tool to get what she wants and can be very persuasive. Parents need to let their Gemini child know they know what is going on in the family and to give explanations for their decisions, especially if they change their minds about something. Young Gemini does not really want to believe she can fool the grown-ups around her, and parents need to maintain firm and realistic expectations of their child's performance in school, or small Gemini may believe she has fooled her parents into thinking she is either smart or dumb.

Being smart is important to the school-age Gemini, who likes to be known for what she knows. She may therefore have difficulty keeping secrets at this age, or she may gossip as a way of letting people know what she knows. Protective parents will explain the maturity required to keep one's own counsel and appeal to the child's desire to appear grown up and trustworthy. Parents will then help their child find other options for intellectual achievement.

Little Gemini is also concerned with equality at this age and is learning about power dynamics. She may appear bossy one moment and subservient the next as she defines for herself the meaning of equality. This is an intense learning period about peer relationships, and for the Gemini child, it is the beginning of feeling like a sister (or a brother) to everyone. She is at this time basically pretty androgynous and begins to be able to fit in anywhere. The young Gemini's need to reach out is so broad that she may have difficulty affiliating with any particular group, and she may not understand the dynamics of commitment or the rewards of affiliation.

*Needs*
Explanations and reasons.
Hassling with humor (playful power struggles and resolution).
Firm limits and gentle rules.

Varieties of experience, role playing, behavior models.
Reminders, repetition.
Moral guidance.
To be held responsible for her behavior.

*Fears*
Force.
Restriction.
Being laughed at.
That she will be able to fool grown-ups.
Feelings.
Labels and being stereotyped; not being allowed to change
her mind.

## 12 YEARS–18 YEARS

Once again, the teenage Gemini continues the behaviors of the previous stage. She is more private at this age, and possibly more tense as she attempts to learn what she needs to learn and still remain socially acceptable. Her need to affiliate with others may be in conflict with her need to be independent and at times solitary. Her curiosity will usually lead her to make peer relationships, but she may have difficulty permitting herself needed private time and instead use sarcasm or wittiness to keep interaction at a superficial level and maintain her privacy that way. She may become quite overextended during this period as she tries to do everything she wants to do, or she may become immobilized at her own expectations or those she thinks others have. She may amaze or intimidate herself with the variety of choices she perceives and try it all—or try nothing. The teenage Gemini's intrigue with opposites and polarities will show up in her behavior and thinking throughout adolescence. She may play devil's advocate or appear contrary as she tests these opposites, or she may seem fickle or disloyal as she experiments with different viewpoints. Concerned parents can encourage their Gemini teenager to explore alternate beliefs and choices without feeling that she has to act on them and value rather than deride their child's intermediate decisions as well as her final ones.

The adolescent Gemini may have difficulty expressing feelings. She may sound increasingly intellectual and cool when stress builds.

She needs a great deal of privacy to figure out what she is feeling and what to do about it. Loving adults should be available and supportive but refrain from forcing their child to explain her feelings. By example, they can show her ways in which feelings are expressed and what purpose they serve. The rest is up to their quick learner, who will take what she needs and ignore the rest.

The teenage Gemini may feel repelled by her bodily changes. Up to this point, she has probably fit in everywhere. Now, to her, her physical changes represent a commitment to a particular group and, possibly, to a way of life for which she may feel unprepared. She may ignore her body and her sexuality or try to control it through vigorous exercise and controlled eating. She is still most comfortable relating to her peers as though she were their sibling; and since there are great rewards from that sort of camaraderie, she is likely to be quite happy in her relationships with friends. She probably does not feel sexual, however, and may rebel against current dating standards in her group. She would rather have a playmate or an intellectual counterpart and much prefers a meeting of minds to a meeting of bodies.

The young Gemini may also rebel against the family work ethic. She usually works hard only at what interests her in school, and she may work for pay only long enough to purchase what she wants. Her adolescent life may feel slightly unreal to her as she explores ways to interact with people more deeply, but this "unreality" may take the form of extraordinary poetry or some other creative endeavor. She remains funny, charming and socially adept and can be counted on to solve her problems responsibly when allowed the time and privacy to do so.

*Needs*

Freedom.

Help in making decisions, setting priorities and setting standards.

Help in beginning things.

Warm and unobtrusive support and encouragement.

Privacy.

Permission to feel her feelings.

Permission not to figure everything out.

Information.

Conversation.

Help in establishing her own ethics and sense of right and wrong.

*Hates*

Being bored.

Waiting, other people's slowness.

Boring forms of repetition.

Noise.

Condescension.

Feeling trapped.

Not knowing what's going on.

Someone telling her what she already knows.

Hypocrisy.

Having to finish one project before going on to the next.

Having only one of anything.

Having to do something over and over again (to get it right).

Personal labels.

Having to choose.

Being treated as unequal or dumb.

Being called flaky, superficial, fickle.

# CANCER CHILDREN

**JUNE 21–JULY 22**

## GENERAL CHARACTERISTICS

*(Note: While many characteristics described below will be accurate for most Cancers, other, sometimes contradictory, traits may also be evident in an individual child.)*

Affectionate and extremely vulnerable, newborn Cancers are able to win over the most hardened and jaded adults. They are serene and open and tug at the hearts of parents and other children alike. Little Cancers bring out the nurturing instinct in all of us and seem truly pleased at our attention and ministrations. Cancer babies are the epitomy of loving sweetness: the Gerber baby was probably a Cancer.

This gentleness can last throughout a Cancer's childhood. They are very sensitive to others, sympathetic, considerate and sincere. They love being helpful and needed. For both girls and boys, being like Mom is a positive and exciting experience, and they are often found helping around the house. Cancer children of both sexes are likely to enjoy playing with dolls as a way of pretending to be grown up. As Cancer children practice their own adult parenting skills, they will keenly reflect the behaviors and attitudes of the adults around them. They are the sign most likely to mimic the behavior of older family members.

This ability to accurately mirror the family environment is both the blessing and curse of the Cancer child. Parents who dislike aspects of their parenting may be very uncomfortable to see those characteristics revealed by their Cancer child. On the other hand, when little Cancer imitates or exposes an appreciated aspect of a parent, he may find himself highly regarded in the family for copying that is second nature to him. The child who smiles just like Daddy may be praised and cuddled; the child who smirks just like Mom

79

may not seem so endearing. Because their behavior is so accurately reflected, parents often have a tendency to act more cautiously and to feel more vulnerable around small Cancers. The Cancer child is not mimicking on purpose. He has no malicious motive. It is an inborn trait and should simply be accepted as part of Cancer's uniqueness.

However, mothers may react more intensely to their little Cancers than to children of other sun signs. Mom may be overprotective or overly distant, depending on the parts of herself she sees reflected in her relationship with the Cancer child. Young Cancers may attempt to live up to, or down to, Mom's expectations in particular. Children of the sign of Cancer have a strong identification with their mother. As a result, the older Cancer child needs permission to be different from Mom and to mature separately from her. He needs to know that he can make his own decisions and mistakes without offending her. Since in his early childhood Cancer may believe only Mom can understand him, he needs warm and positive experiences with other adults to help expand his confidence. Grandparents, aunts and uncles may therefore play an especially important role in the Cancer child's life. He needs them to expand his sense of relationship from Mother to others.

Cancer is a water sign, and all the water signs deal with caretaking and nurturing. Cancer's sensitivity will be obvious in family relationships. Emotional and sometimes moody, the Cancer child has intuitive reactions to the feelings of members of the household whether or not he has been told what is going on. He is extremely vulnerable to other people's feelings and may feel buffeted about by the emotions of others. Cancers tend to assume all feelings relate somehow to them. Confused by their own intuition, little Cancers may decide that family feelings are directed at them or that family feelings somehow originate from them and spread to others. Thus if Mom is angry, little Cancer will most likely feel her anger, whether or not she expresses it directly. Little Cancer may decide that Mom is always angry, that she is angry at him or that he is really the one who is angry and has caused her to be angry by having the feeling himself. In any case, little Cancers are often confused about the source and purpose of emotions.

Young Cancers need honest and open discussions about feelings. They need reassurance that everyone has feelings, that feelings do not always pertain to them and that everyone is responsible for dealing with their own feelings. It will be helpful if a parent who is upset and is holding a Cancer baby will just think to herself, "This is my feeling and does not concern you or interrupt my love for you." Even Cancer toddlers will react intuitively and positively to reassurance about feelings whether or not they understand all of the words. If parents are uncomfortable with their own emotions, they may occasionally be extremely uncomfortable with the volatile little Cancer in their midst.

The Cancer child's acute sensitivity has further implications: his feelings are easily hurt. He tends to be introspective and needs a lot of time and privacy to figure things out. If his feelings are hurt, he will most likely withdraw and deal with the hurt by himself. When a Cancer child intuitively believes he knows what others want of him, he may alter his behavior to either please or irritate them or to resolve family tensions. For example, if Dad is angry, little Cancer may feel anxious and uncomfortable. He may try to relieve his anxiety in several ways: he may blend into the woodwork or deliberately misbehave in order to distract Dad and entice him to release the anger in little Cancer's direction.

Cancer is very sensitive to the type of treatment he receives and the expectations placed on him in the family. He often reacts to unspoken assumptions and labels with either compliance or rebellion. Imply that a Cancer child is artistic and he will either become another Picasso or a car mechanic. In either case, the problem is that Cancer is reacting to external expectations and suggestions instead of defining himself.

Cancer's frequently accurate assessment of other people's feelings and expectations may lead him to believe he can read others' minds, and conversely, that they can read his mind. If the young Cancer comes to believe others can read his mind, he feels he's lost his privacy and individuality. He loses his sense of psychic retreat and may decide to see himself as a mere extension of his parents. Once this occurs, little Cancer's assumptions change. Since he has assumed his intuition is reality and that he knows what others need and feel, he will now expect others to be equally sensitive to what he needs and feels. When others are not equally sensitive, the Cancer child will tend to feel unreasonably punished, ignored or rejected. To correct this situation, Cancer children need encouragement to state their own needs and feelings explicitly. They need to be told, over and over, "I can't guess what you want, you need to *tell* me." And they need to be told, "I know you are smart about knowing how I feel, but you are not always right and you do not need to take responsibility for what I feel."

Because of his emphasis on feeling, all emotions may take on the same importance. The Cancer child may have difficulty distinguishing the important from the trivial. His initial reaction to a lost pencil or a lost pet may be identical. It takes time for him to figure out what he's feeling and its intensity. Because he may appear withdrawn or overly dramatic during this figuring out, Cancer may initially seem to have difficulty expressing his true feelings easily. What is really occurring is a very private and personal mental sorting process.

The young Cancer makes important decisions in the same way he deals with feelings. Afterward he will be able to say exactly what he was thinking and why, but if pressured to explain prematurely, he may give any answer, or none. The Cancer child's conclusions and behavior may appear spontaneous or unconsidered to astonished parents who haven't been included in his long introspection. From the outside, the young Cancer may appear to announce "suddenly" that he's going to buy a puppy, but inside he has carefully, quietly, without giving it much extra attention, spent the past two years considering how he could afford to feed a dog, train it and find the time and energy to care for it.

Because of the intense value placed on introspection, even young Cancer children are surprisingly comfortable with a range of emotions. They may sit placidly in a group where someone is expressing strong emotions and not exhibit discomfort or embarrassment. The exception to this is most likely to be a difficulty in showing their anger and in being frightened of other people's anger. However, Cancers know how to be especially nurturing, supportive and comfortable around people who are sad or scared.

Cancers relate all experience to themselves in order to understand it. Cancer children will share their own similar experiences as a way of proving that they understand someone else's experience. A typical Cancer's idea of sympathy, when comforting a sick friend, is to tell the friend about the time they were sick, too. Sometimes this behavior looks competitive, like a contest for who's in worse shape, and doesn't convey Cancer's intended sympathy. Some people will welcome Cancer's spontaneous sharing, while others will find it irritating. This mixed reaction confuses a little Cancer in the midst of his good intentions. Cancer children need to be taught when their sharing is appropriate and how to communicate empathy without telling their own life story. The Cancer child will continue to make mental comparison because it reinforces and helps him explain his intuitive base, but he can be taught to do it nonverbally and then check out his assumptions with others. He can learn to ask what other people want.

In a similar vein, the Cancer child may not believe his parents understand the depths of his emotion unless they share it with him. If little Cancer is crying, he may want Mom to cry, too. If Mom is not so inclined, she will need to find other ways to show little Cancer she cares, and little Cancer will need to be taught to accept other forms of proof.

Cancer children also need to learn awareness of other people's individual feelings as separate from their own feelings. Since they have an easy capacity to be nurturing, affectionate and caring, Cancers frequently expend much energy trying to take care of the people around them. As part of their general confusion about intuition, mind reading and shared experience, Cancer children often mistakenly believe they can make others stop hurting and feel better. A little Cancer is deeply touched by distress and will often cry with others in empathy or shared frustration. This can sometimes feel very enticing to a tired parent in need of sympathy, even the chirping voice of her four-year-old saying, "Don't worry, Mommy, everything will be all right." However, no child can really alleviate an adult's pain, and to the extent a Cancer child is allowed to try, he is undertaking an impossible task. Once again, he needs reassurance that everyone is responsible for their own feelings and he is not to try and "fix" the feelings in the family.

If little Cancer believes he succeeds in taking care of other people's feelings, he may later assume that his personal worth consists of the nurturing he gives. It becomes difficult for him to stop giving long enough to receive and replenish. If his nurturing is not acknowledged carefully, and if he is not encouraged to receive nurturing in turn, a little Cancer may soon decide that there is something magical or special about his ability to intuit and take care of others. This belief makes it even harder for him to receive nurturing from people he perceives need him or need his special nurturing, and it becomes especially difficult for him to say no to anyone seeking help. He may be attracted only to those who are weaker than he or wounded. While this is a noble trait with injured birds and younger sisters, it leads to difficulties establishing equality with friends. On the other hand, if a little Cancer has taken on this impossible nurturing task and been allowed to feel in charge of making other people feel better and—of course—failed, he may seek out those he believes are stronger, who will help and protect him. Essentially, he may switch from the role of special nurturer to the role of the helpless one in need of special nurturing. In either case, this leads to similar difficulties establishing peer relationships and adds to little Cancer's sense that only Mother, or one other designated grown-up, can understand what he needs and take care of him.

Much of this Cancerian drive to nurture is nonverbal. It occurs quietly within the daily routines of a family and can lead to some rather confusing and unspoken tensions. The simplest way to deal with the drive of the young Cancer to take care of others is to monitor how much he is *receiving* in the family and constantly reinforce the acceptability of *taking* love, of being close and letting himself feel good. On the playground, the Cancer youngster may befriend a forlorn child, but he also needs to have friends who are his equal. A Cancer who is surrounded only by forlorn children may be working very hard for diminishing rewards. He needs encouragement to establish peer relationships and to be taught the joys of give and take.

Little Cancer tends to generalize from himself to others and to give others precisely that which he wants. Cancer children tend to buy for others gifts they themselves deeply desire. If little Cancer is having difficulty figuring out what he wants, parents can teach him to be aware of what he is giving to others. While believing fervently in the golden rule, the Cancer child also turns it around: along with "Do unto others as you would have them do unto you," he adds, "Do unto others and *they will* do unto you." The Cancer child is superstitious. He expects automatic retaliation if he is bad and automatic reward if he is good. He might remember how awful he felt being left alone on the playground and assume that other children feel awful, too. He may believe that if he befriends the child he perceives as an outcast he himself will be befriended in times of need. While this is logical to the Cancer child, he is striking a bargain the world has not agreed to based on assumptions that aren't accurate. The positive aspect of Cancer's ability to generalize from himself to others is a deep understanding of the golden rule. His sense of justice and fairness is based on often unshakable empathy.

This empathy and intuition are inborn Cancer traits that need no further encouragement. A Cancer child will almost always assume he has an intuitive understanding of any situation. Cancer children need to be told what is going on and why so they don't make up their own incorrect explanations and then act on them. They also need to be taught to assess realistically when their drive to nurture and fix things is helpful and when it interferes with what others need to do for themselves. They need permission to resist their nurturing impulses and not feel they have to be involved in every situation that is going on around them.

The tendency of the Cancer child to generalize from himself also includes taking things personally. If Mom is crying, the young Cancer may automatically assume that he made her sad and want to do something about it. If teacher scolds the entire class, little Cancer may feel especially guilty and responsible. The Cancer child may also interpret situations as containing a personal demand or veiled message where none is intended. For example, if Dad says he likes the color blue, Cancer may discard all his pretty red shirts, believing Dad was sending him a personal message. It is therefore important for parents to be direct with their Cancer children and to find the source of assumptions behind what may appear to be odd or unusual behaviors and responses.

If little Cancer thinks people send primarily indirect messages or that they can read his mind, he is not likely to state his own needs and feelings directly and may resent having to state them. He may generally believe: I know what you want; how come you don't know what I want? He may fear being blamed for neglecting his assumed nurturing or his real responsibilities, and he often perceives criticism or discipline as rejection. He may adopt behavior that appears defensive and frightened in order to assure himself of some measure of privacy and peace. For example, if he feels pressure to perform, the Cancer child may procrastinate or leave chores unfinished in an effort to reduce real or imagined adult expectations. Once again, it is important for parents to be specific and realistic with their demands and lavish with their praise when their demands are met. The young Cancer responds best to loving guidance, support and encouragement, with a minimum of attention to his mistakes and shortcomings.

Cancer children need a great deal of love and approval from friends as well as family. They may alter their behavior in order to be liked and not understand when other children refuse to give in to them (that secret bargaining with the golden rule again). Cancers have a tendency to project their intuition onto others and blame others for their superstitions. "Mrs. Thompson doesn't like me anymore. She called on me in class when I didn't have my hand raised, and she knew I didn't know the answer."

As a result of such projections, little Cancers may go through a period of rebellion, refusing to nurture anyone and insisting they don't care about friends, friendship or their acceptance in groups; but they do care. They need a steadfast parent or teacher who continues to offer them affection and challenges their inner assumptions during these periods of rebellion. In response, Cancer children are often like little sunflowers, turning toward the light of other's kindness, soaking it up and hanging around for more.

When little Cancers are sure of the recognition and love of others, they give much love in return and exhibit a spontaneous generosity. Parents will find it rewarding and well worth their while to give small Cancers all the love, support and affection they need. The young Cancer deprived of this bedrock of affection may appear selfish or self-indulgent. He may avoid responsibility except when it suits him, and act generally grumpy and hard to please. A sudden onset of such behavior indicates that the little Cancer is feeling starved for recognition, and a half hour of special attention will most likely restore his sunny personality. Sometimes, instead of looking grumpy and selfish, the Cancer child may poignantly act the clown, making a fool of himself and laughing at his humiliation, preferring anger or ridicule to no attention at all. He may overdramatize his emotions to be sure they're noticed or he may dwell on feelings, looking moody, to be certain he is taken seriously. He needs to know he can get attention simply by asking for it, without the drama.

The young Cancer's love of humor also comes out when he is comfortable. His wit is perceptive and fast, and he is quick to appreciate the quiet and subtle humor of others. Hurt and stubborn Cancer children will often admit humor when other methods of reaching him fail, but he first needs to be certain that the humor is gentle and affirming rather than humiliating.

Cancer children often have difficulty accepting and understanding the use of rules. They tend to ignore the protective functions of limits and perceive rules as controlling. This creates a tendency for the Cancer child to avoid, ignore, resent or misinterpret any constraints. Fortunately, Cancer is a naturally cautious sign; otherwise, the young child may have trouble figuring out how to protect himself when he is so resistant to using the protective rules offered him. Cancer children are also reluctant to identify their own rules and may feel at the mercy of people who are more verbal and direct. As a result, most young Cancers feel they don't quite belong. They see themselves as the black sheep in their families and believe that others know secrets or have a special key to understanding they lack. Often they feel others somehow have access to information and rules that they, the Cancers, neither see nor understand.

The Cancer child may idealistically resent the need for rules at all or, in a form of rebellion, act as though a given rule were permanent and immutable, exaggerating it until the impact is lost. If little Cancer is told not to leave the refrigerator door open while he leisurely surveys the contents, he may refuse to open it again for any reason. As much as possible, Cancers need to have the reasons for rules explained clearly and consequences for misbehavior specifically detailed. Because he is sentimental about, and loyal to, his family, the helping function of a rule will seem most reasonable to little Cancer. The statement "I won't have to defrost the refrigerator so often if you close the door quickly" will have more impact on his behavior than shame or appeals to thrift.

Young Cancers are a virtual catalog of contradictions as they attempt to balance their own needs against the expectations they perceive in their environment. They may act alternately shy and brash, subtle and flamboyant, astute and vague, generous and stingy, tense and serene, cautious and reckless, dependent and independent, secretive and vulnerable, strong and weak. They frequently believe they will receive more attention and approval and less responsibility if they act cute, childish or helpless and may carefully hide their considerable intelligence and skill. They need to be needed but fear being trapped by obligations, so they may act responsible one moment and very irresponsible the next. Though they appreciate predictability in their environment and are often creatures of habit, little Cancers take pride in their own unpredictability and maintain idiosyncrasies in order to assure themselves of their uniqueness.

Little Cancer is often in the position of wanting to belong to the family, to a social circle, to unquestioned cultural norms and, at the same time, wanting to be unique. He wants to stand out in the family and in social circles. He may want to create his own cultural norms based on intuition and understanding rather than knowledge and insight. Similar contradictory dynamics occur in little Cancer's relationship to authority: he needs the approval and validation of authority figures but often fears the control or obligation he believes accompanies their praise.

Cancer children, in all their rich contradictions, are often quite a challenge to parents. These children need to be taught appropriate outlets for their diverse needs and feelings. They need encouragement to talk about their inner assumptions so they can understand that not everyone sees the world as they do. Their most automatic response will be based on intuition, and they will be surprised, and sometimes angry, to discover that intuition is not universally accepted as the way things are.

Cancer children are oddly patriotic. They fervently believe in the abstract concepts of family and land and receive some of their much needed security from the apparent immutability of these institutions, but they may seem to pay little attention to their own flesh-and-blood ties. Young Cancers can be quite tenacious, single-minded and sometimes rather ruthless and stubborn in pursuit of a goal in which they believe. They may act opportunistic or manipulative if their goal is in sight, rationalizing their behavior for the greater good. This goal orientation will show up in even the youngest Cancers as a determination to accomplish what they set out to do. However, having reached their goal, Cancer children are again generous, magnanimous and delighted with themselves. Falling short of their goal, they may rationalize and pretend they didn't care.

Though they dislike sharing, Cancers are quite willing to give. If you borrow a Cancer child's pencil four times in a row, he will give it to you or buy you one of your own. Little Cancers are often quite creative and psychic as well as intuitive. Their deep spirituality frequently carries with it abilities to heal that are channeled through their excellent listening and nurturing skills. Very early in childhood, Cancers may begin to serve as listeners and helpers for their friends. They easily attend to the emotional comfort of those around them and usually freely offer their support and nurturance. Cancer children add softness and humor to their spaces: the air seems to be a little richer when they are nearby.

NEEDS (Cancer's emotional emphasis)

Affection, attention, reassurance.
Unconditional love with limits on behavior.
Demonstrations of love.
Limits, rules, boundaries, protection, consistency.
Reasonable explanations for emotional reactions.
Clear nurturing.
To feel useful and needed: reasonable responsibility.
Encouragement to experiment with different parental behaviors.
Honesty.
Sense of family history.
For adults to act grown up.
Learning the differences between compassion and pity, empathy and overidentification.
Learning realistic assessments of when they can or should help and when they should not.
Not to be rushed into, or prevented from, growing up.
Not to be exploited.
Learning not to take things personally.
Not to be ignored, taken for granted, left out or retaliated against.
Never to be humiliated publicly, criticized, teased or scolded.
Not to be abandoned.
Not to be labeled.
Not to be bribed with or forced to eat unnecessary quantities of food.

COMMON ASSUMPTIONS (How Cancer views the world around him)

Only one person can meet my needs.
If I wait long enough, someone will rescue me.
Family is the primary source of pain or reward.

SENSITIVITIES (Potential sources of misunderstanding)

*Dependence:* Little Cancer is keenly aware of his own and others' dependence or interdependence. He may react to this awareness by appearing passive and adaptable, relying on others' decisions and judgments, or he may rebel against all forms of dependence in himself, perceiving his needs as signs of weakness.

*Nurturing:* Sometimes the Cancer child may be reluctant to offer the nurturing that comes so naturally to him because of the potential dependence on him others may develop. He may try to cope by making conscious choices about when and how to be helpful; but having made these choices, he will tend to define his actions as not "real" nurturing, believing that "real" nurturing is always spontaneous and without self-regard, a spiritual happening.

*Unconditional Love:* The Cancer child may also use his preconceived definition of nurturing to determine the apparent extent and quality of the love he receives. He may use obnoxious behavior to test the love of his parents. If he has not shared his definition of loving behavior with those around him, concerned adults may feel at a loss to give little Cancer the love he wants. The child may feel his needs are met only haphazardly, that he demands too much or that others are unwilling to be kind to him. This situation is corrected by working out a healthy, available definition and expectation of love.

*Rules, Boundaries and Limits:* Young Cancers generally hate both rules and labels and will try to find the exception in any case. Parents will be challenged by little Cancer's unexpected rebelliousness or exaggeration and need to be prepared and unyielding, especially concerning rules that deal with safety. Respectful negotiation on other less important rules may, however, be an enjoyable experience for all concerned.

*Blame and Responsibility:* To avoid guilt and self-loathing, Cancer children may eagerly blame anyone or anything for errors or omissions. Deep down, little Cancers often feel responsible for everything and develop an elaborate system of rationalization to avoid being overwhelmed by their responsibility. Parents can help by maintaining clear standards and by being certain their expectations are explicit and understood.

*Thinking:* The young Cancer appears to prefer living by instinct and intuition to thinking. Frequently he feels stupid and inadequate. In many cases, Cancer children expend a great deal of energy tricking or cajoling others into making decisions and choices for them, thereby avoiding responsibility for the outcome. Often, afterward they realize they knew the answers and feel smarter than those they have tricked into thinking for them. Parents wishing to avoid this game can be clear in their expectation that Cancer children solve their own problems, within reason for their age group. Little Cancers may be especially resistant to this at first, perceiving this expectation as a lack of caring. They may act so slowly that the frustrated adult jumps in and does it anyway: tricked again.


RELATIONSHIPS

Since little Cancers relate to others primarily within their own personal framework, sharing experiences is the easiest and most comfortable way to get to know a Cancer child. Though they appear cautious and slow to trust, small Cancers so desperately want to like others and be liked that any effort extended by others will be met with deep appreciation and loyalty.

*Mom:* The Cancer child expects Mom to be fair, impartial, considerate, tasteful and socially adept. Young Cancer may suffer throes of embarrassment if he believes Mom has made a social error.

Moms who feel they can't live up to these expectations can introduce little Cancer to proper social skills and to one of the greatest joys of Cancer's life: music. Excursions to concerts, theaters, museums and other cultural events will be a positive experience for both mother and child.

Cancer children are the most ambivalent in the zodiac about their mothers. Above all, Mom needs to be true to herself and consistent; chances are that she cannot please little Cancer all of the time. The Cancer child looks to his mom for explanation of those "secret" rules and may simultaneously resent her knowledge. He needs her love and approval intensely and may detest his own need of her. Equilibrium and honest and consistent caring are Mom's best choices in dealing with little Cancer's conflicting demands.

*Dad:* The young Cancer expects Dad to be decisive, strong, angry and not very available. He seeks leadership from his dad and is seldom surprised at disapproval. Dads who feel reluctant to live up to this macho image will find that the easiest way to little Cancer's heart is to play with him: child's games, not skills defined by the parent. If Dad allows his own childlike playfulness and other emotions to surface with the little Cancer, he will find a kind and delighted little playmate and nurturer. Walks in the woods, activities near or on water and doll play are all potential avenues to young Cancer's adoration and admiration.

*Siblings:* Little Cancer sees his siblings as smarter, neater, more thorough and less tolerant than he is. Believing they know more, he may elicit and tolerate criticism from them. The young Cancer may have difficulty feeling equal to his siblings. He may feel weaker than they and in need of their protection, or stronger and therefore needed by and obligated to them. Little Cancer worries about his siblings' health.

*Friends:* The Cancer child is intensely, sometimes blindly, loyal to friends and to those who've been kind to him, and he expects the same in return. He is uncritical and forgiving with friends and may have difficulty distinguishing between loyalty, gratitude and love. He may perceive a friend's lack of exclusiveness as a betrayal and be deeply hurt if someone has friends other than himself. The Cancer child is often attracted to those who seem weaker or needier than he is and may be surprised and hurt when his friends cling, demand, forget or behave in a way that seems disloyal. Little Cancer likes the predictability and comfort of a long-standing friendship and may hang on to one long after he's ceased to get anything from it.


## MIND/INFORMATION/SCHOOL

Much of what little Cancer knows is intuitive and therefore not readily defensible. Cancer absorbs information like a little sponge, soaking up data as it flies around him. A danger in this ability is that information may be incomplete and little Cancer, unaware of the missing pieces, will imaginatively fill in the blanks by making his own creative connections.

Unless frightened or absolutely cornered, young Cancers seldom lie, but their imaginative explanations may sound like untruths to adults. Cancer children need to know "Why?" When an explanation is not offered, they invent one. Little Cancer tends to see details. Only through the details of a situation does he grasp its entirety. However, he may focus on a detail and refuse to see the larger picture, causing nearby adults to feel little Cancer is exaggerating or being stubborn. For example, recalling that Mom served ginger ale the last time he was sick, little Cancer may believe it was the drink that cured him and feel abused or neglected if he doesn't get ginger ale this time. The young Cancer needs to know all the details and must be taught not to stop at the most obvious or expedient point. He also needs to learn how to determine which details are important and which are not. This tendency to focus so narrowly may appear dreamy or beside the point but ultimately leads to the development of Cancer's intense power of concentration and creativity.

The memory of a Cancer child is mostly sensory. He may connect a smell with a feeling, for example, without remembering the actual event. Most little Cancers memorize easily, but later they may not be aware of the meaning of what they've learned. The Cancer child absorbs information first and processes it later. There is a time lag between input and understanding. Consequently, little Cancer may appear inarticulate until he's had time to think, and he may lose faith in his ability to defend himself verbally. He may also believe others are smarter than he is and set about either to prove his superior intellect or give up altogether. If the former, he may appear critical and virtually unpleasable; if the latter, he may appear slow or dumb. He may believe that if learning doesn't come easily, he must be dumb and resent or overlook the effort required to excel in areas important to him.

Little Cancers are gullible and suggestible. Sensing this, they can become extremely skeptical, afraid of being teased, lied to or humiliated. In their eagerness to believe, small Cancers tend to embrace virtually everything. It is therefore especially important that significant adults are honest with very young Cancers, that they not use verbal puns until the school years and that they never use sarcasm. Cancers love jokes, however, and respond to gentle humor when it is not at the expense of themselves or others. Adults will find it worth the investment of time and effort to explain jokes to the little Cancer.

In school, the young Cancer learns best from experience. He is good with his hands and excels at taking things apart. Needing to be outstanding, he may give up when he fails to meet his own standards. He may pretend he doesn't care, become careless or sloppy or drive himself mercilessly. He both expects and fears criticism. Emphasis on the positive will surprise and motivate the school-age

Cancer. He is very perceptive and needs a peaceful and nondistracting environment in which to work. Though preschool may be valuable for the young Cancer's social skills, he is likely to benefit equally from remaining at home.

*Higher Education:* Idealistic about the rewards of higher education, Cancer may be bitterly disappointed by his educational experiences after high school. He needs the structure and protection of formal training but, especially in late adolescence, tends to rebel against it. If he is not overwhelmed by his experience of higher education, he is likely to do best in the arts, humanities or social services. While he values the authority and respect educational credentials afford, he may resent a system that demands or awards those credentials.

## RESPONSIBILITY/WORK/REWARDS

*Responsibility and Work:* The young Cancer is likely to behave most extremely regarding responsibility. He wants total responsibility or none, and he wants to do things his own way, with his own timing. He may be initially enthusiastic about a responsibility and then lose interest, or he may identify so much with his responsibilities that he forgets to play. He is more concerned with process than with goals and can become so involved with the mechanics of a task that he forgets to finish it. The young Cancer who wishes to avoid responsibility can do a miserable job.

Young Cancers are hard workers who tend to do even more than asked when a job interests them. Though they may rebel if someone *tells* them how to perform a task, they welcome and will consider all suggestions. While Cancer children often begin several tasks at once and then have difficulty finishing even one, when working alongside others, they need to feel they have enough to do. They prefer, however, being left alone while undertaking a chore, and if they must work with others, they prefer to lead. If forced to follow, they have trouble mustering much enthusiasm for the job, though they often appreciate the help of close adults. Little Cancers don't work well under pressure.

*Rewards:* The highest reward for a Cancer child is praise, especially in public. Acceptance, being liked and hugs are also important to little Cancer, who loves hearing Mom tell Dad what a good kid he was today. Being permitted to make a choice not ordinarily allowed is another fine reward for the Cancer child. The trust and approval implied in letting little Cancer decide where to eat out or what color flowers to buy are not lost on the perceptive child. Even young Cancers have an excellent business sense and will perceive money earned as its own reward.

## HOME

Home for Cancer is synonymous with security, and little Cancers invest a lot of time and energy in their own space. For little Cancers, home is a haven of safety and comfort to which to retreat after having experimented with the world; even for grown-up Cancers, home is a sentimental haven to return to when the going gets rough.

The young Cancer's space is comfortable, cozy, casual, friendly and pretty, usually filled with special mementos and things of utilitarian beauty. Though Cancer's need for privacy is minimal, he needs control over who comes in and when. He usually welcomes visitors or guests and likes having his friends play in his space. He probably enjoys posters on his walls. Cancers like unexpected flashes of brilliant colors among more generally subdued tones—grays, whites, ivories, pale greens, and turquoise.

## HEALTH

Little Cancers are concerned with the integrity of their bodies and may worry and complain needlessly about minor misfunctions. They may be dramatic about their own and others' common illnesses. In major matters, however, they can be quite stoic and brave, enduring a great deal of discomfort. Illness for a young Cancer may be an acceptable way to be alone or dependent, a way to demonstrate his bravery, to get sympathy or a respite from taking care of others. Little Cancers may use illness as a means of attracting more intimacy, attention or emotional connection with someone important. When sick, most little Cancers like lots of attention and offers of food.

Traditionally, the sign of Cancer rules the stomach and digestive tract. Little Cancers experiencing health problems are likely to feel uncomfortable in these areas. Illness itself is likely to occur in the form of digestive upsets, water retention, loss of energy, problems with eyesight, menstrual irregularities or as the result of overindulgence.

## CHILDHOOD AGES

*(Note: The fears detailed in this section are never to be used as punishment. They are presented as avenues for reassurance and caring).*

### BIRTH–6 MONTHS

The newborn Cancer is loving, sweet and hungry. He appears grateful for whatever he gets. He is very sensitive to his environment and is especially attuned to his mom's feelings and unspoken messages, picking up the slightest changes and nuances in her moods and behaviors. Even as a tiny infant, Cancer may attempt to take care of his mom by altering his own needs, behaviors and responses to suit or to match hers. Mom is clearly the most important person in newborn Cancer's world, and he may be shy with others or resistant to letting himself be cared for by other members of the family or strangers. Little Cancers often have digestive difficulties or problems eating and respond well to being fed on demand and cuddled.

> *Needs*
> Lots of holding and cuddling.
> Reassurances that Mom can take care of herself.
> Positive experiences with other adults and children.
> Adequate food.
> Mom to stay grown up and not compete for attention.
> Sensory stimulation.
> Privacy.
> Private time with Mom.

> *Fears*
> Being too demanding, burdensome.
> Being unprotected or abandoned.
> New and unfamiliar places and people.
> Having to put Mom's needs first.

6 MONTHS–18 MONTHS

The Cancer baby is timid, still cute and cuddly. Both shy and curious, little Cancer may need encouragement to explore his environment actively and to participate in what's going on around him. He is creative and excited by new information and delights in being able to help perform tasks usually done by Mom. He loves nature and water.

*Needs*
Support, encouragement and approval.
Protection, but not overprotection.
Continued demonstrations of love.
Attention and private time with important adults.
To know what's going on.

*Fears*
Being forced to eat.
Being hungry.
Punishment for being curious.
Being a burden.
That only Mom can meet his needs.
Being left out.
Having to be cute to get attention.

18 MONTHS–3 YEARS

The Cancer toddler is erratic and full of contradictions. He is sweet, stubborn, sympathetic, caring, defensive, rebellious, compliant. Emotional and sensitive, he can go from raging anger to winsome charm in a matter of minutes. Still shy and cautious with strangers, he may believe he has to act coy or cute in order to get the approval he needs. He may personalize virtually everything, believing that even the most innocent remark is directed at him or that the most horrendous event was somewhat his fault. A clue to his needs, if he isn't yet comfortable stating them, lies in that which he gives to others, which is usually what he himself desires. Intuitive and sometimes psychic, the Cancer toddler sometimes has an imaginary playmate or special places or things for security. His senses are extremely important to him at this time. He seems to get into everything and learns best by tasting and touching. He tends to be messy.

*Toilet Training:* Little Cancers may be very slow to toilet train but wake up one morning with mission accomplished. He needs a lot of praise and attention during the training period, and accidents should be overlooked or handled in a casual and respectful way.

*Needs*

A security symbol, a safe place.
Approval.
Reassurance.
Calm reactions to emotional outbursts.
Encouragement.
Continued demonstrations of love.
To feel useful.
Opportunities to practice parenting skills.

*Fears*

Abandonment.
Ridicule.
Punishment (in the form of criticism or abandonment) for increased competence or learning.
Lack of standards or overly severe standards.
Being overwhelmed.

3 YEARS–6 YEARS

The preschool Cancer remains volatile, emotional and sometimes defensive. Still periodically tender, loving, sympathetic and caring, little Cancer tends to take things personally and will readily attack to protect himself. Parents may mourn the passing of their gentle and loving baby and resist the child's normal maturing. Tearful one moment and angry the next, little Cancer is dramatic and may appear overwhelmed with emotions. He may enjoy watching grown-ups fight and, while this may be a healthy way to learn skills for dealing with anger, parents need to be certain little Cancer hasn't somehow engineered the argument. The preschool Cancer may continue to have magical fantasies and imaginary playmates in preparation for his rich creativity later on.

*Needs*
  Reassurance.
  Reality checks.
  Compassion.
  Lightness and humor.
  Firm guidance.
  Feeling useful.

*Fears*
  Being able to intimidate or manipulate grown-ups.
  Ridicule.
  Being trapped in a particular family role (usually being seen as the nurturing one or the dumb one.)
  Being taken too seriously.
  Competition from parents.
  Lack of forgiveness: being told, "You made your bed, lie in it."

## 6 YEARS–12 YEARS

The school-age Cancer continues his contradictions. Still cautious, sensitive and defensive, he may sulk and be moody with no apparent cause, continuing to act alternately rebellious and compliant, possibly developing quite a temper. Acting either immature or behaving with pseudomaturity, he may swing between extremes of feeling inferior or superior, acting confused instead of solving problems. He tends to believe that others know some secret he himself does not. Usually it turns out that others know rules little Cancer rejects. He may, however, be very rigid concerning those rules he has identified. The young Cancer is quite conscious of what others think and is likely to be a follower during this stage. Adults therefore need to monitor closely those people, ideas and rules the little Cancer chooses to emulate.

The school-age Cancer tends to be both subservient and inflexible, feeling stuck or sorry a great deal of the time. Apologizing may be a way of forcing reassurance or approval. Cancers need to be held accountable for their actions in spite of apologies. A helpful parental response to an apology is, "I don't need you to feel sorry, I need you to think next time before you act." Self-effacing behavior has the same function; little Cancers need to be taught other ways to elicit support and encouragement.

Energy is very uneven for the young Cancer, who may be full of energy one moment and lethargic the next. However, when not overwhelmed, he remains gentle and full of tenderness, sympathy and caring.

*Needs*

Encouragement to be autonomous.

Confidence in his capabilities.

Time to think before acting.

Time and support for reaching his own conclusions.

Attention and approval from Mom.

Not to be shamed, humiliated or made to feel guilty about behaving in approved ways.

*Fears*

Teasing, humiliation, exploitation.

Punishment for competence.

Pressure to be perfect.

Competition from Mom.

## 12 YEARS–18 YEARS

By adolescence, Cancer has usually resolved earlier contradictions into one of two styles of behavior. Both styles continue to be moody, defensive, sensitive, romantic and nurturing. One Cancer, however, is conservative, considerate, sentimental, ruthless, cautious, pragmatic, responsible and action oriented. The other Cancer is more dramatic, flamboyant, unconventional, rebellious, irritable, resistant and sloppy. Both may be ambivalent about their families, wanting to leave home as soon as possible or to stay forever. Each style challenges the family rules concerning loyalty. Each feels both utterly different from, and hopelessly like, everyone else. Adolescent Cancers tend to punish themselves before anyone else has the opportunity to do so and may be quite severe and punitive. They need an adult nearby who can teach them compassion for themselves by means of both information and example. Teenage Cancers may suffer needlessly to prove a point, to be certain they are taken seriously, to punish themselves or to prove somehow that they are alive.

Cancer's empathy, nurturing and compassion for others continue through adolescence. They easily elicit trust and confidence from others. They may become very attached to one person, group or cause. Their natural flair for the dramatic inevitably leads them toward participation in groups dedicated to improving the world or one of the arts. Such groups can provide powerful and healthy outlets for the Cancer's energy, sense of drama and need for commitment, importance and approval.

Adolescent Cancers may be frightened by their body changes, especially since they tend to develop earlier than their peers. They may ignore their sexuality entirely or utilize their precocious development to get affection, nurturing, power or popularity. They may not truly believe in their own maturity until they've had a child themselves.

*Needs*
Information about responsible sexual behavior.
Encouragement, approval, attention.
Reasonable limits.
To be taken seriously.
Sense of family and tradition (even to rebel against).

*Hates*
Being needed or not being needed.
Feeling unappreciated.
Not being taken seriously.
Being laughed at.
Being teased, humiliated, shamed.
Being called too sensitive, cold, moody, intolerant.
Being forced to make decisions.
Being told, "You made your bed, lie in it."
Being told, "Control yourself."

# LEO CHILDREN

**JULY 23–AUGUST 22**

### GENERAL CHARACTERISTICS

*(Note: While many characteristics described below will be accurate for most Leos, other, sometimes contradictory, traits may also be evident in an individual child.)*

Parents will quickly be captivated by their bright and sunny Leo baby. She will elicit their most tender and nurturing feelings and return a warmth distinctly her own. It is hard for anyone to resist a baby who visibly brightens when you enter a room; and tiny Leo, ruled by the sun, is a baby who loves to shine on those around her. Leo is a baby people practically fight over for the chance to hold and cuddle, and since this infant loves to have attention and affection bestowed on her, she becomes even sunnier. Newborn Leo is a delight to have around and brings a sense of joy into the lives she touches.

The Leo child is usually entertaining and charming. She is strong, friendly, courageous and resilient and will take risks where others are fearful. As a result, families often come to rely on their Leo child for support and approval and to depend on her strength in times of trouble. What is often overlooked in the face of all this apparent and readily offered cheer and confidence is Leo's own need for support and approval. Being taken for granted and not given enough attention are Leo's biggest fears. Though people who assume Leo is doing all right and can take care of herself are often correct, they can forget to acknowledge this child's deep need for recognition.

So great is the young Leo's longing for approval and attention that she may become aware, very early in life, of her vulnerability toward flattery and decide to adopt a reserved or cynical attitude in order not to be easily manipulated every time someone tells her she's a "good kid." If someone pays her too many compliments, the young Leo may wonder what they want from her. If someone pays her too little attention, she may stop what she's doing. Little Leo may hear praise, "What a wonderful job!" as manipulative, or she may interpret lack of praise as disapproval. Caring parents will be consistent with praise and attention, and most important, sincere. Parents can also develop many nonverbal, but meaningful, signals of attention between themselves and their child (a pat on the shoulder, proud, approving glances, tousling little Leo's hair) that give her a sense of support and recognition without constant flattery.

The young Leo feels so internally vulnerable to her need for attention that she nevertheless wants to believe all but the most blatantly insincere compliments. She may believe compliments that other children would perceive as ridicule or joking. And if young Leo cannot get positive attention for herself and her behavior, she will do something to get negative attention: little Leo will be noticed, at whatever cost.

In order to feel safe, the Leo child needs to feel that she has a great deal of control over her environment. She likes to know she has an impact and to believe that what she wants and does make a difference. She does not like to feel that others are attempting to control her and will angrily resist such efforts.

When something needs to get done, the easiest way to engage Leo's cooperation is by appealing to her generosity, maturity or ability with frequent words of encouragement and approval. The hardest way to convince her to cooperate is to order her about. Little Leo does not like to be told directly that she has to do something. Sometimes parents tend to state indirectly what needs to be done and count on little Leo, with her need for approval, to step in and do the task. For example, "Those supper dishes sure could use washing. . . ." This kind of indirectness often works but may put later pressure on the child to continue guessing what her parents want and make her so angry that she does what she has indirectly been told to do but breaks a dish in retaliation. A healthy way to use indirectness with a Leo child is to say something like, "You've been so willing to help this week, would you like to do one more thing? The dishes need washing, and I'd be so glad if you decided to do them." Then while little Leo is washing, a parental cheer and praise for the finished task is much appreciated.

At her most stubborn, the Leo child is a formidable and some-times intimidating opponent who usually appears absolutely certain she is right. Out of her need to experience a sense of control, the young Leo may sometimes feel overly responsible, or she may attempt to manipulate the actions and decisions of those around her. If someone makes a choice that is different from the one she would have made, Leo may be contemptuous of them ("What a stupid decision that was.") or use her considerable powers of persuasion to convince them to change their minds ("If you insist on doing things that way, we'll never get to the movies today, and you will never get to see *Return of the Jedi*. You'll be the only one in third grade who doesn't know who Jabba the Hut is . . .").

The young Leo also likes to control her physical space and may become quite upset if her definite ways of doing things are disrupted. Little Leo will stick to a physical routine and expects others to respect it as well. If the Leo child sits in the middle seat of the front row in music class one week, she will expect to have the same seat the next week and not understand how anyone else could presume to sit in "her" place. This is not the same as Virgo's compulsiveness but is more a part of Leo's need for security. The phrases "first dibs" and "save my place" are Leo concepts.

This conviction of her own rightness and need to get others to agree with her can invite parents and other family members to engage in power struggles with little Leo. Others may want to put her down immediately and try and force Leo back into her less threatening position as approval seeker. This may leave little Leo filled with despair over her helplessness and other family members scared at the intensity of confrontation stirred up. Fathers seem to be in the most susceptible position for getting into power struggles with a Leo child and may need to take a few minutes' "time out" to think about how they want to respond before dealing with their little Leo in a stubborn mood. To balance this difficulty between fathers and the Leo child, little Leos enjoy a healthy sense of competition and will look to their dads for challenge and a race to the top.

One way young Leo can assure her recognition and simultane-ously exercise a great deal of control over situations is to become a leader of peers. Little Leo believes if people are doing what she says, or what she does, they must approve of her. Leo truly believes that imitation is the sincerest form of flattery, and she is seldom offended by being copied as long as everyone acknowledges who "started it." Leo loves giving advice and telling other people what they should do. Before she learns the tact that comes to her in adulthood, however, a Leo child can appear bossy and overbearing. Without followers and the tacit approval they imply, young Leo may simply stop what she's doing if she's not attracting attention for it. Unlike little Aries, who finds followers burdensome, little Leo seeks them and functions best with an audience and among approving friends.

The young Leo best comprehends how she's doing by watching other people's reactions to her, and she will automatically adjust her behavior if their responses are not what she desires. This can make parenting her quite easy in some situations, for when she's not receiving approving signals, little Leo will try on different behaviors until she finds one that pleases both herself and her parents. The young Leo needs other people to act as mirrors of herself, and she may have difficulty understanding another person's preferences or behavior if she cannot see how it reflects or relates to her own preference and behavior. Little Leo's bursts of sometimes astonishing creativity are often another way of testing her impact on an environment, though she may not give her originality full reign if she fears it won't be acceptable.

The young Leo often needs to be the best, the first and the only. She loves and needs to be right. She is frequently a high achiever and may believe she has to excel in order to be noticed or loved. Parents need to affirm their child's excellence while reassuring her that they love the mediocre, nondramatic parts of her as well. The Leo child needs to be proud of herself and wants those she loves to be proud of her as well.

There is so much about a Leo child that attracts positive attention that it is usually easy for parents to be proud of her. However, parents need to exercise caution in not making their pride a demand for "more and better" achievement or drawing attention away from the child who's earning it. Such statements as "That's my kid. I'm Leo's dad" are competitive and distracting, whereas such statements as "I'm so proud to be Leo's dad, what a great job she's doing" are supportive and acknowledging of Leo's achievement.

Sometimes, especially if parents have experienced disappointment with another child, little Leo may feel the need to compensate for the other's lack and prove to the world that not all the Joneses are like that. She may call extra attention to the sibling's inadequacies to look better in contrast or she may push herself harder and harder to perform, not only for her own satisfaction, but somehow to redeem the family honor. Even when such a situation doesn't exist, the young Leo has a tendency to see herself as a model and a representative for groups of people: all the Joneses, all Leos, all redheads or 4Hers. She will monitor her behavior to reflect well on the group, or if she has erred, she may worry that she has discredited an entire group.

In conflict with her need to represent well is her need to be exceptional in some way, to be outstanding and uniquely recognizable at least in one area. For example, if a young Leo who belongs to a minority group, say an Australian exchange student, is caught picking her nose in class, she will tend to worry that the other children now believe all Australians pick their noses in public. But if this same student wins the state spelling bee, she may fear other students will think she's an exception, not that Australians tend to be bright. When young Leos make mistakes, especially public mistakes, they tend toward shame and self-loathing, feeling they have "blown it" for the whole group they represent, as though they have let down the Australian nation. Their frequent statement that they feel "too proud" to accept something, maybe assistance or a gift they can't repay, often means they are really feeling "too ashamed" to accept the offer. Parents need to help Leo children monitor these confusions and develop realistic assessments of their influence in any group.

Part of a Leo child's definition of excellence includes being the only one who can do something. While children of some other sun signs, like Aquarius and Virgo, loathe being the "only one" to do anything, little Leo thrives on her ability to stand apart from the crowd. She will probably guard jealously the opportunities, skills or knowledge that allow her to be exceptional and not want to share the secrets. A school-age Leo who has just turned a triple somersault in gymnastics does *not* want to tell the class how she did it; she wants to bask in the fact that she did it and the other children didn't.

Little Leo likes having people come to her for information or services. She likes being an authority, though she will gracefully acknowledge other people's authority if she respects their expertise.

If she's the best at turning somersaults, she may enjoy teaching others (once she's savored her glory) and look subservient only to the teacher. She is often generous in sharing what she knows in such situations, and may be motivated by her preference that others feel in debt to her. As long as this slight imbalance exists, Leo will feel safe asking for help from those who "owe her one."

Starting at an early age, Leo keeps a careful, secret tally of credits and debits in a "cosmic bank account." She may, for example, help a preschool friend put on his boots, assuming he will help her with her jacket zipper. Later she may work very hard in a friend's campaign for class secretary, fully expecting the friend to work equally hard next semester when she wants to run for class president. Sometimes when Leo doesn't want a return favor she will want praise or affection in return for her work. If she's not running for class president, she may expect gratitude and loyalty from her friend and feel quite hurt if she's criticized in even the most gentle way. Like the Cancer child, Leo may confuse love, gratitude and loyalty and assume that people will have those feelings about her because they owe them to her. On the other hand, she may suspect gestures of affection if she believes they are occurring only because they are owed to her. Adults need to be spontaneously generous to little Leo, rewarding her when she has earned it and also giving her rewards at times when she hasn't earned it—just because they want it.

The young Leo needs to know how things work and may use her information to try to stay in control of a situation. She loves all sorts of tools and gadgets and will fix things herself whenever possible. When she's done the work herself, she knows it's done right and that she's still in charge. If her bicycle is broken, she will try to fix it herself before taking it to a repair shop. Leo has a funny way of being economical and extravagant at the same time. For example, teenage Leo may spend more money buying the right tools to fix her bike than it would cost to have the bike professionally repaired.

The Leo child is usually generous with other people and is a thoughtful and sensitive gift giver. She may have more difficulty purchasing things for herself, however, and frequently wants someone to come with her to act as an expert and help her make decisions about personal purchases. She loves to find a bargain, especially in quality merchandise of any sort.

The young Leo needs to know what things are called in order to make sense out of her environment. If a thing doesn't have a name, little Leo may give it one. She frequently assigns names and nicknames to everything around her. Her bicycle may be dubbed "Pedal-Pal" and her friend Stephanie's name shortened to "Poofie." These names often seem to take on lives of their own and may go through various evolutions. Parents may have a hard time keeping track of what little Leo is calling the kitten this week. Young Leo likes secret names and code words and is highly creative and entertaining when she reveals this part of her private world. A Leo preschooler seriously explained to her mother, "All my shoelaces have a name. This is Lolly and Louise, because they're on the left shoe, and this is Rita and Rainbow, they're on the right shoe. No matter how hard I try to be fair, I always forget and tie my right shoe first and then Lolly and Louise get mad and won't stay tied. See, they're already untied again. They like attention, just like me."

The school-age Leo is often a kind and benevolent leader, enthusiastic, dramatic and able to motivate others. These are often years when the Leo personality shines brightly; when one's greatest need is to have the approval and following of others, one often is amazingly good at leadership. Leo is responsible, engaging, frequently funny and entertaining. She excels at identifying what appears and is important to others. Teachers usually like putting Leo students in charge of group projects: they know they can count on completion of the task with minimum discord in the group. If her leadership is challenged, however, this schoolroom charmer can become quite dictatorial and self-righteous, believing she knows what's best for everyone and wanting things her own way. A challenged Leo may feel her whole sense of identity is being called into question and rise to defend herself or sulk. She is ambitious and likes the power that accompanies leadership. She is not likely to relinquish her power gracefully unless she foresees a later gain from doing so. For example, "I won't run for president again this term if I can run again in the spring."

The Leo child who doesn't feel she can lead, who for some reason inhibits this quality in herself, may feel isolated indeed. She needs to belong and fears being left out. One small Leo never closed the door while she was going to the bathroom for fear her family would leave the house while she was unable to join them. The young Leo always needs to know what's going on and may feel betrayed if information is not shared with her or if she thinks others have secrets. She likes to be on the "inside track," to be privy to exclusive knowledge. Little Leo likes knowing more than anyone else, and since she may believe this gives her special power or authority, she can scare herself if she believes she knows more than the grown-ups do and that they will not be able to take care of her adequately. Leo may need to talk through her understanding of situations to be reassured that the adults she's depending on have as much as or more information than she does.

The young Leo is often deeply connected to her family. Her need to belong is so extensive that she may perceive her friends and their families as part of her personal family group. Little Leo thinks about family in a sort of tribal sense, expansive and inclusive with many interconnecting bonds. A young Leo of either gender in a leadership position often perceives followers as his or her "children," people for whom she is responsible. This is not arrogance but a way of defining position and identity that allows her to remain distinctly separate in the midst of this tribal grouping. When she feels superior or even only equal to those around her, little Leo is assured that she will not be swallowed up and lost in the mass.

While this assumption of quasiparental role may be irritating to other children and sometimes also to adults, in effect the Leo child provides a temporary environment that allows others to play, enjoy the situation without having to feel responsible for it, and generally behave more spontaneously and creatively.

The young Leo likes challenge, and she especially likes winning. She enjoys conquering difficult tasks and is often more interested in the conquest than in what follows. For the Leo child, the conquest itself is the reward for her efforts. In her intense search for new things to conquer, Leo may appear grandiose, but her large schemes and dreams often work out, much to the astonishment of onlookers. Throwing herself into various tasks, Leo may eventually admit exhaustion, but not for long. This child has stamina and endurance that will accommodate all but the most severe stress.

The Leo child is usually healthy and confident. Even when scared she is full of bravado and often achieves in situations where others give up. Though she takes her work seriously, she allows herself time to play and plays as hard as she works. Leo is aristocratic and generous, with a flair for the dramatic. She sees all the world as her stage and treats the world with the respect due any theater. Families with a dynamic little Leo in their midst find themselves participating in her exciting and challenging life. And since the Leo child is so generous with the rewards of her efforts, other family members often find themselves benefitting emotionally and socially as well.

NEEDS (Leo's emotional emphasis)

Attention.
Approval, support, honest praise, encouragement.
To be listened to, taken seriously.
Humor.
Reasonable responsibility.
To be included.
Good examples and role models.
Not always to have to be strong and cheerful.
Permission to have "negative" needs and feelings.
Mirrors: people who will reflect back accurately, respond honestly.
Permission to be different or the same.
Honesty.
Center stage much of the time.

COMMON ASSUMPTIONS (How Leo views the world around her)

You're nobody 'til somebody loves you.
Laugh and the world laughs with you; cry and you cry alone.
All the world's a stage. . . .

SENSITIVITIES (Potential sources of misunderstanding)

*Drama:* Because the young Leo usually lives intensely, she may believe her needs and feelings will go unnoticed unless they are enormous. She may either wait to have feelings until they feel enormous to her, or she may exaggerate feelings ahead of time in order to have help ready. The young Leo may create her primary emotional connections with people through complaints or crisis. Parents need to monitor the very young Leo to be certain her needs do not reach crisis proportions, and they need to show the older Leo child how to get people's attention without being highly dramatic. Since the young Leo may see lack of drama as boring, she also needs to be shown alternative ways to excite and entertain herself and to learn to see challenge and excitement in both safety and comfort.

The Leo child who is constantly dramatic runs the risk of not being taken seriously when a real crisis occurs. Leos in this mood are prone to wide, sweeping statements such as, "I was never so thrilled/embarrassed/angry/etc. in all my life!" The little boy who cried "Wolf!" was probably a Leo. While these histrionics can be quite entertaining, concerned parents need to respond appropriately rather than join in the drama. They need to offer their attention to little Leo when things aren't at a crisis stage and teach her to ask for and accept nurturing without having to have a crisis first. Nurturing should not become associated with reward for having lived through the latest drama.

Positive outlets for this Leo characteristic exist in theater and politics, and Leos often spontaneously enter both fields, both on a child and adult level.

*Impact:* Little Leo loves to make an impact and often says or does things simply for effect. Often she does not realize the impact of her behavior until there is a response and she counts on the people around her to respond to her presence and actions. If, however, other people's response is negative, little Leo's feelings are easily hurt.

Teaching the Leo child the ability to watch herself and respond to her own actions is the beginning of autonomy and a childhood-long task for both parents and child. She may resist this self-sufficiency at first, assuming it will cut her off from others or that it's having to accept second best. As she realizes the independence that accompanies being able to see and trust her own responses, Leo will become increasingly delighted and self-confident.

Especially if she feels she is hiding parts of herself, the Leo child may never quite believe others like her. She may decide they like only her facade, her mask. While, for example, the Libra child wants everyone to like her, the Leo child concentrates on getting the approval and affection of people she respects. And yet, once she gets this approval and appreciation, she may be confused about its sincerity or afraid it carries hidden obligations. Young Leo needs attention in all her moods and especially needs reassurance that she is delightful and valuable when she is "weak" and needy as well as when she is strong and confident.

The young Leo loves an audience and does her best when people are watching. Since many people dislike being watched, non-Leos may discreetly look away just when Leo is most hoping to grab their attention. And others may be embarrassed to find the Leo child watching them so openly and closely. Permission for little Leo to watch and be watched is an important part of her learning process and will add to her good feelings about herself.

*Confidence:* Leo children tend to look quite self-confident and high in self-esteem, especially when performing and having fun with their own dramatic flair. Some parents respond to this exuberance by deciding that their child thinks too well of herself and trying to curb her personal enthusiasm. This is entirely unnecessary and damaging. Parents need not worry about providing "too much" support, attention or approval for their Leo child to handle. It is not the child with high self-esteem who acts superior or spoiled; it is the child with low self-esteem who desperately tries to compensate for feelings of worthlessness.

*Control:* Little Leo likes to take charge of things and may appear quite bossy as she attempts to make things go her way. She will refine her leadership skills throughout childhood, but she may go through periods of acting superior or arrogant while she experiments with this skill. When she doesn't know what else to do she will act like a little replica of her father or another father figure.

A bossy Leo child is probably frightened. She may believe no one else is taking charge, or they are not as smart as she is and will lead her into unsafe situations. Parents need to reassure their Leo child that they know what they are doing and will competently take care of both themselves and her. If parents reassure little Leo and then make a mistake, however, they may have an indignant child to contend with. The child needs to be taught that everyone makes mistakes, that mistakes are not the same as lack of control and that she too will be supported when she makes mistakes. This permission will relieve little Leo of some of her anxiety about responsibility and allow her to pursue her wilder schemes and challenges.

## RELATIONSHIPS

Since the young Leo often doesn't know how she's behaving until someone responds, relationships with other people are a matter of survival for her. She is intensely aware of others' expectations and reactions and will usually take their opinions into account as she makes decisions for herself. She wants to be noticed and included and may alter her behavior in order to get the attention she needs. She constantly changes and polishes her behavior and appearance until it feels like a fine performance. The effect is not one of changing her patterns as much as of refining them and putting the finishing touches on a work of art. Little Leo may use drama, humor, complaints or crises to begin or maintain intimate attachments to other people.

The Leo child is attracted to power and tends to see people and systems as hierarchies. She will ordinarily choose to affiliate with either the most powerful or the one with the most potential. She likes the equality possible in such relationships and believes some of the power may rub off on her. Her attraction to power, however, can cause her to overlook other important attributes in a person, and little Leo needs to be reminded of other significant areas worth her inspection.

Little Leo will offer her absolute loyalty in exchange for attention and powerful support. She will adamantly stand by a friend, right or wrong. Once her loyalty is given, it usually remains, unquestioned, and she is quite willing to be noisy and active in defense of someone she loves. However, once she feels betrayed, she may never forgive the offender. Since she sometimes awards others her loyalty in return for a small favor or brief support, little Leo can find herself defending a relationship that is draining or dangerous. Parents need to emphasize degrees of loyalty and to help their Leo child to reassess periodically her feelings toward and obligations to various people. "Don't you think you've paid Billy back adequately?" is one way to challenge the absoluteness of the Leo child without minimizing her sense of values.

*Mom:* While the Leo child often feels very secure with her mother and comfortable because she can so easily predict Mom's responses, she may also perceive her mom as private, mysterious and possibly unreachable. When Mom does reach out to little Leo, the child may feel pushed or intruded upon. Mom's own need for privacy may be used by little Leo as permission to go her own way, or it may be seen as neglect.

Moms who are not excited about this way of interacting will take cues from their Leo child. Since small Leo is very sensitive to control, being pushed and issues concerning pride, moms of Leos need to strike a fine balance in order to give the approval this child needs without making it sound like a demand or an intrusion. "I'm so proud of you!" can, at different times, sound like praise or a demand, and Mom herself needs first to know which it is and then to be prepared to explain it to little Leo. Small Leo is also suspicious of interactions that appear automatic and will be skeptical and on guard if Mom always praises or always condemns her work (especially if Mom always uses the same words).

*Dad:* The young Leo usually perceives her dad as affectionate, solid, stolid, reliable and strong. She may think he's unmovable and rigid and see him as moody and defensive, someone to charm and cajole. She may get into power struggles with him if she feels smarter than he is or if she feels he is unfairly controlling her life.

Dads who don't want this image need to remain open-minded about their Leo child. They need to listen carefully to her and give her extra attention without encouraging her to act cute or phony. The Leo child responds well to sensitivity, attention and willingness to cooperate and will usually award Dad her adoration and loyalty if she feels he "deserves" it.

*Siblings:* Opinionated and flamboyant, little Leo may perceive her siblings as weaker, more wishy-washy and less exciting than she is; however, she is usually committed to taking care of and protecting them. Often a strong bond forms between Leo and at least one sibling, if both agree that young Leo is the boss. While the Leo child is often very creative, it is frequently one of her siblings who is called "the artist" in the family.

*Friends:* The young Leo likes to have things her own way and often chooses friends whom she can lead or who don't seem to care about or notice power dynamics. She may have two sets of friends, each very different. One set often consists of children as powerful as or more powerful than she is. Little Leo is loyal and generous with her friends and is usually an exciting companion with whom to hang around. She is often popular and sought after, especially if she also has the power to make a difference in their lives. For example, if she's student body president, even more people will want to be near her.

## MIND/INFORMATION/SCHOOL

The Leo child usually sees school as a place in which to perform, win approval and be appreciated. She may be especially competitive at school and have a strong need to be one of the best students in at least one area. While she is often visual and learns well by reading, she also responds to being shown things and to actual experience, and she may learn a great deal through conversation. Like young Libra and Gemini, she learns best by comparing things and by learning opposites and polarities. At its best, school and play intermingle for young Leo, and she finds herself playing at learning and learning as she plays.

Appeals to the little Leo's heart rather than her head are more effective. If she has an emotional reaction to a piece of information, she will understand and retain it better. Little Leo is also very good at adapting other people's ideas both for entertainment and as part of her own creativity. She may be highly opinionated once she has considered all sides and made a decision. She is as loyal to ideas and causes as she is to people and will defend an ideal as quickly as she does a friend.

*Higher Education:* The older Leo youth is usually initially quite excited about further education but may become bored and move around a bit once the newness has worn off. She excels at what interests her and frequently becomes involved in cause- or socially-related groups. She likes to take newly developed courses and courses about new things and enjoys being the first to learn or master particular areas.

## RESPONSIBILITY/WORK/REWARDS

*Responsibility and Work:* Little Leos take responsibility very seriously and will work hard, especially if there are people nearby who might be impressed. She needs praise along the way or she may not finish the job, and, like Taurus, she needs her own territory. She is patient and will usually see things to their conclusion, and though she definitely has her own way of doing things, she respects the boundaries, goals and limits set for her.

If, on the other hand, no one is watching or if she feels the job she is doing is menial and beneath her talents, young Leo may become quite lazy about finishing it. At these times she is like Tom Sawyer, motivating others to whitewash her fences, delegating responsibility like a pro.

*Rewards:* The Leo child is usually willing to work hard to get things, most notably, recognition and money. Public praise delights her. She likes getting paid for what she does, and if she is being Tom Sawyer, she may even pay her employees. The social interaction of someone else helping her with work is often seen as a reward by the young Leo, and she eagerly accepts affection, additional privileges and toys as rewards for jobs well done. She also loves to eat out and enjoys having such a promise to look forward to while working.

## HOME

Little Leo's home is her castle. It is often a showplace for those treasures she values most, and it is tastefully and, if possible, creatively and expensively decorated. The young Leo likes little nooks and crannies and may store things in unexpected places. The Leo child needs to have her space and privacy respected and will often request a lock on her door or a solid barrier for her part of the room.

The Leo child may spend a great deal of her nonsocial time happily alone in her space, sometimes on the phone. While she will also invite special friends in, she chooses carefully whom to entertain and why. She may decorate her area with a theatrical or sports theme and usually chooses bright, sunny colors for her decor.

## HEALTH

The young Leo usually enjoys fine health. She is robust and strong and can endure for incredibly long periods. She is often matter-of-fact about health and responsible concerning her own habits. Though she loves being treated as a grown-up in most areas, she may fear growing old and watch carefully for symptoms that she believes indicate aging.

If the Leo child gets sick, it's usually because she has overextended herself and needs a rest. Illness may buy time for her or relieve performance anxiety, or it may take her (or her family's) attention away from other distressing problems. When ill, little Leo needs a label for her malady, then she needs a competent and trustworthy adult to take over her care. She likes to sleep a lot when sick, to read and to catch up on all the pleasurable and quiet things she's neglected.

Traditionally, Leo rules the back, bones and chest. A little Leo experiencing health problems may faint, feel weak or get stitches in her side. Her heartbeat may be arrhythmic, and she may have fevers or problems in the area of her eyes or with vision. Leo children are particularly vulnerable to sunstroke and heat exhaustion.

## CHILDHOOD AGES

*(Note: The fears detailed in this section are never to be used as punishment. They are presented as avenues for reassurance and caring).*

### BIRTH–6 MONTHS

The Leo infant is sunny and loving and often unusually healthy. She is amusing and charming and loves being the center of attention. She is vocal about her needs right from the beginning; if her needs are not met within what she deems a reasonable amount of time (usually right away), little Leo may become even more vocal and demanding. A strong child physically and emotionally, tiny Leo may offer parents an immediate challenge to discipline her.

The Leo infant loves games that elicit laughter or attention. She likes being bounced moderately and rituals that involve babies and grown-ups who magically appear and disappear. Gentle tickling and parental mirroring also delight this usually happy baby. Baby Leo makes a wonderful role model to teach other children about babies.

*Needs*
Attention.
Laughter.
Visual stimulation and feedback.
Praise and approval.

*Fears*
Being ignored, overlooked, neglected.
Lack of response.
Hostility from Dad.

## 6 MONTHS–18 MONTHS

The Leo baby is alert and curious. She loves to share her excitement about discoveries with other people and will show off mightily for an audience. She needs lots of interaction with all sorts of people and seems to soak up applause and approval. Even at this age, she likes to make things happen in her environment, and she will begin to choose her behavior for the effect it may have on others. She may seem a charming clown or an angry tyrant, but she is always aware of the nature of the responses she elicits.

*Needs*
Attention, approval, applause.
Feedback, appropriate response.
Social opportunities.
Someone to share things with.

*Fears*
Being ignored, left out, unnoticed.
Disapproval from those she loves.
Reproach.
Limits on her explorations.

## 18 MONTHS–3 YEARS

The Leo toddler is bright, entertaining, delightful and generous. She is tender and can often be seen mimicking her most nurturing parent with her dolls as she learns how to take care of herself and other people. This little Leo is often quite dramatic and may tend to exaggerate the importance of events or people. She may need guidance in deciding when to elaborate a little for the sake of a good story and when to stay with the exact facts. She continues to need lots of attention and approval and is beginning to become skeptical of praise she feels is insincere. Little Leo girls of this age often want to be boys.

Though little Leo is normally cheerful, she may appear extremely controlling and cranky when she cannot have her way. She may be rebellious or contrary as she tests the limits set by her parents and can appear quite bossy with other children if she feels she is powerless in her family. Nevertheless, little Leo can usually be reached through gentle humor, even at this age, and extra effort to kid or cajole her out of a "bad mood" is likely to pay off.

*Toilet Training:* Little Leo responds better to Mom for training than to Dad. While she is fastidious and tends to keep private about such matters, she loves having a fuss made over her and will respond to delighted exclamations from Mom and others alike. If the response is strong and consistent enough, young Leo may train herself all in one day just to experience the resounding approval and appreciation from those she loves.

*Needs*
> Attention, approval, support.
> Encouragement to be curious and to lead.
> Reasonable limits set by parents.
> Reassurance that others are smart and in control.
> Reassurance that parents will protect her.

*Fears*
> Being ignored, replaced, left out, forgotten.
> Being overwhelmed by her own and others' expectations.
> Losing control.
> Public humiliation.

### 3 YEARS–6 YEARS

Although preschool Leo enjoys acting grown up, mature and in charge, she still may suddenly feel little, and alert parents will give equal attention to the mature and immature parts of their child. Little Leo continues to enjoy drama and is beginning to use exaggeration as a tool of entertainment and attention. She may also copy and exaggerate the behavior of her parents, and adults who do not like the mirror small Leo presents need to do something about their own behavior, not Leo's.

If small Leo believes she is more valuable or worthy when she is cheerful and responsible, she may wait until her feelings and needs reach crisis proportions before she talks about them. She may hang on to feelings for a very long time, and her behavior may appear quite erratic until she figures out how to handle her feelings. Concerned parents will ask little Leo what is going on and patiently wait for her to find a way to verbalize her emotions.

Leo of this age is often quite loving and generous, and her social and outgoing nature is very evident. While she is initially friendly toward nearly everyone, her earnest efforts to find an identity she is comfortable with may lead her to behavior that appears arrogant, snobbish or condescending, especially in peer groups. Leo may tease or order other children around as she tests her leadership skills, and she may encourage fighting between peers. She likes to compare herself with other people and "win." For Leo girls, this often means being as good at boys' sports and games as they are.

*Needs*
To be included.
Approval, praise, support.
Compassion.
Honest reactions.
Not to be dismissed.

*Fears*
Being left out or overlooked.
Being publicly (or privately) humiliated, discredited or scolded.
Feeling invisible or unimportant.
Being caught setting up fights and disagreements.
Having to act too grown up or accept too many responsibilities.
Being wrong.

6 YEARS–12 YEARS

The school-age Leo is often responsible and capable. She is in the midst of her conflict concerning how to be a leader and still remain equal, and she rapidly learns leadership and management skills. If she takes on a lot of leadership during this period, the young Leo can be rather rebellious and inflexible and have difficulty empathizing with those around her whom she views as her "children." Leo may exhibit a false cheerfulness that she thinks will win her support, or she may act quite superior or defensive to convince others she is capable of the jobs she wants. She may act quite argumentative as she sorts through her own values and ethics. When she is very busy, what work she does may be sloppy; parents will need to teach young Leo how to prioritize her activities and how to do what she says she'll do.

This child may be loud, boisterous and intensely physical. She is extremely loyal to friends and may be aggressive in their defense or her own. Simultaneously, she is learning to be charming, and parents watching their little Leo's experiments may have to suppress smiles at her abrupt tactical changes. Especially during this period, the young Leo needs to feel a sense of control over her environment in order to feel safe. She may arrange and rearrange things, herself and other people endlessly toward that goal.

During this time it's easy for parents to begin to feel that little Leo is ready to live out their dreams. They may become quite intrusive or demanding, expecting their Leo child to behave in certain, specific ways or to make very specific choices based on what the parents themselves want. The school-age Leo is very sensitive to even covert demands, and while she may indeed try to live up to these expectations, she sacrifices part of her identity and spontaneity to do so. Parents at this time need to exercise extra caution to be sure they allow young Leo to determine her own identity, goals and preferences.

*Needs*

Approval, encouragement, support, praise, applause.
Firm structure and limits; protection.
Playtime.
Learning cooperation.
Attention from Dad (for both boys and girls).
To be accountable for what she says she'll do.

*Fears*

Invisibility, being left out or ignored.
Humiliation.
Having to live up to an unrealistic standard; being found imperfect.

Having to be too competent or responsible.
Disapproval or competition from Dad.

## 12 YEARS–18 YEARS

The adolescent Leo is quite individualistic and often very courageous. She is intensely aware of other people's responses to her and
may appear brash, loud, flamboyant or even outrageous as she tests
her impact. Because she is dramatic and often seeks center stage,
her behavior may appear self-important, grandiose, egotistical or
controlling; in reality, she is reflecting the variety of behaviors she
has witnessed throughout her short life. Her need for support
continues, and she may cover her feelings with laughter in order to
win approval or change her perception of something that didn't turn
out as she planned. Thus, if she loses the election for president, she
may insist that she never really wanted it at all; if she says something
a person important to her disagrees with, she may pretend she was
joking. It is hard during this time to know when young Leo is serious
and when she is joking, and she is not likely to tell. Theater is
obviously a wonderful outlet for the Leo adolescent. She also
benefits from jobs working with children.

The teenage Leo may feel she *has* to lead, that everyone is
watching her for cues. She may feel like a role model and become
extremely self-conscious as she tries to live up to others' expectations, especially if those expectations are in conflict with her internal values. She is loyal and stubborn and may align herself with a
particular side simply to relieve the pressure she feels to please
everyone, or she may insist that the idiosyncratic way she has
chosen to handle conflict is simply "her way." While she is proud,
her "pride" is often a cover for deep insecurity and feelings of being
an impostor that no one really knows. Parents often need to bypass
Leo's proud and self-confident front to reach the little child who still
lives within. She is likely to rebel against precisely those things the
family is proud of; parents need to remain aware that a new, more
substantive pride is building and permit their Leo offspring to make
her own choices and decisions.

Relationships are very important to teenage Leo, and she seems
to be involved in everyone else's business. Though she is loyal, she
may also gossip if she feels this will earn approval. She may try to

obtain friendship through compliments, gifts or favors, and she may feel betrayed and lost if her gifts are refused and dismissed. She wants to be adored, desired and loved by everyone. She may anguish for hours if she believes someone important doesn't like her or she may pretend she doesn't really care. For Leo, a steady partner is often a badge of success and desirability: either a best friend or a beau or, preferably, both. She may flirt outrageously with many people and seem to offer a great deal, but sexually Leo is shy and romantic and probably not behaving as brazenly as others believe or fear. Young Leo usually welcomes her body changes as evidence of increased maturity and competence. Both genders frequently like the way their bodies feel and decorate themselves with care.

### Needs

Approval, etc.
Firm boundaries and limits and rules.
Honest feedback about appearance and behavior.
To be held accountable for her behavior.
Parental pride but not overinvestment in her choices.
Support for new behaviors and endeavors.
Permission to experiment with new behaviors.
Leadership skills and opportunities.

### Hates

Being called petty, impersonal, overdramatic, egotistical.
Feeling ashamed or humiliated.
Pressure to perform.
Being left out, excluded, ignored.
Secrets.
Being told, "You're too young to know about . . ."
Being reminded, "But you always . . . before."
Being asked to "Do it for me . . ."

# VIRGO CHILDREN
**AUGUST 23–SEPTEMBER 22**

## GENERAL CHARACTERISTICS
*(Note: While many of the characteristics described below will be accurate for most Virgos, other, sometimes contradictory, traits may also be evident in an individual child.)*

Parents will regard newborn Virgo as one of the sweetest, most gentle babies around. The Virgo baby is alert and quiet, shy and sensitive to his environment. He loves affection and cuddling and responds with an intense gaze and slow smile to attention that is all for him. Since later on young Virgo may act quite self-sufficient and think he has to reject demonstrations of love and affection in order to maintain his independence, Virgo's affection-loving infancy is a good time for parents to establish a base of warmth and trust in their relationship with this child. Virgo loves to be talked to, cooed at and played with. He will respond in astonishingly wise ways, even as a tiny tot.

Affection and playful touch help the Virgo child of any age stay in touch with his body. More than children of other signs, little Virgo values his bodily integrity. He has a concrete sense of physical boundaries and fears intrusion or getting hurt. Unnecessary explorations of young Virgo's body, such as probing for new teeth or fussing over regular bowel movements, may feel particularly intrusive to the Virgo child. Parents who are overly concerned with the Virgo child's health or growth may inadvertently teach him to regard his body as fragile or to assume there is something wrong with him physically.

At the other extreme, parental neglect of small Virgo's health or bodily needs may support unrealistic expectations about physical stamina or disregard for bodily functions. Even on his own, the Virgo child will tend to see himself as either physically invincible or frail. He may jump on his bicycle the first day of spring and head off on a twenty-mile trek or be afraid to pedal around the block without training wheels.

A young Virgo therefore needs time and privacy to get acquainted with his own body and to develop realistic expectations about his physical limits. He needs careful guidance from parents in learning what to expect of his body and how to read signs of fatigue or illness. Throughout his growth, he will need help understanding what is enough, what is too much, and what is reasonable to expect of himself physically.

If he cannot get this guidance from adults, little Virgo will devise his own ways of protecting himself and guarding his physical integrity. He may develop patterns of angry, bullying behavior to keep people far enough away so they cannot hurt him. Or he may become docile and passive in attempts to reduce the possibility of other people behaving aggressively toward him.

Young Virgos seek perfection in all things. Virgo children will try mightily to be perfect children and often feel inadequate when they fail at impossible tasks or self-expectations. People who love Virgos need to be sensitive to this internal disappointment and fear of failure. No one is perfect, but it seems harder for the Virgo child to accept his imperfections than for children of most other signs. Parents who want to help reduce little Virgo's sense of inadequacy can reassure him that perfection is not expected and help him set realistic and easy-to-meet standards. Just as Virgos need help setting realistic expectations for their bodies, they will need help understanding what is enough, what is too much, and what is reasonable to expect of themselves in general. Left to decide this issue alone, Virgos tend to think they can do anything they put their minds to or assume they will fail at anything they try.

There are several behavior signs parents can watch for to know when their Virgo child is struggling with his expectations of perfection. One typical response to his sense of inadequacy is to give up without trying. He may have difficulty starting or finishing things: projects not started cannot fail, and projects not finished cannot be judged poorly. Virgo often assumes he can't actually do something as well as he imagines doing it in his mind's eye. He may thus refuse to become very involved in projects or attached to anything as a way of dealing with his predicted disappointment.

On the other side, Virgo may decide to drive himself mercilessly, to fret and worry over tasks until they meet his standards (or the standards he assumes others have of him). It is very hard to convince a Virgo in this mood that what he is doing is already good enough. He may come close to finishing a project and become so frightened by his internal pressure that he messes it up at the last minute and insists on starting over. He may fluster easily or become suddenly disorganized in the midst of a methodical routine. Contradictory impulses can occur simultaneously. For example, the same Virgo child who completes his homework with excruciating care may crumple it into his lunchbox to take to school.

Parents need to intervene with clearly stated limits and expectations, with approval, feedback and reassurance during any major task. Told to clean his room, the Virgo child may make it a day-long chore, become overwhelmed with details and lose sight of his overall plan. Mom may find him using his toothbrush to clean off carefully all the book tops while the rest of the room still awaits dusting.

Parents can provide their little Virgo with both nurturing and realistic assessment of how he's doing and what could be improved. Even as a young child, Virgo is introspective about his shortcomings, or his projects' shortcomings, and wants thoughtful, respectful adult feedback. While he needs to be taught that everyone does not have the same standards and allow himself to modify his own standards, he does not want to believe he can fool grown-ups into accepting things that do not live up to his ideals.

Young Virgos enjoy being shown how to do things and helped to produce satisfactory results. They would rather accept respectfully offered assistance than waste time making mistakes and having to learn everything the hard way. The key word to helping a Virgo child in the midst of a task is *respect*. Parents who notice when their Virgo child looks frustrated and say, "That won't work, here's how to do it," will earn little Virgo's gratitude, respect and loyalty. However, little Virgo often has definite ideas about the way to do things and should be allowed to follow his chosen course whenever possible. The Virgo child doesn't mind being told what to do or having goals set for him, but he does mind being told *how* to do something unless he has specifically requested the information.

Virgo is the most efficient sign of the zodiac. If anyone can figure out the least wasteful way to get things done or the straightest distance from here to there, it is little Virgo. The Virgo child's precocity in this area will surprise even the most efficient adults.

Since small Virgos are usually quite modest, adults may tend to underestimate their abilities. Occasionally, the Virgo child may appear overly humble and use false modesty to elicit reassurance from adults. Once again, realistic assessment will give the Virgo child a sense of security and perspective. Emphasis on analysis and constructive criticism teaches small Virgo how to appraise situations realistically and set manageable goals. Parents need to remember to provide data for their little Virgo and avoid opinion, teasing remarks or empty praise.

Though his standards are high, the Virgo child generally has a pretty accurate assessment of what he can and cannot do, and he will respond honestly to parental inquiries. All parents need to do is ask, "Do you want to do that yourself or do you want me to help you?" One serious three-year-old Virgo, when asked to retrieve something from the basement, told his father, "I am big enough to reach the light switch and go downstairs, but I'm not big enough to reach the hammer." When father and son went to the basement together, the boy was right; he was three inches too short to reach the required tool. Letting little Virgo set his own pace is the most successful and comfortable way to parent him. A Virgo will efficiently tell or show observant parents what he needs from them. The only areas in which it is not safe for parents to wait for Virgo's clues are those already discussed—understanding his body and coping with his drive for perfection.

The Virgo child is observant, watchful and wise. Little passes by him unnoticed. He sees flaws where others have overlooked them, but he also sees redeeming qualities in areas others have ignored. He is an inventor and innovator and will often use these talents to heal himself or others or to make things more safe or organized. His criticism is offered in the service of efficiency or beauty and appropriateness and is seldom used as a weapon. He is not cruel.

Since the Virgo child seeks perfection, he may become quite disappointed when events and people don't meet his expectations. A Virgo planning a day with grandma at the zoo will have a very concise image in his mind of how the day should go, what would make it perfect and what he should do to contribute to this perfection. Not being able to wear his favorite T-shirt, a cloud in the sky or grandma suffering from a head cold are all blemishes that mar his ideal image. To reduce the possibility of disappointment, a Virgo child tends to sound cynical or pretend to have lower expectations when planning future events. He is simply preparing himself to cope with the difference between his fantasy and reality. "Grandma says she can go on Tuesday. It'll probably rain." "What do you mean, it's in the laundry. I *told* you I was going to wear that shirt . . . Now I don't care what I wear."

If these comments begin to sound familiar, look up the character Eeyore the donkey in *Winnie-the-Pooh*. Reading these stories aloud will give the young Virgo a character to identify with, someone he understands perfectly.

"Good morning, Eeyore," said Pooh.

"Good morning, Pooh Bear," said Eeyore . . . "If it is a good morning, which I doubt."

Grown-ups who react defensively to the verbal cynicism and critical attitude of the Virgo child need to remember that these statements reflect the quieter criticism little Virgo imposes on himself. Rather than fighting with Virgo to change his attitude, parents will be better off showing him through patient and loving examples. Parents who tolerate life's little disappointments with poise will teach their child to do the same. Parents who emphasize the positive aspects in people, especially in themselves, will teach their child to celebrate himself—even if he isn't perfect.

Little Virgo cannot be easily lied to. He detects falsity in people and in their reactions to him. The Virgo child is especially attuned to rationalization and denial in people and will demand honesty and truthful appraisal within those relationships he values. Virgo is in relentless pursuit of accurate data and carries on a lifelong search for honest information.

The Virgo child's need for data and his willingness to challenge other people's information may annoy those who are more careless with facts and reasons. For example, a parent trying to exaggerate the size of a fish caught on a recent trip will have trouble doing so in the hearing of his very accurate Virgo child. A small Virgo who has been misinformed may assume he was intentionally lied to and pursue sorting out truth from falsehood with great single-mindedness.

Virgo children are intrigued by details and categories and need lots of specifics. They also want to develop a comprehensive understanding of the overall picture. This is not only the way Virgos think but the way they talk. Ask a Virgo of almost any age how his week went, and watch his way of processing information in action. While this seemingly endless analysis and synthesis of information may appear trivial or unproductive to less patient adults and children, it is an urgently needed and necessary gift in our highly technological society and is not to be dismissed lightly. People often seek out even young Virgos to verify information or to help them remember the exact details of an event. Little Virgos love being asked to share their collected data, and may offer much more information than is asked for. Virgo children need to be taught to answer only the questions they are asked; adults need to remember not to punish honest little Virgo for what he knows or for accurately giving the information requested.

A similar dynamic occurs with the Virgo child's efficiency and task orientation. If you want something done, ask a Virgo. Young Virgos are often invited to parties or club meetings when there is a task to be accomplished. The Virgo child will usually settle down to finish the business at hand before relaxing into playtime. People nearby need to remember that one of the reasons they invited little Virgo was to assure that the work would be done. It would, therefore, be unfair to criticize the child for being a "party pooper" or in other ways embarrass him about his work talents.

Little Virgo often needs permission to play and to receive satisfaction from playing. He tends to postpone pleasure indefinitely, until "after this is done" or "when I'm through with school work." He may make play into work or expect even his casual productions to be perfect. Conversely, a Virgo child may choose not even to play if he feels he cannot participate well. A Virgo on the Little League team expects himself to be a valuable and appreciated team member and may need some private coaching to improve skills before he's willing to join in activities in which he's not sure of excelling.

Virgo needs to be productive and wants to have something to show for his efforts. Work is very important to Virgo, even at an early age. He can often be found hanging around parents, sincerely wanting to help in adult tasks. Being helpful seems to be little Virgo's mission in life, and he is often happiest doing something important well. He is more willing to do repetitive work than children of other signs and will work long and hard when he believes his task is meaningful and contributes somehow to the quality of his own life or the lives of those around him. Young Virgos will often do the chores no one else in the family wants to do. Parents need to be careful not to take advantage of their Virgo child's willingness in this area, but to make sure chores are evenly divided among children or other family members.

The Virgo child is careful, methodical and reliable. He will organize things and people until they are "just right." He may eat only one thing on his plate at a time—usually going from worst to best. His sense of appropriateness is nearly flawless, and when this is combined with his sense of perfection, he is seldom in error. Parents can count on their young Virgo to handle himself well in social settings, to ease family gatherings with behind-the-scene work and to know how to behave around adults and authority. However, Virgo may seem finicky or slow while he does things in his own way, at his own time.

Though clean and organized, little Virgos are not necessarily tidy. Their own rooms may overflow with projects and seemingly disorganized clutter. However, a small Virgo can locate anything in his chaotic environment at a moment's notice. There is, indeed, a system to how he does things that may not be apparent to astonished adults. Young Virgo loves categories and lists and will somehow always manage to know where things belong and where they are, both physically and mentally. Though he enjoys the freedom to leave his own space in creative chaos, young Virgo is very respectful of other people's environment and will usually leave someone else's space exactly as he finds it—or a little bit neater.

The Virgo child's way of thinking is intensely process oriented. He pays attention to the means as well as the ends. In other words, *how* he gets there is as important to a Virgo as *where* he is going. Planting the garden carefully is as important as harvesting the vegetables later. He tends to be thorough, carefully completing one step before going on to the next. He is intrigued by how things work. Virgos of both genders often show early mechanical or technical skills. Little Virgos are equally intrigued by how people think and feel. They are interested in emotional process as well as actual feelings. It's not sufficient data to tell a young Virgo, "I'm angry."

He also wants an explanation of what happened, what caused the anger, what needs to be done to solve the problem and how the anger is going to be dealt with.

As part of this attention to process, young Virgos are often intrigued with change and growth and are comfortable and adept around all small forms of life. They know how to treat kittens, plants, baby siblings or butterflies. Virgo children intuitively understand cycles and patiently watch for changes in direction and repetition of events. They may compare each birthday with former ones or catalog how the family has celebrated Christmas or the Fourth of July for the past five years. They like to have four seasons and five weekdays and are especially drawn to rhythm: music, poetry that rhymes and chants.

Since he accepts cycles so well, the Virgo child is usually quite adaptable and matter-of-fact regarding life changes. Though he dislikes surprises that seem to affect him adversely (like rain on the day he's going to the zoo with grandma), he will generally adapt well, even to events that appear disastrous. For example, if the garage burns down, he will become fascinated by the process of clearing debris, rebuilding, blueprints and what the new garage will look like. In spite of this inborn adaptability, little Virgo will react more readily to events if he is prepared in advance with careful explanations. This is not a child who should be tricked into visits to the dentist but who will accept the necessity of dental care once it's been explained to him.

When making his own decisions, young Virgo tends to be conservative. He is cautious and practical and will realistically assess a situation and avoid risks when possible. Virgo is quite discriminating and can find nuances of difference in choices that seem identical to others. He likes to think, ponder and consider options and then to apply his judgment concretely. Because he takes time to process information mentally before acting, he may experience several changes of mind before making a final decision. The Virgo child tends to go with the tried and true. He is skeptical and literal. He likes proof. He likes to test things and to experiment. He will frequently rely on his own experience as the best teacher and believes if he can't touch something, it doesn't quite exist.

Virgos try new things only at their own pace. It may be difficult for adults to convince a Virgo child that riding the Ferris wheel would be fun, but on the next trip to the amusement park they can share in his readiness for the experience and his delight at his courage.

Despite this apparent skepticism, little Virgo remains curious and intensely interested in the world. His search for perfection is ultimately a spiritual journey that can lead to an intense interest in nature, the arts or healing. Virgo is interested in things other people overlook and in people others dismiss as unimportant. The Virgo child can talk with equal comfort to an autistic child, a senile relative, a frog he just found or a pine tree.

Virgo is a survivor. He is committed to making things better, and this commitment includes healing whenever he can. Young Virgo will bandage a wounded bird's wing or try to hatch an abandoned egg. He may take an early interest in the curative (or poisonous) properties of plants, or be able to rattle off information on herbs and their uses. He may later become interested in formal aspects of health care and function well in medical professions, due to his innate respect for the human body. Little Virgo loves fixing things.

Though the Virgo child's humor blossoms early, it is often such dry wit, and sophisticated beyond childishness, that parents miss it altogether and fret that their child is humorless. Virgo children usually love words, and their humor often takes the form of puns, plays on words or occasional sarcasm. They are bright and articulate, and often find outlets for this skill with words through poetry, debate, reporting or critical analysis.

Parents generally enjoy having a clever, considerate and helpful little Virgo around. Virgo children seem to bring a sense of order into families, which makes life a little easier and more rewarding for everyone. They are well behaved, responsible and reliable children who are eager to please and respond instantly to kindness. Their innate efficiency and organizational abilities make them attractive to people who are less attentive to details. Virgo may quickly become the family member most counted on to handle chores of daily maintenance or to keep track of schedules. Little Virgo's subtle humor, caring and flexibility are delightful in any situation and especially appreciated in times of stress. Though usually quiet and gentle, young Virgo is Johnny-on-the-spot, willing to help and to fix things.

## NEEDS (Virgo's emotional emphasis)

Information.
Explanations.
Permission to play, relax, be unproductive.
Permission to fail.
Permission to get dirty.
Permission to be proud of himself.
Order, predictability.
Rules, limits.
Affection and control over touching.
Recognition.
Social activities.
Help nearby and available.
Help starting things.
Respect for idiosyncrasies.
Frequent rests.
Conversation.
Not to be taken advantage of.
Not to be stuck with only menial chores.
Not to have to grow up too soon.
Not to be forced.
Not to be physically hurt.
Not to be held responsible for other people's pain.

## COMMON ASSUMPTIONS (How Virgo views the world around him)

I'm strong; I should not need protection.
If only things were different . . .
Perfection is a worthy goal.
Anything can be fixed; everything needs to be fixed.
If I allow myself to really want something, I won't get it.

## SENSITIVITIES (Potential sources of misunderstanding)

*Health:* If young Virgo grows up with a distorted view of his body, he may feel unable to determine accurately when it is in need of extra attention and care. He may therefore react either with apparent disinterest in his bodily functioning or with preoccupation with signals he regards as potential symptoms of illness. The young Virgo is often quite frightened at the loss of control illness represents and may act very passive or agitated at the prospect of his own or others' sickness or injury. Little Virgos appreciate learning correct hygiene habits early and may voluntarily adopt healthy eating and exercise patterns while still quite young. Knowledge of bodily systems and functions often reassures little Virgo, and participation in the care of younger siblings or animals helps him identify physical malfunction and keep his own body in perspective.

*Criticism from Others:* Though Virgo children are extremely sensitive to criticism from those they respect, they much prefer honest evaluation to rationalizations or lies. Generally, young Virgo knows when something is wrong and may often know what it is. What he seeks from others is validation of his own perceptions and help in correcting the situation. Adults in positions to judge little Virgo's behavior and achievements would do well to rememeber to give advice as well as criticism or to help young Virgo find his own better way.

*Criticism from Himself:* Criticism serves a variety of functions for the Virgo child. He uses self-criticism or self-critique to exercise and challenge his restless young mind. Criticism reflects little Virgo's search for perfection and his subsequent disappointment upon discovering that all is indeed not perfect. Criticism also serves the Virgo child's need for efficiency: he will most often criticize that which is wasteful, ineffective or inappropriate. In his pursuit of appropriate and effective options, the young Virgo can be an excellent troubleshooter or arts critic, and he is nearly always socially adept.

The young Virgo may also use criticism as a way to reassure himself that others are indeed as human as he is. He may identify a flaw without really wanting it to change. Adults who become defensive at his catalog of imperfections need to ask little Virgo what reassurance he really needs. The Virgo child seldom uses criticism to maintain feelings of superiority; more often it soothes his feelings of personal inadequacy. Adults who teach little Virgo to accept what he must and to change what he can will be setting their observant little child on an easier and more rewarding path.

*Order:* More than children of any other sun sign, young Virgos need order in their lives. They are methodical, thorough and erratically fastidious. Though they adapt well to most situations, they appreciate knowing in advance what will happen, how and why.

Virgo is a natural pacifist who sees order in chaos and looks for a spiritual sense of perfection in the midst of change. He may explain politics or religion with an insight beyond his years. He presents a vision to those around him of what the world might someday be and works toward that inner vision in ways both large and small.

Young Virgos usually devise their own system of organization, both in their lives and with their possessions, and may become quite upset if others tamper with their affairs or belongings. They may appear quite intolerant of other people's less careful arrangements. They also usually hate noise, perceiving it as but another sign of a disorderly environment.

*Reality:* Practical, pragmatic and sometimes quite literal, little Virgo often refuses to have fantasies. Disappointment can be a shattering experience for the Virgo child. Once he has experienced a reality that fell short of his expectations, young Virgo may decide to try avoiding disappointment by refusing to hope for better things in the future. He may act bitter, sarcastic or skeptical. He may try to eliminate all expectations and pretend to be content and grateful for anything he receives. Adults near an unhappy little Virgo need to offer him other options for handling his distress: alternative plans, trying again or sometimes simply allowing the disappointment to run its course with the aid and nurturing of compassionate grown-ups.

Little Virgos are often deeply spiritual but may suffer the same sort of disappointment when their idea of God appears to let them down or things happen that they find incomprehensible. Concerned adults need to affirm the disappointment and help little Virgo accept that no human being can ever understand or justify everything that happens. Young Virgo also needs to know that his unmet expectations were not foolish and their lack of fulfillment is not a reflection of his worthiness as a person. He needs to know he is not being punished by fate and that he has the right to continue to hope.

*Survival:* Virgos of all ages are keenly aware of the requirements for survival at a mundane, daily level. Young Virgos often notice changes, unusual events or variations in patterns that others overlook. They may appear hypersensitive, overreactive or just touchy.

They may seem to worry more or start worrying earlier than those around them. The Virgo child may be the first to notice that the family is running out of milk or the first to smell smoke coming from the basement. It is important that adults respond to his perceptions and teach him what to *do* with this stimuli. Since the Virgo child is usually quick to shoulder responsibility, he needs to be able to tell an interested adult who will take him seriously and assume responsibility for action.

*Pleasure and Play:* Small Virgo may believe he has to earn the right to relax or play; and since he never feels quite perfect enough, he may withhold pleasure from himself or put himself in situations where relaxation is impossible. Virgo tends to see pleasure as reward and will forego the pleasure if he believes he has not earned the reward. As mentioned earlier, the Virgo child may postpone pleasure until he thinks he's earned the right to it or make his play into work, seeking some "redeeming" quality for the apparent frivolity. Virgo children need plenty of permission to relax, take time out, reward themselves on the way to their goals (not only after they've reached them) and to enjoy themselves even when they haven't been perfect. In other words, young Virgos need to be taught to eat their desserts first.

## RELATIONSHIPS

Socially, young Virgos are often quite cautious, preferring to relate to living things other than humans. They may test social skills on pets and dolls before venturing out into the world. While they can be witty, charming and quite adamant with those they know and trust, Virgo children may appear shy and aloof around strangers and behave with quiet compliance, especially near those they wish to impress. They may extend their high standards to those around them and experience either chronic disappointment or eternal gratitude for whatever attention they get. As adults acknowledge and explain (rather than defend) their own imperfections, little Virgo will also gain permission to be less than perfect himself. Young Virgos need to feel safe, however, and if they perceive that adults' imperfections threaten their safety, they may believe they have to become even more perfect to accommodate the lack. Frank discussion of the relationship between safety and perfection will make life easier for all concerned.

*Mom:* Virgo children see their moms as quite similar to their dads: knowledgeable, restless and easygoing. Young Virgos are also likely to value Mom's humor, warmth and honesty and to have a firm belief in Mom's acceptance of them. On the other hand, moms of Virgos are likely to have strong and unshakable beliefs and opinions concerning the ways of the world and of children. These moms may therefore encounter problems with their child's probing and analytical challenges to those beliefs. Moms who do not perceive in themselves the warmth, acceptance and humor their child values may want to reassess their self-concepts and relax around their offspring. Explanations of her occasional cool or humorless days will help little Virgo align his expectations with reality. Moms of young Virgos tend to trust their child's instincts and behavior but need to exercise care to avoid giving the child too much or too little responsibility. Moms of little Virgos may not have a lot of patience with their child's learning process and need to be reminded periodically that their sweet, curious, helpful little child is indeed still a child.

*Dad:* Little Virgo often has—or needs—two father figures and sometimes feels caught between their conflicting values. Nevertheless, Virgo children expect dads to be knowledgeable, witty, funny, charming and easygoing. Sometimes the Virgo child may seek more intimate interaction from Dad than Dad feels capable of giving, and occasionally young Virgo may appear quite disgusted with the apparent superficiality—or lack of accuracy—of Dad's information.

Fathers of Virgo children may feel quite nervous or inept around their observant little offspring. Acknowledging their discomfort and discussing and implementing ways to increase comfort for both parent and child may alleviate some of Dad's concern. Dads will please and reassure little Virgo most easily and least self-consciously simply by talking to or working beside the child, giving small Virgo the information and responsibility he requests. Virgo children respect dads who honestly acknowledge the limits of their information and who are willing to seek out answers to their endless questions. Young Virgo needs to know Dad is smart and knows what he is doing and/or that he will seek the information necessary in a particular situation.

*Siblings:* Young Virgo is often an only child or the only child of that gender. Somehow he feels unique and different from his siblings. If someone else in the family has problems, little Virgo will often try to compensate with exemplary behavior, thereby becoming the favorite or the scapegoat (or both). Virgo needs to be reminded that he cannot make up for another's real or perceived shortcomings and that each person is valuable in his or her own unique ways. The Virgo child usually has intense feelings toward at least one sibling and frequently the atmosphere is highly competitive.

*Friends:* The young Virgo usually seeks friends who are at approximately the same social level as he, rather than those who are the same age. Thus, Virgo may have friends much older or much younger. Often his friends are as introspective as he is, though frequently noisier. They share the same values, often a mutual interest in learning or in nature. A shared criticism of something exernal is often enough to bind Virgo to his friends. Virgo children and friends tend to exchange a great deal of nurturing and information. Together they may seem more critical and rebellious than either is alone. Since little Virgo's standards for friends are nearly as high as those he has for himself, he may periodically encounter difficulty making friends or keeping playmates.

## MIND/INFORMATION/SCHOOL

Virgo children are highly analytical and exploratory. Curious little Virgo is pragmatic and practical and often will remember only useful or interesting information. His thinking is usually quite linear, and he needs to have information organized in a logical manner. Though he has the ability to synthesize disparate bits of data into a cohesive and meaningful whole, he tends primarily to recall only details, sometimes neglecting the larger picture. He is a reliable little data bank and can be counted on to give accurate information.

The Virgo child enjoys routine but dislikes repetition once he has learned the assigned task. He learns unevenly, in great bursts, often at inconvenient or surprising times. He may become quite passionate about a new interest, and that intensity generally remains until he has mastered the area to his satisfaction. He knows a great deal intuitively and may collect data and files to verify what he already knows. He loves categories and often has scrapbooks and cubbyholes filled with things even while very young.

The young Virgo responds best to experiential, hands-on learning and dislikes sitting still and listening. He is usually adept with mechanical and technical skills and masters techniques with remarkable speed when physiologically ready. His ability to criticize becomes an asset at school as he handles and evaluates vast quantities of data. This critical quality may not, however, endear him to teachers or classmates who do not like having their information challenged.

Little Virgo loves learning useful things, generally enjoys school and is quite proud of his abilities and accomplishments. If school is the only place in which he feels competent and secure, pressure may mount for him to continue his high level of achievement. He is likely to read about a subject before it's even taught, to complete assignments ahead of time and to worry about the amount of work he feels compelled to do. He may become quite competitive at school and feel threatened by others' equivalent skills. Or he may give up in hopelessness at meeting his own expectations and decide to do only enough to get by. Parents and teachers alike may be perplexed by the resulting "underachievement." Making certain rewards are forthcoming in other areas of young Virgo's life will help alleviate some of the pressure he feels at school and free him to dare to fail. Young Virgos often believe mistakes equal failure and will avoid risking error if it threatens their self-esteem. Adult acknowledgment that successful people make mistakes and learn from them will be reassuring and enlightening to the Virgo child.

*Higher Education:* The young Virgo's pursuit of higher education usually depends heavily on family values in that area. Often Virgo's additional education is interrupted. If and when he does choose to continue, he usually just barges through. He likes the promise of increased income and security. He still enjoys experiential activities and does best in apprenticeships and internships. Since his need to be excellent also continues, he is usually as meticulous in his advanced learning as he was in previous years.

## RESPONSIBILITY/WORK/REWARDS

*Responsibility and Work:* Young Virgos take their responsibilities seriously and are usually conscientious in carrying out tasks. With their attention to detail, they may spend inordinate amounts of time in areas that seem insignificant to observing adults and need to be guided back to original goals. In their efforts to have things "just right," Virgos may have difficulty starting or finishing tasks. With these exceptions, little Virgo can be counted on to carry out expected chores with a minimum of supervision by parents.

Since Virgo children often do not mind doing chores no one else wants, they may feel exploited, ignored, and sometimes ridiculed. Rewards are especially important for this little child, who carries on regardless. Like the young Aquarius, the Virgo child does not like being the only one who knows how to do something and will cheerfully share whatever information and skills he has.

Virgo children love to be helpful and get a great deal of satisfaction from a job well done. They may want to offer help to others when help is not wanted and need to be reminded that people nearby will ask for help if they need it and that he can ask if they want it before he pitches in.

Little Virgos often enjoy tasks, play at working and feel proud and useful when they've accomplished something. Their tendency to sometimes perceive work as more important than play may make for a rather unbalanced childhood. Concerned adults need to encourage little Virgo to take time off for "frivolity." The young Virgo also usually prefers to do two tasks at once. Since he is likely to do both well, adults need not be concerned that performance on one will suffer and can encourage the child to develop his own style.

*Rewards:* The Virgo child sometimes feels that he—or his environment—will go out of control if he allows himself too much playtime or relaxation. A wonderful reward, then, for the young Virgo is permission, encouragement and sometimes even the means to relax and play. Young Virgo sometimes needs to be reminded that he does not have to earn the right to play or be loved. Affectionate demonstrations of love and effusive statements of approval and appreciation are rewards little Virgo soaks up. Virgo children also like rewards of money, clothing and items relating to whatever interests them at the time.

## HOME

The Virgo child likes his space orderly, comfortable and fairly traditional. While the order of his space may not be immediately apparent to interested observers, the young Virgo can usually locate any of his possessions at a moment's notice and becomes quite upset if things are rearranged without his permission or knowledge. Little Virgo has special places for special things and is often surrounded by items or pictures from nature. In later childhood he may add collections of mechanical things that interest him. Virgo children most often prefer earth tones and deep blues. They like durability and may become impatient with furniture that is fragile or easily broken.

Though Virgo children are excellent and adaptable travelers, frequently the best part of the journey is coming home.

## HEALTH

Virgo children are very curious about health and illness. They are usually intrigued by others' ailments and seek as much information as possible about body systems and malfunctions. Though they may choose not to use the information they have, they usually have an excellent grasp of ways to stay healthy and of general hygiene.

A sick or injured Virgo child needs immediate attention and reassurance. In some respect illness is the worst thing the young Virgo can imagine, and he has either avoided it altogether or has actively embraced that which he most feared—"to get it over with." Virgo children may therefore ignore their bodies or pay detailed attention to each symptom. The young Virgo may use illness as a means of avoiding the pressure of responsibilities and to get permission to take care of himself, or he may get sick as a reaction to stress and chaos. When sick, he likes some activity and select attention from friends. He likes his privacy but fears being left entirely alone.

Traditionally, Virgo rules the small intestine and the nervous system. A young Virgo experiencing health problems may act restless and irritable. He may have minor accidents due to carelessness. He may not handle small aches and pains well, though he can be quite stoic with intense discomfort. Young Virgos are also prone to digestive problems, colic, ulcers and allergies.

## CHILDHOOD AGES

*(Note: The fears detailed in this section are never to be used as punishment. They are presented as avenues for reassurance and caring.)*

BIRTH–6 MONTHS

Parents will find sweet and serious newborn Virgo hard to resist. This gentle infant is usually undemanding and adaptable. He loves being held and cuddled and needs to sense that the stroking is just for him and not a reward for good behavior. Little Virgo cries only when in physical distress. He likes to be clean and may squawk earlier than other babies at dirty diapers or wet sheets. If his environment is stressful, tiny Virgo may experience stomach problems or become finicky; parents who remove the source of distress will often find that infant Virgo returns quickly to his placid self. Tiny Virgos are quick to notice changes in their environment and respond well to explanations and preparation even at this age. As they get older, this characteristic becomes more pronounced, but even the newborn Virgo is observant and alert.

*Needs*
Cuddling for pleasure.
Clean, orderly environment.
Preparation or explanation for changes.
Eye-to-eye contact.
To be played with.
Soft clothing.
Consistency.
Contact with a variety of adults and children.

*Fears*
Physical discomfort or neglect.
Being pushed beyond physical capacities.

6 MONTHS–18 MONTHS

The Virgo baby is methodical and loves taking things apart and putting them back together again. He enjoys stacking things and toys that nest or fit together. Alert and curious, he notes all that is occurring around him and is quick to see deviations from patterns. He frequently begins talking early and is intrigued with labels. "Blue" often is not enough for him. He wants to know the shades of blue, like "turquoise" and "cobalt." The Virgo baby loves nature and, even at this age, begins to show a deep tenderness and respect toward plants and pets. Though he likes to be outside, he reacts intensely to temperature extremes. Physically the Virgo baby is cautious in his explorations. He fears hurting himself and will generally be quite conscientious and careful.

### Needs
Permission to explore.
Stimulating but not necessarily complex toys.
Parents who are not overanxious or overprotective.
Someone to talk to.
Cuddling.
Exposure to other live, growing beings.
Labels.
Choices.

### Fears
Accidents or hurting himself.
Making mistakes.
The unexpected.
Feeling lovable only when quiet.

## 18 MONTHS–3 YEARS

The Virgo toddler is shy but curious, quietly going about finding the information he needs. He is intelligent and intense, asking questions, synthesizing and integrating information, testing what he knows. Still cautious, he values organization and may devise elaborate systems and rituals for himself and others. This little Virgo may be tidy and meticulous, almost compulsive, or he may rebel and experiment with chaos and disorder. A perfectionist in either case, he may delay attempting new tasks until he's certain he can do them well. If little Virgo hasn't talked early, he may wait until he can converse in complete sentences. The Virgo toddler loves to be helpful and is satisfied with, and actually grateful for, routine tasks. His attention span is short, so it would be a mistake to count on his help to completion. Little Virgo is also very curious about health and illness and may be fascinated with his own body and other people's bodies and functions.

*Toilet Training:* The Virgo toddler responds well to explanations and reason. He is usually very eager to complete toilet training in order to stay clean and comfortable. So unless there are physiological difficulties, toilet training for little Virgo usually proceeds easily and quickly. There may, however, be periodic accidents well beyond the training age as the young Virgo tends to become so involved with projects that he forgets his physical needs. Such accidents are best treated with little fuss. If the young Virgo is expected to clean up after himself quietly, he will soon learn to pay attention to his physical needs on a more timely basis.

*Needs*
Reasons and explanations.
Cuddling.
Permission to experiment.
Permission to play and get pleasure.
Permission to make mistakes.
Limits.
Encouragement to dream.
Choices: two yeses for every no.

*Fears*
Chaos.
Injury.
Lack of information, limits or order.
Germs.
Unreasonable demands.
Having to do it over and over until it's right.
Being pushed beyond developmental limits.

## 3 YEARS–6 YEARS

The preschool Virgo is usually modest and cautious but, once comfortable, may appear arrogant, overconfident and critical. He loves figuring things out and fixing them and is quite willing to share his ideas with anyone nearby. Often his ideas are excellent. Parents who need to be more right than their child may be nonplussed by their little fountain of information and suggestions. Generally, the preschool Virgo is rather stoic and prefers sharing ideas to sharing feelings. Since he may seem irritable or fidgety when he's scared or nervous, he needs to be taught to express his feelings and to feel comfortable with his child needs. At this age, it is very easy to frighten Virgos into compliance so they look super appropriate, well behaved, etc. This is not a wise course of action. Virgo needs to build a solid experience of being himself in the family and in the world.

The preschool Virgo embodies many apparent contradictions as he tests various roles. He is nurturing and tender, especially with the physically sick or wounded, but he may feel uncomfortable or seem critical around emotional suffering. He may be loud one moment and withdrawn the next; compulsively tidy, then messy; whiny, then cheerfully adaptive. He may seem finicky, not easily pleased, then sweetly grateful for what attention he receives. He may expect nothing and then everything, alternating between contentment and utter dissatisfaction. He may be aloof one moment, cuddly the next; considerate, then critical; highly focused then apparently scattered; helpful, then resentful; a miniature grown-up, then a big baby. Little Virgo often does not know quite how to get what he wants or how to situate himself in the world. He remains kind and gentle through it all, however, and merely needs to be reminded of the value of those parts of himself when he gets into a snit. Adults who perceive preschool Virgo as basically sweet and considerate will have no problem guiding the confused child back toward behavior that feels safest and most rewarding for all concerned.

*Needs*
> To experiment.
> To be allowed to do things his own way.
> Honest responses.
> Compassion.
> Guidance and help when requested.
> Relief from internal pressure.
> Choices and alternatives.
> Humor.

*Fears*
> Criticism.
> That parents will take his shifting behavior seriously and
> reject him.

Disappointment.
Settling for less than he really wants; having to be "grateful."
Substitutions.
Being stuck with chores no one else wants.
Physical injury.

6 YEARS–12 YEARS

The school-age Virgo pretty much continues the patterns begun in preschool years. Still cautious and careful, he may be confused by his emotional ups and downs, alternately hassling and challenging nearby adults and testing the limits of his own behavior. Compliant one moment and independent or rebellious the next, the school-age Virgo continues his contradictory behavior. He is extremely persistent but may become frustrated at odd moments when his performance does not match his expectations. A solitary child, young Virgo may feel inferior to others and compensate by expecting miracles of perfection from himself—or by giving up altogether. He may appear exclusive in his choice of activities or friends. He may be overly concerned with (or defiant about) rules and details. His abilities to question, test, synthesize and evelute information becomes apparent during these years and may seem especially bothersome to parents who had grown quite comfortable with an adaptable and compliant child. He is practicing thinking, disagreeing and conversing.

Ever practical and pragmatic, efficient little Virgo likes to manage and will systematize even the most unlikely things. Though the school-age Virgo may become impatient with activities that seem without purpose, he is a hard worker when interested; and his compassion permits an unusual understanding of other people's differences. Since it usually takes him only one try to learn any lesson, he may expect similar efficiency from others and may feel superior or become impatient with other people's repetitive errors. Boy and girl Virgos may rebel against sexual stereotypes (and want to define their own ways of looking and of acting male or female). By this age, the young Virgo's humor is apparent, and he can often be kidded out of his frustration at things he cannot control. Laughing, helpful, pragmatic little Virgo continues to be a delightful and unobtrusive companion most of the time.

*Needs*
Labels and categories.
Respect.
Explanations and reasons.
To know the rules.
Permission to enjoy, to take pleasure and to play.
Preparation for changes.
Social skills and rules.
A variety of experiences.
Compassion and understanding.
Permission to dream and ways to cope with disappointment.
Moderate responsibility.

*Fears*
Criticism.
Having to be perfect.
Disorganization.
Surprises.
Illness and body malfunction.
Being the only one who can do something.

## 12 YEARS–18 YEARS

The teenage Virgo can be astonishingly shy and insecure. He keeps a sharp eye on the activities of his peers and is quietly responsive to their pressure, either following their lead without appearing to do so or becoming apparently "superior" and very critical of what his classmates are doing. He may stay aloof and detached from peer group activities or become a quiet leader in task-oriented activities—or both. He may agree to edit the school paper and, while outwardly grumbling at the ultimate insignificance of the task, be secretly quite pleased at the recognition and authority bestowed upon him. An idealist at heart, he may also attempt to use his position of power to improve something in a fairly traditional and approved way: writing an editorial about the flagrant misuse of grades by particular teachers, for example.

Virgos in general tend to react to stress by attempting to make things more orderly. As adolescent Virgo crosses the very stressful bridge between childhood and adulthood, he often becomes extremely thorough, careful and organized. Minor details become very important, and he may overlook large concepts as he pursues obscure details. Some Virgos experiment with rebellion and chaos during this period, challenging their bodies and external authority, but most take the conservative route through adolescence, saving rebellion for later. This caution may add to the teenage Virgo's feelings of isolation and not belonging. Though they are often quite popular, precisely because of their sense of order, willingness to work, humor and modesty, adolescent Virgos often overlook evidence of other people's fondness as they examine their own small imperfections. Parents who offer sincere reassurances, not platitudes, can alleviate much of Virgo's discomfort.

During adolescence, young Virgos reach the height of their criticism of themselves and others. They may make decisions about hopes and expectations that affect the rest of their lives. They may appear irritable, critical, picky, finicky, compulsive and sarcastic, and they certainly act as though nothing can please them. They may look for imperfections in others in order to reassure themselves that no one is perfect but feel crushed and betrayed to discover that those they love have flaws. In what appears to be modesty, Virgos often criticize themselves before others can. Parents and other adults need to confront this critical behavior and teach young Virgo other ways to get reassurances and deal with imperfect reality. Permission to be idealistic, acceptance of disappointment, information about dealing with expectations are all parenting needs of the adolescent Virgo.

Virgos's heightened awareness of the flaws of the world usually leads to renewed resolve to improve things. In adolescence, Virgos often find idealistic activities or causes to work in. Parents need to provide adequate outlets for this idealism and acknowledge the sincerity in their desire to improve things.

The adolescent Virgo is also a realist and often a cynic, refusing to believe or to hope until he has proof and guarantees. He is analytical and sees himself as extremely reasonable. While he may appear impossibly uncompromising to exasperated adults, he is, in reality, quite willing to negotiate and needs only to be taught how. His emphasis on literal practicality may cause him to overlook his own emotional needs or the needs of those around him. He needs to be taught to regard emotional needs as having the same urgency and importance as practical "necessities." In the family, more emotionally oriented members can challenge Virgo's assumptions that feelings aren't as real as tangible projects and guide him toward an awareness of his own feelings, even while he is busy working.

In spite of their acceptance of other people's bodily needs and functions, teenage Virgos may be particularly uncomfortable with the body changes that accompany adolescence. They may simultaneously fear and welcome this evidence of approaching maturity. Modest young Virgos may suffer agonies of self-doubt if forced to expose their changing bodies; and, particularly, if they are unprepared or don't understand what is happening, they may become disgusted with signs of puberty. Parents need to remember Virgo's need for information and see that their child has all the explanation he wants for accepting his "new" body.

Close relationships may be particularly threatening to young Virgos. They are likely to find motherly or friendly roles preferable to romantic relationships. Sexual activity may seem scary to them, though they love affection and cuddling. Virgo adolescents are also particularly aware of health matters and may postpone close relationships for real or imagined health reasons. They may use cynical behavior to disguise a basically idealistic stance, and teenage Virgo may ultimately find work preferable to close romantic ties.

It is in the areas of health or tidiness, however, that adolescent Virgos may rebel. Parents who are rather casual about cleanliness may find that their offspring washes his hands several times a day. Parents who eat only health foods may be appalled to find their son smuggling in candy bars and potato chips—purchased, of course, with his own money.

Crafts are frequently an acceptable outlet for painstaking Virgo's energies during this period. Since Virgo children of any age often prefer the company of nonhuman beings, an attachment to a pet or plants may assume intense importance during adolescence and provide numerous rewards. Offered adequate constructive outlets for the drive for perfection, the Virgo adolescent continues to be a delightful companion. His humor and willingness to pitch in are valuable assets to families and other groups, and others often benefit as well from his Virgo need for order.

*Needs*
Preparation for changes.
Information about body functions and changes.
Social skills.

Reassurance of personal value and self-worth.
Only moderate responsibility.
To be reminded that no one is perfect.
Skills in coping with disappointment and disorder.
Negotiating skills.
Fast attention to physical ailments.
Acceptable outlets for idealism.
Not to be the only one who can do something.

*Hates*
Platitudes.
Feeling as though he's settled for less.
Being forced to expose his body.
Disorder, lack of logic, impracticality.
Having to do things over and over until he gets them right.
Being bored.
Criticism, unless given as information in order to do a job more perfectly.
Waste.
Sentimentality.
Having his personal things rearranged.
Information or conversations that don't make sense.
Being pressured to be sexual or to form romantic relationships.
Being told, "If it's worth doing, it's worth doing right."
Being told, "You're never satisfied . . ."

# LIBRA CHILDREN

**SEPTEMBER 23–OCTOBER 22**

## GENERAL CHARACTERISTICS

*(Note: While many characteristics described below will be accurate for most Libras, other, sometimes contradictory, traits may also be evident in an individual child.)*

From the start, parents will most likely be delighted with their social little Libra baby. She is easy to care for and seems innately aware of what is "acceptable" behavior—even acceptable baby behavior—right from the beginning of her interactions with the family. Libra is friendly, open and generous with her smiles and gurgles. Parents and other family members may find themselves going out of their way to simply say "hi" to this social infant.

Social adaptability and social skills are among the strongest assets of the Libra child. She has a keen sense of the appropriate and will find a way to fit in anywhere, and she will make others feel comfortable as well. Libra has wonderfully expressive eyes, and even before she is able to talk, there will be little doubt that she is communicating with her gaze alone. Young Libra lives to interact and will begin talking as soon as she can. Before she can speak any intelligible language, Libra will entertain herself and others with melodious baby talk, and as soon as she's speaking English, Libra will find lots to say. One three-year-old Libra commented to her parents at the supper table, "I wish I had two mouths, one for eating and one just for talking."

This is a child who will be easy to manage in public, and when practicing her social skills, she may enjoy the company of approving adults more than that of other children who couldn't care less about little Libra's poise.

The young Libra shares a keen sense of duality with children of the signs of Gemini, Pisces and Scorpio. She, too, needs to know both sides of an issue, and she will tend to think about things in terms of opposites and polarities. The young Libra will be helped greatly by having a context in which to learn things. She will understand "X" only by comparing it with "Y"; without "Y," she cannot fully comprehend "X." For example, if Aunt Sally is talking about big dogs, Libra conjures up a picture of the smallest dog she's ever seen and tries to imagine another dog that is as comparatively big as the one she's imagining is small. If little Libra is told never to go into the woods alone, she may well imagine being trapped in the woods and unable to get out. In other words, Libra tends to swing from one extreme of an idea to another before getting to the middle or being able to comprehend exactly what it is others are talking about. The Libra mind has a true understanding of the law of physics that states: "For every action there is an equal and opposite reaction." Libra needs time to have her reaction before she makes decisions or states her case.

The young Libra defines who she is by first identifying who she is not. She may also make decisions by first deciding what she does not want to do. For example, if asked what she'd like to do next, little Libra may initially answer, "Well, I don't want to take my nap, and I don't want to take a bath." As a result of this method of internal thinking, Libra is often keenly aware of who she isn't and what she doesn't want to do. She may spend a lot of time and energy doing things that have no real interest to her simply because the thing isn't on her list of "don't wants," and she hasn't yet clearly defined a list of "do wants."

The Libra child excels at comparing and contrasting. She always knows what is bigger, better, bluer or stronger. As an older child and adult, she will also know what is more expensive, desirable, exclusive, valuable or trendy. This knowledge does not necessarily mean she embraces the values she perceives or that she feels the need to represent an extreme or look exemplary, but she does take note of such things. Sometimes onlookers interpret little Libra's skill in this area as competitive, and sometimes she is, but most often this is merely her way of putting information in order.

Also along the lines of comparison and contrast, little Libra may not hear a compliment as complimentary unless she is also told how bad something could have been. A mother's saying, "I'm proud of how well you behaved at Grandma's house," may not communicate the compliment to Libra. Mom may need to say, "You could have been noisy and insisted on eating more cookies after I told you to stop. Instead, I knew I could count on you to be careful, quiet and follow my advice. Thank you." In contrast, a Libra child may not recognize her uniqueness or talent in a certain area until she meets someone who is quite different. She may think all six-year-olds can play Chopin on the piano until she hears a friend struggling through "Twinkle, Twinkle, Little Star."

Sometimes little Libra's talent for comparisons may cause her unhappiness or cause her to want to control a situation. She may complain that her sister got the bigger piece of cake. She may hear her mother's compliment on how she does the dishes as a demand that she always do the dishes or do as careful a job every evening. If she doesn't get the highest grade on a test, young Libra may challenge herself to do better, or she may simply acknowledge the circumstances and let herself be exactly where she is. Libra is the sign of balance, and Libra is the sign most skilled at moderation. Despite her mental awareness of extremes, she feels less inclined to pursue them and will naturally gravitate toward a stance of "moderation in all things."

Despite the gentleness of a sign that seeks balance, the Libra child who constantly compares herself to others and falls short of the standards she has devised for comparison may needlessly suffer a sense of inferiority and insecurity. Little Libra may become quite apologetic, both to relieve some of the guilt and tension she feels and possibly to elicit praise and reassurance from those who are important to her. Parents who want to help their Libra feel better about herself need to remind her of her good and incomparable traits and to teach her not to make assumptions about other people's performance or expectations of her.

The Libra child frequently believes the grass is greener wherever she isn't, and she may keep a close watch on things to make sure she's not missing something. She may try to be all places at all times, and part of her varied and busy interest in things may stem from a fear of missing out on some experience or relationship. She will probably need reassurance that being in only one place at a time is good enough. "Sometimes," laughed the father of a ten-year-old Libra, "I get the urge to nail his shoes to the floor, just to make sure he's stopping long enough to know where he is."

Libras like to be liked; it's part of their social adaptability. This social adaptability leads to precocious social skills even in very young Libra children. Charm and poise are second nature to them. They are consistently liked and approved of by grown-ups and get along well with other children. As part of their need to be liked, however, Libras may modify opinions or behavior to assure social acceptance. This malleability may seem fickle to those counting on them and become a source of problems, especially in the school years as Libras learn to balance their social needs with a sense of reliability.

A young Libra is most comfortable identifying how she is like other people, noting what she and other people have in common. While she often accepts and even fights for another's right to be different, she basically likes people to agree with her and with each other. Libra tends to surround herself with people who share her values and beliefs, and she may perceive someone's disagreement with these values as personal rejection or anger. When a friend disagrees with Libra in an area she feels is important, her feelings are likely to be hurt, and she may feel personally criticized. If a dog-loving Libra discovers that her best friend prefers cats, she may feel personally insulted and rejected. Since little Libra dislikes unpleas-antness and certainly categorizes such disagreements as unpleasant, she often learns to keep her opinions to herself, to avoid certain topics or, in extreme circumstances, to end a friendship rather than endure the discord.

Libra is a cardinal sign, which means it is oriented toward action. Some Libra children, despite their high need for social acceptance and display of social skills, do not appear malleable at all. They have a need to "do" something: to take a stand. They are not content appearing noncommittal, and often they fear their own indecisive-ness or feel that any action is better than none. These are children who will bring up the most uncomfortable topic first "just to get it over with" and who will stoically accept consequences rather than live with ambiguity. These are children who will openly fight for what they believe, and they may appear very different from their quieter Libra cousins.

For this second type of Libra child, being well liked is not quite as important as being fair or respected, and asserting her identity is more important than being socially skilled. Underneath the behavior, however, the same motivation remains true for both types of Libra child: they want to be valued for their knowledge and consideration and careful handling of people and situations. In this case the consideration is usually expressed for groups of people, while in the earlier type, consideration is focused more on individuals. Noisy Type B Libras have often made a commitment to certain ideas or causes, more like an Aquarian child, and decided to take their popularity and social acceptance from a more select group of people than more compliant Type A Libras. In either case, their need for interaction and approval remains, and they will have more in common than in difference.

Young Libras believe that nearly any problem can be solved reasonably through rational communication. They can often be found mediating and negotiating, from preschool through corporate management. Most Libras have a great desire for calm and pleasantness and will do anything they can to help avoid a scene; that they are very good in such situations is an added bonus. Sometimes the noisy type Libra will create a way for hidden tensions to come to the surface, to get them released and dealt with, but most Libras will avoid public displays of emotion and are uncomfortable with dramatic emotional reactions in others.

The Libra child often has a strong sense of justice. When this sense is combined with responsibility, compassion and empathy, the young Libra exhibits a great deal of conscience. So much conscience can lead to confusion with guilt, and little Libra may feel personally responsible when things go wrong, even if she wasn't present. If the family runs out of peanut butter, young Libra may take it on as her fault, feeling bad about herself because she didn't remind someone to buy more. Parents need to make sure their Libra child doesn't take on guilt for such incidents and that she gets reassurances about accidents and mistakes not being her fault.

Balance and harmony are key words in young Libra's life. She does not like things to be out of kilter and will willingly exert effort to maintain harmony in the family and later in school and other social settings. She needs symmetry in her life and environment: to be valued for this trait as well as for that, and to have blue pajamas at her own house and red pajamas at her grandparents' house. She may adjust her own wishes to accommodate her needs to the desires of others around her. When family decisions are being made, little

Libra needs an extra unpressured minute to decide what she wants before other family members chime in and the young Libra simply agrees with their opinions.

So great is the Libra child's need for peace that she may interfere in areas that do not involve her personally simply in an attempt to restore harmony. If two other friends are arguing, the young Libra may try to get them to make up, even though the fight has nothing to do with her and she hasn't been invited to mediate. Unfortunately for bewildered and sincere little Libra, such interventions can turn the anger of both friends on her. They may indeed make up by directing their deferred anger at Libra as a way to reconnect, but at the cost to young Libra of their friendship. The Libra child needs parental guidance about using her mediating skills, guidelines on what is appropriate intervention and when such intervention is not a good idea. She will need discussions on the nature of her own responsibility and how to limit her sense that she ought to be or can be in charge of the harmony in her environment. When she has been through an experience where her intervention failed—and every Libra child will go through such experiences—she needs nurturing, relief from guilt and nonjudgmental conversation on the lessons to be learned.

Little Libras may also feel guilty if they do not intervene and help solve problems, for deep down they believe they *can* make a difference and that they must try. Parents in the midst of a family quarrel may be quite surprised at their Libra child's insistence on mediation and should not let her try to negotiate problems far beyond her age or understanding. With their strong need for equality, small Libras may put themselves in the position of sacrificing what they want in order to maintain balance or peace. For example, a Libra child may say to a sick brother, "If you can't go, I won't go either." Or if her best friend isn't hungry, little Libra may decide not to eat either.

Occasionally, adults count heavily on their little Libra to maintain peace and harmony within the home. Sometimes little Libra assumes this role without anyone being aware of what is occurring. The child becomes increasingly careful, moderate and present in family problems and problem solving and more and more reluctant to state her own needs emphatically. Without anyone consciously planning it or supporting the role, a little Libra can start looking more like the U.N. peacekeeping forces than an active child. This situation needs to be corrected with much reassurance from parents that they will step in and help maintain family harmony, while Libra can go about pursuing her many interests. Children have the right to be passionate, unreasonable, opinionated, to get their own way sometimes, to be the one the rest of the family adjusts to—and little Libras will have the rest of their lives to be moderate, considerate, skilled negotiators. While the moment is ripe and the Libra is young, a little excess here is a lesson this child needs: three scoops of ice cream with all the toppings, a day at the amusement park with all the rides she can handle, a stylish outfit of stripes and polka dots in contrasting colors.

The Libra child may find herself in the middle a lot. This tendency probably originates with her mediation skills and spills over into other areas of her life. The young Libra may socialize in small groups and triangles where her negotiation skills and social charm are called on by the group and validated. Later she may have difficulty believing she deserves a person of her very own, or that she can maintain one-to-one relationships where the balance or imbalance is accentuated by there being only two people involved. Libras are often the second-born child, or they act like second-born children, or are the second-born of that gender.

The young Libra's attention to what is appropriate often leads to behavior that is decorous and proper. She looks so socially comfortable that parents and other family members may not question how such decorum feels to the child herself. The main problem encountered by the Libra child in her ability to anticipate the needs and expectations of others, to be socially at ease and conversational beyond her years, is that much of this behavior occurs in response to outside stimulus rather than being generated by the child's own inner needs. Libra may worry needlessly about what other's think and may inhibit herself unnecessarily. She may do things because she thinks she should rather than because she wants to. If she's rebellious, she may do the opposite of what she thinks she should, but the problem remains that she's reacting instead of initiating from within herself.

The young Libra needs permission to make her own choices regardless of what others think. Parents may need to provide special encouragement in this process and help her learn to distinguish and listen to an inner voice as clearly as she anticipates and listens to the voices of others. Basically, she needs to be taught "selfishness," putting herself first. There is enough sense of balance in Libra that this child will not abuse such permission but will have to learn a level of self-interest most people take for granted in their personalities. Libra needs to learn to focus on herself so that external circumstances do not exert such a powerful influence on her thinking and behavior and to be less sensitive to the goings-on around her. Parents of young children can help their Libra in this development by getting her opinion first, by making a game out of it and by not responding judgmentally or allowing others to respond judgmentally when Libra voices her own wants, needs and decisions.

One way the Libra child retains her inner sense of peace and balance, regardless of what's happening around her, is through appreciation for art. In the arts Libra finds tangible expression of the harmony she so deeply values. Even if she is not interested in making art herself, she is nearly always captivated by things graceful, elegant, beautiful, tasteful. Early exposure to the arts is a joy for little Libra, and the opportunity to make her own art, including music and performance, is often an exceptional gift for this child. She will probably be more interested in trips to art museums, concerts, dance performances, etc., than many other children. She is a good candidate for art lessons, either privately or as part of her school program. She will usually endeavor to make her surroundings as lovely as possible, even if the rest of the family doesn't follow her sense of artfulness. While her siblings may have Star Wars and Garfield posters in their rooms, hers is more likely to have art posters, a carefully arranged display or collection, and she may take an interest in classical music.

Libra often finds the ritual associated with art or with traditional religion reassuring and harmonious. She likes the pomp and circumstance of ritual and the appeal it makes to all her senses at once. Little Libra may establish little rituals of her own around the home, developing a certain routine about going to bed or getting dressed in the morning. For example, in order to do her homework most effectively, she may first turn on some special music, set up her work area and light a candle. She may have secret words she says to herself in times of stress, and the Libra child, far more than children of other signs, is careful not to step on sidewalk cracks.

The Libra child needs a great deal of privacy, and because she attunes herself so carefully to others, it's often hard for her to feel she's getting enough time or space alone. Like all air signs, she can pull her consciousness into her head and detach herself when she feels overloaded with environmental stimulation. The Libra variety of this detachment may appear simply as a lack of attention (noticeable in one usually so attentive to others) or a continued sense of cordiality that feels impersonal to those around her. "She keeps on smiling and talking to the relatives," said one mom of a Libra teenager, "but suddenly I get the feeling there's no one home inside. When I pick up that signal, I excuse her and see that she gets some uninterrupted privacy. When she comes back, I have my lovely, charming daughter again."

Reading is usually an important source of artful harmony, information and acceptable detachment for the Libra child. Her love of books gives her permission to develop a fantasy life and contributes to her creativity. Starting with bedtime stories in the early years, this child soaks up information through reading and being read to. She has an enormous capacity to take in information, especially from the printed page, and learns more easily from reading than from experience. Libra is a fountain of information, and she can be counted on to share it in the most tactful way. She loves to give advice and is often extremely helpful resolving areas of misunderstanding or correcting misinformation.

With so much ability to take in and put out information, communication is of key importance to the Libra child. She tends to filter nearly all input through her ears. She listens well and may need to read out loud when learning new data. She takes what she hears very seriously. Libra needs and prefers verbal attention, reward and affection. Parents who are not accustomed to verbalizing their good feelings about others would do well to learn to do so in order to help their Libra child. Libra may appear indifferent to physical affection but will accept and relish verbal praise.

The entire family benefits from a little Libra's tact, diplomacy, love of beauty and peace. It is the Libra child who will see to it that things don't get too extreme and that they remain fair. Often young Libra champions the rights of others, and she will take action that bears out her words. Libra cooperates and shares willingly, and is usually delighted to be part of a team. Parents and siblings alike can count on this moderate and responsible little child and will find her vision of the world satisfying, reassuring and full of noticed beauty.

NEEDS (Libra's emotional emphasis)

> Privacy.
> Audience.
> Beautiful environment.
> Affection and approval.
> Permission to be passionate
> Permission not to mediate.
> Skills in making decisions and taking a stand.
> Permission to say no, to defend herself.
> Private space.
> Permission to be exclusive.
> Chances to be included.
> Information.
> Support for involvement in the arts.
> Peer support and interaction.
> Help not comparing herself with others.

COMMON ASSUMPTIONS (How Libra views the world around her)

> You're nobody until somebody loves you.
> You are known by the company you keep; birds of a feather . . .
> Turn the other cheek.
> If it looks good, it must be okay.

SENSITIVITIES (Potential sources of misunderstanding)

*Anger:* The young Libra can be extremely uncomfortable with anger, both her own feelings and those of others. She values pleasantness and may feel ashamed when she's angry, preferring to let the problem go undealt with rather than face her discomfort. Little Libra may let things reach crisis proportions before dealing with an issue. She may believe that if she understands the other person's point of view, she has no right to get angry, or she may tell herself that her own needs aren't as important as the other person's needs. Having put off dealing with the feeling as long as possible, the young Libra can be quite frightened by the enormity of her anger once it surfaces. She may have guilty thoughts that if she'd done everything right she could have prevented the situation from happening. Parents may note this pattern in their Libra child as long periods of apparent calm followed by sudden rages followed by little Libra's contrite apologies and withdrawal.

Young Libras often believe that anger, as well as other emotions, need to be justified and explained. Since young children usually haven't the capability for explaining themselves, a Libra child may think her anger is not worthy or not real. With this confusion between feeling and rationalization, the Libra child may fear that she or others will go out of control when anger is expressed. There is enough balance and control in Libra to make her fear basically ungrounded, but it feels real nevertheless.

Little Libra often equates anger with hatred: if she is angry at someone, she must hate them, and if she hates them she has to leave them. Since she is not ready to take such a risk, she may not allow herself the anger. She may also think that when someone is angry with her, they hate her and will leave her. She will need additional reassurance and teaching from angry parents when the inevitable family stresses occur.

The Libra child needs to be taught the function of anger and to separate feelings of anger from angry behaviors. She may literally have to be taught how to be angry and how to use her anger to get a problem solved. Typical problems include little Libra getting angry with a smile on her face and not being taken seriously or feeling angry inside and assuming her anger is communicated when she's sending out no signals at all. The young Libra needs reassurance that feelings do not hurt herself or others and that she can express feelings in ways that get her and the other person what they each need to resolve the problem. Above all, she needs reassurance that other people's feelings do not come before her own, that her role is to get her needs met by parents, not to act like a parent herself.

The rebellious Libra child may be able to get angry more easily but may still have difficulty solving the problem represented by her anger. She seems to know something must be done about the feeling but not know quite how to do it. This child needs guidance for thinking about problem solving and in learning alternative ways to get people's attention:

*Comparison:* The Libra child who compares herself with others and uses other people's standards finds herself in a win-or-lose position rather than with the sense of equality that is so important to her. While she is busily comparing herself with others, little Libra confuses their goals and dreams with her own goals and dreams. If the young Libra decides she's going to tap dance as well as her friend Maureen and achieves that goal, she finds herself in the confusing position of having achieved something she wasn't interested in in the first place. If Maureen keeps moving ahead of her, little Libra may never reach her goal, and she may expend all kinds of energy and disappointment in the process instead of defining for herself what is as important to her as tap dancing is to Maureen. With a little extra guidance during initial goal setting, a Libra child can be taught to define her own dreams and to separate them from the wishes of people around her.

The Libra child needs reassurance of her uniqueness, and parents need to resist comparing her with other children. Since the Libra child is exceptionally sensitive to comparisons, acknowledging her excellence without comparing her to anyone is the safest way to praise this child.

*Appearances:* The young Libra is concerned with appearance both in terms of how she looks and how she behaves. She likes to "look good" socially and physically and is extremely vulnerable to shame in these areas. She should not be teased or humiliated for this concern; it's simply part of her nature and is often a part that other people enjoy and can learn from. Libras often serve as role models for other children about styles of dress, cleanliness and personal hygiene, manners and art appreciation. Brand-name jeans may be especially important to the Libra child, and she may not want to blow up balloons for a party if she thinks it will make her face look funny in front of others.

Often the young Libra believes that if something "looks good" it is good. She may be fooled by appearance or tend to take things at face value more than other children do. She may prefer friends who dress well or like a certain teacher because he is so handsome. Even the Libra child who is oriented to social causes will be at least privately aware of how good it looks to be so involved. While this concern with appearances adds to the young Libra's social poise and ease in belonging, the Libra child also needs encouragement to look beyond the obvious.

## RELATIONSHIPS

Relationships are extremely important to little Libra, not only relationships between people but also relationships between concepts. However, people's relationships are of special importance and the Libra child devotes a great deal of time to friendships and other relationships. She is responsive and willing to alter her behavior to assure her place in a group. She is grateful for whatever love and attention she receives.

*Mom:* The young Libra sees her parents as having switched roles in some respects. She may see Mom as the primary disciplinarian or believe Mom is the stronger one and the rule maker in the family. In any case, Libra expects her mom to be a fairly traditional mother, conservative and predictable. While she expects Mom to meet her needs effectively, she may be surprised when affection accompanies efficiency.

Mom needs to share her softer side with a Libra child to give young Libra a role model for emotional warmth that is combined with efficiency and rationality. Moms of little Libras may want to spend some additional time with their youngsters simply talking and working together on projects. Little Libra, while needing nurturing and protection like any child, loves to be treated as an equal and is especially fond of times spent with Mom doing "grown-up" activities like shopping or seriously discussing important topics of the child's choosing.

*Dad:* The young Libra expects to receive the most nurturing from Dad and often sees him as a family man, regardless of his actual behavior. She may believe Dad is more emotional than Mom and may be especially drawn to or repelled by him, depending upon how she feels about her own emotions at the time.

The Libra child expects Dad to be permissive and loving. Fathers of Libras can feel free to cuddle and play with these infants and to build an affectionate base on which to add later verbal expressions of love. It is important that Libra does not believe *only* Dad can be supportive and warm, that both parents take extra care to show their affection and, if necessary, talk to their child about the different ways of caring and the validity of each parent's style.

*Siblings:* The Libra child may not feel much connection to siblings except through play. Little Libra is often the mediator in families, and siblings of all ages will come to her for advice on justice and fairness. This attention may surprise the young Libra, who tends to believe her siblings are smarter than she is.

*Friends:* The young Libra likes pairs and often has a best friend to whom she is devoted and loyal. She also tends to have many acquaintances and is a cooperative team member. She likes rather flashy individualists, as long as they meet her standards for "looking good," and will often bask in the associated glory of their daring and quietly support their adventures. With her need to fit in, the young Libra may appear to be rather easily influenced and persuaded by peer pressure; once the attention is off her, however, she is most likely simply to go her own way. Libra is generous with friends and often receives a lot in return.

## MIND/INFORMATION/SCHOOL

The young Libra has a rational and logical mind. She is concerned with dualities and opposites and sees things primarily (if not entirely) in relationship to other things. This means she needs a lot of verbal data to understand a concept and will seek out everything related to that concept in order to make sense of it. For example, she won't be content to study Italian painting without also studying Italian history, politics, religion and geography. If she can eat some Italian food and learn a few Italian songs, she will be delighted with herself. The more extensive her knowledge, the more interested she becomes. A young Libra scholar doing a simple school paper may come home from the library with a dozen books vaguely related to the topic at hand. Interdisciplinary studies were invented for little Libras, and they love crossing academic boundaries in search of additional data and interconnection.

The Libra child weighs things and needs time to sift through the large amounts of information she gathers. She can absorb a great deal of information at a time and sort it out later. She loves to see patterns and connections in what she is learning. She will often make her learning politically or culturally relevant, applying learned principles to groups of people and maintaining a keen awareness of what is fair and unfair in the world around her.

The young Libra loves to learn and loves to read, but she may not take school very seriously. The right teachers can make a great deal of difference to the Libra student. She needs a teacher who allows her to follow tangents, who listens to her and values her information gathering. In exchange, Libra will often become quite devoted to the teacher and allow herself to be studiously motivated. Libra is very curious about what is happening and why. Especially as a toddler, she seems to ask "why?" endlessly. She is visually oriented and may need to see information in print in order to fully retain it. The young Libra likes to teach others and becomes more certain of her knowledge as she shares it (hears herself saying it) with others. Making her a classroom assistant in certain subjects is a way to motivate her.

*Higher Education:* The young Libra is as likely to be attracted to college as much for the social lessons it provides as for the academic lessons. She may join a sorority or political group and is interested in how people interact at all levels and the impact people have on each other. Her choice of majors may well reflect this orientation, and she is inclined to study areas that allow her to connect with people or with art. Most Libras attend at least two schools and have several majors before settling on one thing. Their attitude is one of simply collecting data, and they will frequently change emphasis in their continual absorption of new information.

## RESPONSIBILITY/WORK/REWARDS

*Responsibility and Work:* Little Libra takes work and responsibilities seriously. She finds security in doing well and often does more than is required, especially if the task involves helping someone. She likes to feel useful and needed and particularly enjoys chores that require her to take care of things and communicate with others.

Sometimes the Libra child fears that if she is too good at her work people will assume that she wants to be totally self-sufficient and stop helping her. She is afraid of being alienated from others by too much excellence, of being the target of competition or resentment or of simply being abandoned if she doesn't seem to "need" anyone. Parents need to remember to offer their highly functional Libra child the same care, nurturing and attention all children need. They need to be careful not to burden her with more than she can handle because little Libra will try to live up to their expectations rather than complain.

The young Libra likes explaining and giving advice and works best in the company of others. She is extremely cooperative and willingly shares both tasks and rewards. With her tendency to compare herself to others, the Libra child may need special guidance to learn to work at her own speed and to motivate herself rather than counting on other people's goals to motivate her.

The young Libra is very sensitive to criticism of her work and may become quite defensive when she thinks she is about to be judged or criticized. The most successful way to criticize little Libra constructively is for parents and other concerned adults to emphasize the positive, start by telling her the good parts and speak tactfully of those areas they are not pleased with.

*Rewards:* Libra responds best to words of approval, appreciation and recognition. She likes being granted time off to do whatever she wants and, of course, likes to receive beautiful gifts or money. Though she may seem indifferent to physical affection, loving touches, pats, and hugs usually make a little Libra feel all warm inside.

## HOME

Young Libras like their homes to be tasteful and lovely. If they cannot carefully select or afford what they want around them, they may not care at all. The one area in which Libra children can be extreme is in the decoration of their living space, and if they can't have it all, they will often opt for nothing. Regardless of their budget, however, their space will often be decorated well, in pastel shades. Since it is frequently used as a place for working on projects, as well as for socializing, the room is likely to be utilitarian as well as beautiful.

Libra children expect their homes to be a safe place—a haven—and may have a lot of rules about how one is supposed to behave there. They like to travel and to come back carrying things they have gathered or learned and nestle back into the comfort of familiarity.

# HEALTH

When Libra gets sick she is a dramatic invalid and expects the maximum in concerned care, compassion and special treatment. She may worry about hospitalization, regardless of the ailment, and need reassurance that her illness is not that serious (though she wants adults to take it seriously). Once the Libra child is convinced that everyone is sufficiently concerned, she is generally content to be left alone to read or talk on the phone with periodic check-ins.

Young Libras get sick for a variety of reasons. Illness can add drama and interest when little Libra is bored, or it may allow her to relax and let herself get cared for. Sometimes if the young Libra perceives a problem in the family, she may get sick to create a crisis she believes will unite family members and distract them from the original problem.

A Libra child can be rather cavalier about health, with a tendency to romanticize her susceptibility or immunity to health problems and to identify her self-image with frailty or super strength. She can be evasive about what ails her or perhaps not be able to identify the problem, even to herself. While some Libras are intensely interested in matters of physical health, most are not or limit their interest to mental and emotional health.

Traditionally, the sign of Libra rules infections, blood, kidneys and bladder. Little Libras experiencing health problems may find themselves more susceptible to blood poisoning, equilibrium difficulty or diabetes, or they may have bladder problems, including bed-wetting or cystitis. Libras have a rather notorious sweet tooth and may also have difficulty controlling their weight.

# CHILDHOOD AGES

*(Note: The fears in this section are never to be used as punishment. They are presented as avenues for reassurance and caring).*

### BIRTH–6 MONTHS

Tiny baby Libra is pleasant to have around and easy to please. She is observant, chatty and responds to attention immediately. She is usually a pretty baby who welcomes interaction with other people and is a charming companion even at this early age. The Libra infant loves ritual and finds comfort and security in having the same things done the same way at the same time. She seldom tires of her favorite lullaby, and she will be content to be rocked for hours. Early on, she will probably demonstrate preferences, and she may have a favorite article of clothing before she's even six months old.

*Needs*
Social interaction.
Firm physical support.
Pretty and comfortable clothes.
Visual and auditory stimulation, including music.
Being around what's going on.

*Fears*
Being ignored, isolated, neglected.
Being dropped.
Sensory deprivation.

6 MONTHS–18 MONTHS

Baby Libra continues to seek social interaction and often welcomes and needs the presence of playmates. She is curious and wants freedom to explore and look around. She may begin talking and labeling things early. The Libra of this age loves choices, and she is at her happiest when ruminating over which rattle to chew, what toys to play with, what to do next.

*Needs*
Support for her curiosity and love of choosing.
Physical support for her little body.
Freedom to move around; clothes that are attractive but utilitarian.
Interaction with other people, including peers.
Physical and verbal affection.

*Fears*
Restriction.
Abandonment, isolation.
Competition.

## 18 MONTHS–3 YEARS

The Libra toddler is still eager to please. She is social and curious and usually willingly reaches out to other people, even during what is usually a shy period for babies of other signs. She continues to appreciate ritual and loves celebrations, "remember when" stories and fairy tales. She is likely to drive her parents to distraction with her love of hearing the same stories and songs over and over. Already at this age, she is concerned with appearances and how she looks, and she may be easily impressed by others. She begins comparing herself with others now. While this may appear to be an easy way for parents to control her behavior, if comparison is used for that purpose, it will backfire later: "Eat your food now because Johnny does," will later become, "I won't eat my food because Johnny doesn't have to."

The young Libra is beginning to connect with her artistic abilities and is learning about competition and fairness. She is interested in all relationships but is especially drawn to marriage and may begin asking pointed and sometimes uncomfortable questions about her parents' relationship(s).

*Toilet Training:* Since little Libra seeks approval, likes to look good and likes to be appreciated, she is often easy to train. She responds well to bribery and reward: the promise of special new clothes or outings may be enough to motivate her. The bed-wetting that sometimes occurs in young Libra's life should not be taken as evidence of faulty toilet training; it is more often a health problem that will be outgrown naturally.

*Needs*

> Opportunities for social interaction, particularly with peers.
> Approval, appreciation, support.
> Information, conversation.
> Cuddling.
> Lessons in autonomy; permission to be different.
> Firm limits and rules.
> To know appearances aren't everything.

*Fears*

> Being compared with others.

Lack of limits; everything is okay and there's no one to push against.
Being too different.
"Looking funny."
Being valuable only because she's cute.


### 3 YEARS–6 YEARS

The preschool Libra is friendly and flirtatious, willful and bossy. She may be considerate and loving one moment, blaming and sarcastic the next. Since she is exploring different social roles, her behavior may range from coy to rebellious, and she may seem very volatile and changeable. She excels at comparing things during this period and may become quite competitive or indecisive as she attempts to establish her values in light of the opposites she perceives. She may tend to see things or people as "better than" or "worse than" at this age and may therefore have difficulty maintaining the sense of equality she deeply needs.

Libra at this age becomes more consciously aware of choices and is sometimes more uncomfortable making decisions. She may try to get other people to make decisions (think) for her or she may seek someone else to blame if she feels she has made a wrong choice. Ever more aware of the dynamics involved in relationships, this little Libra may experiment with setting up fights between people (to see what will happen) or in various ways, including teasing and bullying, to get other people to do what she wants them to do. While learning about tact and about her own intelligence, the young Libra may appear particularly evasive, stretching or denying the truth or the reality of a situation. Parents need to offer acceptable outlets for little Libra's creativity and to provide firm limits for acceptable behavior during this time.

Preschool Libras are also very interested in prescribed rules and will eagerly explore behavior traditionally attributed to their gender. They are wonderful daddy's and mommy's helpers during this period and may be quite amusing as they accurately imitate the sex-role behavior they see around them. Amused parents need to hide their amusement and continue to offer their child discussions and examples of other possibilities beyond mimicry.

*Needs*
>Affection.
Awareness of in-between gray areas.
Help, not pressure, in making choices.
Firm limits, rules and boundaries.
Permission to "dress up" literally and to try on new roles.
Not to be allowed to manipulate others.
Lessons in social behaviors.
Appreciation and praise for jobs well done.
Reality checks.

*Fears*
>Being laughed at.
Too much responsibility.
Being forced or hurried.
Being isolated, left out.
Being a bother.

## 6 YEARS–12 YEARS

The school-age Libra continues the patterns established from ages three to six. Even more conscious of her peers, she may become extremely concerned with status and appearances. She may appear very slow to make decisions, waiting to see what others are deciding; her tendencies to compare herself with others manifest now, as do the external standards that go with it. Parents may find they have almost no influence over their little Libra in the school years and feel concerned that she is being unduly influenced by her friends. Since little Libra needs to experiment with a wide variety of behaviors, parents can be reassured that she will probably move on to another behavior soon enough; the real challenge is not in controlling who her friends are but, rather, teaching the Libra child how to hear her own inner voice. The Libra child both seeks and resents parental interference; she counts on parents to provide realistic limits but may complain mightily when that occurs. Parents need to be firm with their limits and secure in their confidence to make wise decisions for their still-young Libra.

The young Libra is also concerned with appropriate behavior at this age, and because she compares, she may feel that others are getting along better than she is or that they know something she doesn't know. She may spend a fair amount of time trying to psych out her peers, whether she ultimately chooses to follow or rebel against them. The youthful Libra is concerned with rules, both the rules of society and the more covert rules of her friendship groups. She is usually excellent at identifying and following these rules. She may experience great confusion if the rules of society are in conflict with the rules of her friendship group, but she is usually rather conservative and will generally stick to established rules and traditional sex-role behaviors.

The school-age Libra is becoming very aware of the concepts of fairness and equality. She has a keen eye for inequity and may temporarily experience a conflict between this growing need for equality and her tendency to compare herself favorably or unfavorably with others. She likes to be with people and during this age especially likes close personal contacts. At earlier ages Libra was content to sit beside someone and do her own thing; she is now learning to truly cooperate and share to be part of a productive team.

*Needs*
Reasons, explanations, information.
Social experience.
Support and approval.
Balance, harmony, symmetry, moderation.
Permission to learn things her own way.
Close platonic relationships.
Permission to continue acting childlike.
Firm rules, limits, boundaries.
Support for creativity.

*Fears*
Winning and losing.
Making a fool of herself.
Losing love and support of parents.
Having to choose between parents and friends.
Abandonment, isolation.
Having to sacrifice her wants to gain harmony or equality.

## 12 YEARS–18 YEARS

Believing "you're nobody until somebody loves you," the teenage Libra usually throws herself into relationships and expends most of her adolescent energy in that area. Everything may come second to relationships where the teenage Libra is concerned. She tends to pair up with one person at a time as well as become involved in groups. The young Libra may suddenly become shy or appear aloof; since relationships mean so much to her, she may try to look uninvolved if she feels she wants them *too much* and foresees disappointment. Libra is convincing, socially competent and usually attractive whether or not she recognizes these traits in herself, and she remains concerned with appearances and status.

The adolescent Libra's intense concern with dualities and polarities may make decision making exceedingly difficult, and she may appear disloyal to friends as she attempts to hear all sides and gather all information on behalf of "fairness." She often challenges her family's definitions of what is fair. The young Libra is at the apex of identifying herself according to who she isn't and may place high priority on being associated with people who are like her or who represent what she wants to be. Since she continues to need to know the "other side" in order to have something to resist and to push against, she may place her parents in the role of adversary. Responsible adults need to be prepared to identify and defend their limits and rules clearly and reasonably.

The teenage Libra may seek to make herself indispensable to those she cares for and expend a lot of energy helping others, sometimes at her own expense. She may make sacrifices in order to preserve her vision of equality. She may believe she is not lovable if she is not needed, and she will often use all of her mediating skills to attain the approval and appreciation she equates with love and acceptance. Somtimes the teenage Libra uses concern with other people's problems as a way of avoiding her own problems, or she may insert herself into the disagreements or relationships of others to be noticed and valued. Parents who wish to broaden their child's basis for self-esteem can support and facilitate her explorations of any of the arts or guide her strong helping instincts toward volunteer activity at a nearby hospital or nursing home.

The adolescent Libra's quest for relationships may take some unusual turns. She is usually easy to get along with, even during her difficult periods, and even for parents. With peers, she loves intellectual intimacy and physical affection but may confuse those needs with sexual behavior. She seeks a playmate and a soul buddy but may consent to being sexual if she belives that is the rule or the price. Loving and concerned adults will share with the young Libra their beliefs about appropriate sexual behavior and their methods of setting boundaries and limits. The young Libra may feel left out, however, if she is not paired with someone, or she may worry that there is something wrong with her. Once again, activities designed to build her self-esteem in areas that do not require another person are most likely to be rewarding.

*Needs*

Support and approval.

Information.

Discussions about setting limits, making decisions.

"How-to" information.

Discussions about love.

Encouragement for pursuing art activities or volunteer work.

Permission to be autonomous, to make her own decisions (and commitment to let her live with the consequences).

Social activities.

Being liked, appreciated.

*Hates*

Not knowing or representing a current style.

Feeling as though she looks funny.

Being left out.

Being compared.

Being forced to make a choice.

Feeling ugly.

Being called competitive.

Feeling unloved, unappreciated, unnoticed, unwanted.

Being told, "Why can't you be like . . ."

# SCORPIO CHILDREN

## October 23–November 21

## GENERAL CHARACTERISTICS

*(Note: While many characteristics described below will be accurate for most Scorpios, other, sometimes contradictory, traits may also be evident in an individual child.)*

Parents will be intrigued by their solemn, attentive and responsive newborn Scorpio. Though infant Scorpio sleeps a lot, his awakenings are characterized by intense interest in all that surrounds him. He smiles infrequently, but the wait is worthwhile. The dazzling effects of a baby Scorpio's grin cannot be overstated, and the recipient knows it's directed at him or her. Open and vulnerable, the Scorpio infant is sensitive to the slightest nuances of feeling in those around him. This sensitivity is a pleasure when parents are enjoying their child and their lives, but may be disconcerting during periods of parental preoccupation and stress. Scorpio's inborn intuition, observable from infancy on, helps make him one of the most considerate children of the zodiac, but parents need to be careful not to take advantage of even the infant's willingness to put the needs of others before his own.

Scorpios are often born believing they have to make up for something lost by their parents during, just after or just before pregnancy. Thus, if the birth was difficult, they may try to be extra good in order to prove the pain was worth it; if Uncle Henry just moved out of town, young Scorpio may try to fill the vacancy left by his departure. While this belief is certainly below consciousness, the tendency toward compensatory behavior is very real for young Scorpios. Parents may also notice that their little Scorpio sometimes exhibits extreme behaviors; chances are the child is compensating for the opposite behavior present somewhere else in the environment. A Scorpio child with highly verbal parents may communicate largely nonverbally. If his brother is already a Little League star, Scorpio may excel in art or music. Scorpios catch on quickly to both verbal and nonverbal messages and tend to believe that current status is endless reality. If things go wrong today, then things will remain wrong tomorrow.

Extremes are very much a part of the young Scorpio's life. This is the most complex sign of the zodiac. Scorpio has no major themes— or all of its themes can be considered major. It is a water sign; so, like Pisces and Cancer, action will be based more on emotion than on thinking. However, especially in young Scorpios, this complexity often does not show on the surface. Scorpio children tend to be intense, friendly and watchful, withdrawing into their Scorpio complexity only when they are frightened. Parents need to exercise a special gentleness with Scorpio children. Much of the information in this chapter will be a guide for helping non-Scorpios comprehend and interact with these subtly complex children.

Often a Scorpio child knows who he is *not* before he knows who he is. He nearly always knows what he doesn't want before he knows what he does want. Parents may need to offer their Scorpio child more options than they offered their other children. Their child's rejection of one option after another is not a personal rebuke of the parents or spiteful rebellion but his way of sorting through the "don't wants" until he finds what he does want. The unhappy Scorpio infant may continue crying even after he's been changed and fed, and only when he's cuddled by a particular favorite person does he realize that's what he wanted all along. Caring parents may find themselves still offering options to their Scorpio infant even after their patience has run short. In the early years of parenting a Scorpio, parents may need to spell each other off while supporting this child's option-sorting process.

Scorpio children tend to think in terms of opposites as well as in extremes. If an adults says "hot" to the child, little Scorpio will think "cold." If the young Scorpio is complimented on his nifty new T-shirt, he may wonder what's wrong with his trousers. If young Scorpio believes everyone thinks in opposites, he may hear compliments as veiled criticisms. He may think a favorable remark about his smile is a demand to comb his hair. When this belief is unconfronted, the Scorpio child adopts these behaviors himself and frequently appears to say the opposite of what he means. A parent who says, "You have a lovely smile," may notice the Scorpio child fussing with his shirttails. Scorpio needs to hear the compliment repeated over and over until he has settled for himself that no hidden meaning or opposite was intended.

Because of this tendency to think in opposites, even well-meaning family teasing may deeply confuse a young Scorpio. On an emotional level, he may learn to deny or contradict his true needs and feelings, thus making it very difficult for adults to satisfy him. From the start, the Scorpio child needs to be taught to let his needs be known directly. And parents need to refuse to play guessing games with their little Scorpio, no matter how winsome his behavior. The older Scorpio child will occasionally play a game of "Come and get me," whereby parents and other caring adults are supposed to sense the child's distress and pursue the child until he consents to having his needs met. This behavior puts parents and others into an extremely frustrating position: they cannot win, up against the internal Scorpio complexity, unless the Scorpio is ready to let them win. Rather than follow their child into the maze, an easier technique is to consistently invite little Scorpio to stay out of it through statements such as, "I can't guess what you want from me but I will try to provide it when you tell me what it is." Though a few Scorpio children take this behavior to an extreme and want only what they cannot have, most will share their wants and needs if they are certain they will be listened to and taken seriously.

Scorpio's ability and, in fact, his need, to consider opposites makes him an excellent devil's advocate, debater and strategy planner. Considering opposites is also partly responsible for his compassion since it often leads him to put himself into another person's shoes. However, the need to consider both sides may make decision making difficult. The young Scorpio may take a long time to figure out what he's feeling since he has to consider all the options first. During this option sorting, the Scorpio child may appear uninvolved or secretive. In reality, he needs to examine all the possibilities in order to feel secure in stating which one he chooses. Since this takes time and privacy, parents may want to ask Scorpio a leading question and then leave him alone to sort things out.

Little Scorpio's automatic awareness of opposites makes him vulnerable to manipulation. When parents know it will get them the results they want, they may be tempted to adopt a style of parenting through opposites. To get their Scorpio child into bed, they simply forbid him to go to bed. Little Scorpio's automatic compensation for other people's behavior is another way in which he can be manipulated. Siblings who fear that little Scorpio will be more popular need only be excessively verbal and charming, and their Scorpio sister or brother will automatically become less verbal and charming. Scorpios who are manipulated in this manner as children often grow up to be calculating and conniving adults, intensely aware of power dynamics. After a while, most Scorpios will choose to seize control of manipulations rather than remain the brunt of them, and then the whole family dynamic will shift. One cannot outmaneuver a Scorpio, even a child Scorpio, who has reached the end of his willingness to be other people's pawn.

Scorpio often seems to have an innate good sense of timing. This is another manifestation of his ability to compensate for any imbalance in his environment. The Scorpio child may wait until just after his sister has been given a new doll to ask for a new bicycle. He may quietly watch his parents' reactions to a brother's illness before admitting he doesn't feel too well himself.

Since the young Scorpio is seldom direct, he may look for clues to other people's preferences in their behavior and then alter his own behavior to conform to what he thinks they want. If Scorpio's best friend announces that she's about to begin acrobatic lessons, little Scorpio may feel compelled to take lessons also, assuming he will lose value to his friend if they cannot share the excitement of backward somersaults. Since the young Scorpio needs to excel, this child may ultimately be a better acrobat than his friend. He reasons, "If she likes someone who's good at acrobatics, she'll love someone who's great at it." To observers, little Scorpio may appear driven or competitive. He thinks he is merely trying to live up to standards he presumes others have.

All young children think of themselves as the center of the world and assume the world really is as they perceive it to be. Learning to expand this sense of reality is a long process that continues throughout childhood and later life. In a sign as complex as Scorpio, one of the major parenting tasks will be to help these children think consciously about their assumptions and beliefs. Since their complexity is an innate part of the sign, little Scorpios don't perceive their complexity as different and don't readily ask for help in understanding it. Quiet, nurturing conversations about daily activities, friendships and feelings will help parent and child sort through this process together.

The young Scorpio needs and loves approval. He loves praise, especially in public, but may develop a distrust of kind words. The young Scorpio may believe that other people know his need for approval and are merely trying to manipulate him instead of meaning what they say. Since the Scorpio child is not usually a good judge of sincerity, he may ultimately become suspicious of all praise, wondering what strings are attached. As with compliments, praise needs to be appropriate, specific, moderate and repeated consistently.

The Scorpio child can be quite critical of himself, and he usually has a pretty good idea of the quality of his performance. Parents need to be extremely honest in their assessment of little Scorpio's work or behavior and respond accordingly. A parent who shows equal enthusiasm for a scribble that took thirty seconds and a drawing that took three hours will earn only the Scorpio child's contempt and distrust.

The young Scorpio often prides himself on his loyalty and may remain attached to a possession or relationship long after it has served its usefulness, and even after he has been hurt. It may be difficult for parents to convince their Scorpio child to throw things away or to give up on a losing cause. His definition of loyalty may include beliefs about enduring pain and despair. Concerned parents will want to teach this loyal child ways of offering support without making personal sacrifices and when to let go.

The young Scorpio is usually efficient and resourceful. He believes he can nearly always find a use for things others discard. He may therefore be quite a pack rat. While this may be irritating to other family members, he does have an ability to turn his collected treasures into gold: to come up with the missing piece for a sibling's project or to have just the right wrapping paper when the family is hurrying to Aunt Josie's birthday party.

The young Scorpio's efficiency may sound critical, but his resourcefulness will nearly always sound helpful. Often, however, the Scorpio child can see only one way to do things, and he may have difficulty letting others do things their way when it's not as efficient as his own. Parents who teach compromise to their Scorpio child will be rewarded with his expanded creativity and gentleness. As with the Virgo child, little Scorpio may use apparent cynicism and criticism to mask disappointment, and he may appear angry when his feelings are hurt. The young Scorpio loves the predictable and may resent even wonderful events if they are unexpected.

Scorpio children are often cautious and methodical. They value control in themselves and others and fear loss of control on any level. They never need to be taught to control themselves—control comes naturally. Instead they need to be taught to relax. Scorpio children will often test themselves, particularly in areas of self-discipline. Sports requiring endurance and art projects requiring intense coordination and concentration were made for Scorpio children. Since small Scorpio's distinction between self-control and self-punishment is often unclear, the Scorpio child needs to be taught to use his incredibly focused energy in positive ways. He needs to be encouraged to relax and enjoy the rewards of his intense effort.

Permitting a young Scorpio to determine his own punishment is a dangerous venture. He's certain to be harder on himself than an adult would be. Light-handed discipline, with acknowledgment and discussion of the transgression, is all this child needs. If punished too heavily, he will learn to dodge responsibility; and if adults won't punish him, he will take over his own disciplinary action with far more vengeance than an adult would permit or expect.

The Scorpio child is intensely aware of the power dynamics in any situation. In new circumstances, be it a new school or gathering of people, little Scorpio will first note where the power lies: who's calling the shots. Since frequently the person with the power is not the one labeled as powerful, the Scorpio child is adept at knowing whom to ask for what he wants. He may know intuitively to ask the teacher's aide for more crayons and return to his desk with a fistful of colors while classmates wait in line to ask the teacher. Though this behavior may occasionally appear sneaky or manipulative, Scorpio children have a great deal to teach children of other signs about how to get what they want.

Scorpio is a very emotional sign. Scorpio children usually feel their emotions all the way down to their toes. When this intensity of emotion is combined with their knowledge of power, Scorpio children may develop particular ideas about the power of emotional expression. They may fear others will have power over them if they show their emotions or that they have given something away. For example, a Scorpio child who's been teased may refuse to show his anger. He will not "give" his teasers the satisfaction of knowing they have affected him. Unfortunately, a child who carefully guards his emotions may not be treated as if his emotions are real. People may see only what Scorpio wants them to see, while his real feelings go unnurtured and unacknowledged.

The young Scorpio often feels two emotions simultaneously; and being sensitive to other people's expectations, he may show the appropriate one and hide the other. He may assume others do the same and develop a distrust of emotions shown by others or assume others are hiding something. Thus, the Scorpio child is adept at reading the nuances in people's words and behavior. He must be cautioned about assuming too much or assuming that other people are as conscious of what they are communicating as he is conscious of interpreting these communications. He also needs to be encouraged to express the feelings he has chosen to hide. It may take him a long time to do this, and he may need to do it first outside the family and then try it at home.

Though little Scorpio may be reluctant to show what he's really feeling, he does not lack drama or animation. He very much needs to be noticed and cared about, and may exaggerate the events of his life to assure attention. His reactions to a lost sock or lost kitten may initially look identical, though the real feelings he has for the kitten will last much longer. It may be difficult for parents to determine what is really important to their child. Once again, quiet, reflective conversation with the Scorpio child can teach him to accept attention without drama and to sustain closeness without having to take the other person's feelings into account.

The Scorpio child wants to see what is underneath, inside and hidden, and will usually not stop until he has his answer. He loves to take things apart and cut things open. He is often intrigued with bodies and how they work and may be ambivalent about bodily functions. Things that disgust others are often intriguing to Scorpio. He's the child who will examine the dead mouse carcass, turn over moldy leaves, feel immensely drawn to a handicapped classmate. This interest is not detached from feelings and often has a healing component. The young Scorpio is likely to try to fix what he or another has broken. Since he is a very adept, creative fixer who is proud of his work, people often rely on him in this area. This may indeed become his area of greatest personal reward.

Crisis plays an important role in the young Scorpio's life, as it allows his talents to shine. The Scorpio child needs intensity and intimacy and loathes superficiality. In a crisis situation, or while working under pressure, little Scorpio has the opportunity to use all his healing and organizing skills, to be intense and intimate in a limited and structured way, and to get all the approval he needs. This is a time when he knows he is most alive. As a result, he is often given rather large amounts of responsibility, and peers and adults alike frequently seek him out during stressful times.

Pain also occupies a special place in the life of the young Scorpio. He frequently relates better to people who are in pain, since he feels needed, useful or somehow superior or relieved that he is not the one in pain. The intimacy that comes through shared pain may also be attractive to the young Scorpio, though others may be bewildered at the child's abandonment when their pain is past. For example, little Scorpio may befriend a child with a broken leg, but the friendship loses importance when the cast is off. Scorpio needs to be taught how to value happy periods as well as crises, and how to interact with happy people as well as those in pain.

Through the distress of others, little Scorpio may find permission to have his own distress, or he may find reassurance that his needs are also within the range of acceptability. He often believes he can fix discomfort and he sometimes prides himself on being able to anticipate and meet the needs of others. While this gentleness and concern is admirable, young Scorpio needs to be reminded that he is welcome even when he's not "needed."

Scorpio's pride in his ability to anticipate the needs of others may ultimately interfere with his relationships. If the Scorpio child believes he *should* have guessed his mother's needs, then he may interpret her request for a neck rub or for help putting away groceries as humiliating criticism. Scorpio loves to surprise others and may be deeply offended if his surprise is not well accepted, even though the recipient may feel more controlled than loved. For example, Dad may not want to take the bath little Scorpio just prepared for him and feel resentful at having to choose between hurting the child's feelings and interrupting his schedule. Ironically, the young Scorpio himself usually loathes surprises.

Since this ability to react to other people's unspoken needs is an inborn Scorpio trait, the child is often confused about how to use his skill in moderation. When people say, "I don't want you to second-guess me, I'll tell you what I want," little Scorpio hears a reprimand not to be himself. Parents can help by following a request, to not "second-guess" them, with a brief explanation that this intuition is a *skill,* separate from the child himself.

During adolescence, the Scorpio teenager and his family can more easily work to separate intuitive skill from self-concept and teach Scorpio that just because he guesses what another wants, he is under no obligation to provide it. A family structure where both adults and children have healthy permission to state what they do and don't want will be of great help in raising the Scorpio child.

While the young Scorpio is quite willing to deal with other people's needs, he is more ambivalent about having needs of his own. He may perceive his own physical and emotional needs as signs of weakness and feel contempt for himself. He may react with shame or feel exposed when someone identifies his unspoken needs and offers help. He may wait until his needs or feelings reach monumental proportions before he admits to having them. If he is not stating his own needs and is withdrawing or rebelling when someone guesses them, he is in the awkward position of ensuring that his needs will not be met. This is hard on parents who want to feel adequate in caring for their Scorpio child. Parents need to remain sensitive to this dynamic and remind their recalcitrant child that he is indeed like everyone else, and everyone deserves to have his or her needs lovingly responded to. In other words, it is just as blessed to receive as it is to give, though it may take Scorpio a long time to figure this out and to let it be okay.

Generally, the Scorpio child's sensitivity works in favor of everyone. Sweet and considerate, he uses his healing energies to improve his environment. The young Scorpio can organize and manage things with astonishing style, and he will stick to any project until it's done. Though he is introspective and sometimes self-indulgent, he is passionate about those he loves, loyal and devoted to things and people he cares about. His awareness of natural cycles and his depth of insight and resourcefulness create a commitment to return to life at least as much as he takes. He leaves any environment different, and often in better shape than he found it. He is creative and observant. Parents will come to rely on their Scorpio's intense concentration and sense of responsibility, and the entire family will be delighted at his infrequent, but on-target, flashes of humor.

## NEEDS (Scorpio's emotional emphasis)

Appreciation.

Privacy.

Challenge.

Intensity.

Permission not to compensate.

Permission to fail.

Permission to be honest.

Permission to show fear.

Permission to explore, eliminate, refuse, exclude.

Permission not to react; help in identifying own voice.

Quiet periods.

Options and choices.

Tempered approval.

Light-handed discipline.

Guidance in speaking directly.

Guidance in including other influences.

Guidance in discovering neutral, in-between reactions.

To be taken seriously.

To learn humor.

To differentiate the relative importance of events.

Honesty: to be told as much truth about family dynamics as is
appropriate to his age and understanding.

Not to be teased, shamed, humiliated, manipulated.

Not to be told to control himself.

Not to be pushed or coerced to expose emotions.

Help relaxing.

## COMMON ASSUMPTIONS (How Scorpio views the world around him)

All or nothing: half a loaf is not better than none.

An eye for an eye.

Suffering is a measure of love.

Pain is the measure of living.

SENSITIVITIES (Potential sources of misunderstanding)

*Fear:* Possibly the most difficult emotion for the young Scorpio to acknowledge is fear. He tends to be especially fascinated and attracted by precisely that which scares him. He believes that if he can figure out how it works or how to control what threatens him, he can make his fear go away. He is also very proud of his courage. The Scorpio child needs to be taught the purpose of fear; that it is a warning signal necessary for survival. If he persists in being attracted to fearsome things, he is likely to put himself in rather dangerous situations and to be a poor judge of safety.

*Sharing:* The young Scorpio may experience difficulty sharing. Though often generous, he is territorial and prefers having things of his own. If he offers to help wash the car, he is being generous with both time and energy, but he will work better having a side of the car designated as his own responsibility and working on it by himself. On a more abstract level, the Scorpio child is often confused about sharing concepts like blame and responsibility. He does not know how to do things halfway and tends to take all or nothing. Parents who exercise caution in assigning blame will do a great service for the Scorpio child. Teaching the child how to divide responsiblilty and that he is not responsible for the behavior of others—including siblings—will also help to relieve little Scorpio's distress.

*Shame:* The young Scorpio is particularly vunerable to shame. Since he is a perfectionist at heart who needs to do things "just so" and have things "just right," the Scorpio child is likely to feel quite ashamed if events do not go as planned, whether or not he had any direct responsibility for the outcome. Little Scorpio may compulsively organize things in order to avoid the shame of disarray. He may also feel ashamed of his body, needs or feelings. Concerned parents will make extra efforts to reassure their frightened child that he is adequate and lovable just as he is, that everyone misbehaves and errs occasionally, and that his behavior is not connected to his worthiness.

Because of his intense need to do things right, the Scorpio child often assumes the position of either the favored child or the scapegoat in his family. In either case, he feels isolated and increasingly fearful about his performance. Whether parents are saying, "Be like Scorpio" or "For heaven's sake, don't be like Scorpio," everyone is invited to vent their frustration on this little child. Parents need to acknowledge their Scorpio child's essential humanness and sameness and to avoid comparing him with others. Like any child, he is sometimes good and sometimes obnoxious, and he doesn't need to be trapped in either role.

## RELATIONSHIPS

Relationships are the most important area to the Scorpio child. He defines himself by comparing himself with others and identifying areas of similarity and difference. It is urgent for him to converse intensely with those nearby in order to make these comparisons, and small Scorpio therefore has little patience with chitchat. Once having interacted at that deep level, however, the Scorpio child feels quite invested in the relationship and may have difficulty sharing that person with others. The small Scorpio who has just had an intimate conversation with his teacher may feel betrayed or frightened when he sees her five minutes later talking to another student. Thus, the Scorpio child may appear jealous or possessive and needs reassurance about the continuity and importance of his relationships and the concern of the other party.

Little Scorpio tends to be both loyal and exclusive. His attention is usually directed to only one person at a time, and he expects the same in return. Others sometimes find this exclusive attention unnerving. A young Scorpio who is forced to share someone's attentions may feel betrayed or ashamed and is not likely to forget the incident. In compensation, he may try to hurt the offending person as he was hurt. He feels that only after the situation has again been equalized can he resume the intimacy.

On the other hand, little Scorpio may not acknowledge when he feels slighted, instead giving the other party "enough rope to hang themselves." At this point, the young Scorpio assumes the other person knows what he wants and is deliberately behaving in a way contrary to his needs. Finally, though the Scorpio child's external behavior may not change, he closes off his openness to this person and alters the status of the relationship by releasing his investment. Parents need to teach little Scorpio to articulate his needs if a relationship is important to him and not to let it fail for lack of insight. Young Scorpios may wait patiently for proof of someone's concern, interpreting their ignorance of his needs or respect for his privacy as disinterest or punishment.

It is the Scorpio in any of us that is competitive or not. The young Scorpio can be extremely competitive and needs to be taught positive outlets for these energies. Small Scorpio may use comparison with the achievements, behaviors, decisions or gains of others to motivate himself toward more difficult goals or to make himself feel bad, but competition in a close relationship prevents the intimacy he so fervently seeks. The young Scorpio may also use this behavior to make himself feel more important (if he's "winning") or to scare himself (if he's "losing"). In either case, he deprives himself of equal relationships. If the young Scorpio believes that others are like him in this regard, he may have difficulty trusting other people or believing in their unconditional goodwill.

The Scorpio child may also believe there needs to be a purpose to any relationship. He may have difficulty justifying an ongoing friendship if he is not getting or giving something. Learning to appreciate people for exactly who they are without changing them (or himself) will be a valuable lesson for this child.

Little Scorpio's standards for himself are so high he often seeks someone else to blame in order to reduce internal pressure. He may use the word "you" when he really means "I," as in, "You can really get grouchy when it's hot." He may become terribly ashamed of himself and defensive if he has no one else to blame for his imagined or real transgressions or if he is caught in the act of blaming. Parents need to remind little Scorpio exactly who is responsible for what and to approach difficulties as problems that need to be solved rather than as events to which blame must be assigned. A father who shouts, "Who forgot to put gas in the car?" is teaching his children to attribute blame rather than to solve problems.

Once committed to a relationship, the Scorpio child is loyal and determined. He will stand by others in all circumstances and is often the one with the most stamina and endurance. His ability to perform well in crisis and his comfort with other people's distress assures deep and lasting contact once his trust is earned.

*Mom:* Scorpio children expect Mom to be more intellectual than Dad, more erratic and less accessible. They may treat Mom more like a friend than like a parent.

Moms who want to nurture their Scorpio child more directly will make an effort to be consistent and predictable and to follow through on what they say they will do. Though they may feel personally intimidated by the intensity of their child's feelings, moms of little Scorpios will endear themselves to their child by listening carefully to the emotions and not asking too many questions or trying to solve the child's problems. While Dad and the Scorpio child are equally strong and may have to vie for position, Mom and little Scorpio have the potential to be true equals in a way that does not require proof or struggle. It is important that moms remember to function as parents, however, and not demand the child's equality too soon.

*Dad:* The young Scorpio sees Dad as reliable, strong, authoritarian and mostly predictable. He usually appreciates Dad's humor and feels safe near him.

Since dads of Scorpios tend to be strong, and since little Scorpio is also quite powerful, these two members of a family may form a remarkably productive alliance, or find themselves engaged in a subtle battle of wills. Both parties may need to be right, and both strongly resent being bullied. The young Scorpio will probably test Dad's strength, endurance and intellect. Dad needs to remember that he is battling with a child and to continue being his usual generous and magnanimous self without condescending.

The young Scorpio may make a particular effort to keep an ailing family together, or he may utilize the discord as an opportunity to subtly set one parent against the other. Parents need to exercise great care to avoid being manipulated by their little Scorpio and to help him maintain confidence in their maturity and abilities.

*Siblings:* The young Scorpio will often try to keep up with his siblings, especially older ones. He may become frustrated at what he perceives as their privilege or expertise, or he may form a strong bond with a favorite. Since Scorpio children cannot tolerate teasing and are very sensitive to blame, parents of little Scorpios need to maintain vigilance around the interaction between Scorpio and his siblings.

*Friends:* Little Scorpio is a loyal and enduring friend. He is helpful and reliable and will often patiently remain involved with a friend when all seems lost. He likes people who share his values and outlook and will often form a close bond with someone who also agrees with his rather cynical view of the world and appreciates his dry humor or sarcasm. The young Scorpio may be popular but usually has only one or two close friends at a time with whom he is intense and exclusive.

## MIND/INFORMATION/SCHOOL

Young Scorpios are inquisitive and persistent and often have minds like steel traps. Most Scorpio children have fairly complete recall but often choose to remember only those items that are, or may be, useful. They are practical and serious students who frequently exhibit precocious mechanical ability and remarkable skill with metaphor. While Scorpio students often appear to be intimidated by authority, they may spend considerable time figuring out ways to avoid or subvert those in power.

The young Scorpio is intuitive and perceptive, and may not always be able to identify the source of his data. He learns well by means of opposites and often needs a contrary idea or person to react against. He himself will frequently play devil's advocate in order to understand a concept more clearly, to irritate or engage others or to hide his true beliefs. While young Scorpio can be extremely blunt and incisive, he seldom tells all he knows. Little Scorpio is a wonderful keeper of secrets.

Young Scorpio is especially curious about human behavior. He wants to know what motivates people and why they act as they do. He dislikes anything superficial and tends to probe beyond the obvious. He likes reading between the lines, looking under things and hearing what's not spoken. While the danger exists that the Scorpio child will assign a meaning to events or interactions that does not exist, he needs to know the meaning and application of all he learns.

*Higher Education:* The young Scorpio likes the safety of credentials and will usually eventually pursue whatever certification is required for his chosen field. He may choose a career that permits him to manipulate things, people or money, and he often believes education will help him be a more effective and productive worker.

## RESPONSIBILITY/WORK/REWARDS

*Responsibility and Work:* Even the young Scorpio is capable of intense concentration and focus. This energy, applied to any task, assures it will be done and done well. While the Scorpio child will usually finish any task he begins, he may become resentful if the task is long, arduous or unrewarding. If he perceives beforehand that he will dislike the chore, he may begin complaining early so that when he's really fed up, the adults around him are already well prepared. Or he may become a silent martyr, carrying his anger at the imposition silently for a long time. Scorpio children are very good at getting others to do their work for them. Nevertheless, if they want a task done properly, they will insist on doing it themselves. Or they will supervise the others closely.

Scorpio children have a very strong sense of responsibility and take their efforts seriously. They feel safe when they are in control. Scorpios expect others to take their efforts seriously as well and may be quite hurt if their achievements are overlooked. Sometimes young Scorpios assume responsibility that is not rightfully theirs, feeling guilty about events they think they caused or could have prevented or becoming quite insistent about the proper way for others to do things.

*Rewards:* Little Scorpio needs recognition, approval and acknowledgment of effort. Ever wary, the young Scorpio is keenly aware of the relative importance of various tasks and is sensitive to the relative magnitude of the reward. He distrusts large rewards for small efforts and is hurt by small rewards for large efforts. He likes gratitude and payment in kind, and very much appreciates money or privilege for tasks completed. Especially with the teenage Scorpio, it is important to discuss the terms of reward prior to the undertaking of task.

## HOME

The Scorpio child prefers a room, or at least an area, of his own. He likes privacy and entertains only those people he explicitly invites in. He likes somber and subdued colors and new quality brand-name furnishings. He will periodically instigate a sudden and complete change of decor. He is usually proud of his living space and careful with his selected possessions.

Little Scorpio often prefers staying at home to traveling and needs a home base for security. While he likes traveling to a place for the second time (then it is familiar), he most loves coming home.

# HEALTH

When the young Scorpio gets sick, he likes a great deal of respectful and unobtrusive attention. He may see illness as a way of getting attention and approval, or he may use it as a means of avoiding or expressing anger. Little Scorpio may also use illness as an excuse to speak the truth or possibly as a means of discouraging others from speaking the truth.

The Scorpio child is interested in bodily functions and eagerly participates in his own treatment. He needs explanations of all procedures and may become frightened or resentful if information is withheld.

Traditionally, Scorpio rules the excretory and sexual organs. Little Scorpios experiencing health problems are likely to have bowel or menstrual irregularities, or to suffer from exhaustion incurred while pushing themselves too hard.

# CHILDHOOD AGES

*(Note: The fears detailed in this section are never to be used as punishment. They are presented as avenues for reassurance and caring.)*

BIRTH–6 MONTHS

Newborn Scorpio is serious and intense. He is cautious and self-contained until he is certain he feels safe and his needs will be met. Once assured of his survival and comfort, however, he opens like a flower, and his extraordinary smile and attention illuminate his entire environment.

This is a private little baby who is extra sensitive to personal violations. He needs never to be tickled, teased, exhibited or controlled by means of shame. Even at this tender age, little Scorpio needs to be prepared in advance for changes whenever possible. Problems with digestion or bowels usually indicate that infant Scorpio is feeling unsafe or unprotected, and more attention should therefore be paid to his comfort and security. Cuddly and affectionate entirely on his own terms, little Scorpio quickly trains sensitive parents to take their cues from him and rewards them amply with smiles and loyalty.

*Needs*
Privacy.
Unconditional love.
A lot of attention.
Stimulation.
Touching and holding entirely for him.
Respectful touching without intrusion.

*Fears*
Invasion.
Deprivation.
Punishment.
Fear.
Dependence.

## 6 MONTHS–18 MONTHS

Baby Scorpio continues to be intense and serious. Intuitive and capable of deep focus and concentration even at this age, little Scorpio is aware of his surroundings and is already interested in taking things apart, getting to the bottom of things. Baby Scorpio becomes more aware of his impact on others at this age and begins exhibiting behavior designed to elicit predictable results from nearby grown-ups. He also shows budding awareness of the dynamics of opposites and delights in games that include rudimentary concepts of opposition, such as fitting pegs into the right shaped holes and later identifying opposite colors, etc. Baby Scorpio may also be precociously interested in sexual matters and may ask probing questions about death or sex as soon as he can talk.

Little Scorpio loves water and wet things and begins at this age his lifelong love/hate relationship with things that other people may define as dirty or gross. He loves mud and finger paints and should not be discouraged from this kind of involvement, which helps both his creativity and his comfort with his own body later on.

*Needs*
Privacy.
Sincere approval.
Structured cuddling and affection.

Limits.
Interaction.
Light joking, playing, laughter.
Permission to get dirty.

*Fears*
Teasing.
Shaming, humiliation.
Punishment.
Disapproval.

## 18 MONTHS–3 YEARS

The Scorpio toddler is sensitive, emotional and private—bordering on sulky. He may not talk until he feels he has something to say. Creative and volatile, this little Scorpio reacts to a variety of stimuli in ways that are often original, unexpected and sometimes quite delightful. The family will be amply supplied with anecdotes of little Scorpio's behavior and responses. Such delights provide a pleasant balance for families of Scorpios as these may be competitive, compulsive, controlling years for this toddler. Scorpio wants to test his power, and parents may occasionally become quite exasperated with their sometimes stubborn, rebellious, resentful, contrary child whose concern with opposites also includes answering "No!" to all suggestions and commands. The Scorpio toddler was doubtless the model for the "terrible two's."

The intense Scorpio curiosity continues in this child and now includes deep interest in both sex and death. The toddling Scorpio is also confronting his own fears, usually by scaring himself. He is exploring cause and effect and, especially toward the end of this period, wants to set his own boundaries and mete out his own punishment. Both the boundaries and punishments are likely to be too severe, and watchful parents will put strict limits on the extent to which young Scorpio is allowed to set his own boundaries and punishments.

*Toilet Training:* Little Scorpio is extremely vulnerable to decisions about his body, and it is during this period that he learns pride or shame concerning his physical being. He is very interested in his bodily functions and will usually respond to reasonable explanations or to appeals to his pride in his self-discipline and ability to control himself. If this approach is successful, he may virtually toilet train himself. If, on the other hand, he feels rebellious or is currently fascinated by things that repel other people, he may be very resistant to toilet training. Since Scorpio cannot be forced or coerced into any behavior, power struggles are best avoided through patience on the part of parents and minimal attention to the task.

*Needs*
Explanations and reasons.
Permission to do things his way.
Privacy.
Outlets for competitive energy.
Outlets for creative energy and fantasy.
Support and approval.
Persistent and consistent caring.
Permission to be dependent.
Preparation for changes.

*Fears*
Teasing.
Criticism.
Shame (especially in public).
Force.
Intrusion.

3 YEARS – 6 YEARS

The preschool Scorpio continues to be intense, dramatic, volatile and, often, frightened. He is quite concerned with comparing everything with everything else and often pushes himself to be the best, the most, etc. He may want the biggest or the newest or the most expensive, though seldom does he seek the ostentatious. Little Scorpio may precipitate crises just to see what will happen by instigating fights or acting out of control or depressed to test his power and impact on others. In testing various roles, he may copy and reject a variety of behavioral styles and, at any given time, may appear quite critical of all roles other than the one he currently espouses. He may test the effectiveness of sarcasm during this period, especially if he has been teased previously, and this is the age at which he learns to smirk. He loves secrets.

The preschool Scorpio needs to know that grown-ups are not afraid of him and that they will not let him hurt himself. His natural sweetness, creativity and sensitivity will be evident only when young Scorpio believes that the adults around him are both smarter and stronger than he is. Adults need to monitor their reactions to the emotional expressions of their Scorpio child and to make firm decisions about not meeting drama with drama.

*Needs*
Approval.
Compassion.
Appropriate reactions to emotional expression.
Help evaluating relative importance of things.
Feedback.
Limits and boundaries.
Information, especially about sex and death.
Help sharing.
Adults willing to make extra effort to know the Scorpio child.
Responsibility appropriate to his own level.

*Fears*
Coercion.
Isolation.
Being too powerful.
Loss of control.
Lack of supply.
Being laughed at.
Retaliation.
Humiliation.
Being blamed.
Being teased.

## 6 YEARS–12 YEARS

The school-age Scorpio is private, sometimes secretive, and cautious. He is very aware of other people's views and opinions of him and will often alter his behavior to achieve a desired result, whether it's to shock people or to gain their approval. He may believe he and his behavior represent his family, ethnic group or some other group to which he belongs and therefore push himself harder and harder to perform. His sensitivity and perceptiveness may prevent him from accepting the very approval he longs for. Since he is acutely aware of his vulnerability to manipulation through flattery, he may discount approval as simply the way others attempt to control his behavior. Whether he rebels or attempts to comply, he is very conscious of status.

His fear of being blamed, or otherwise held responsible, for actions other than his own may lead to behavior that appears defensive or rigid. The young Scorpio may secretly believe that others know some magic way of behaving that he doesn't know; he may act condescending or superior, as if he knows some magic others do not. He may insist that things be done his way or not at all. He may pretend that if he does not have a particular thing, that thing is meaningless. The young Scorpio may occasionally seem particularly manipulative and controlling to adults who want their own way.

The young Scorpio may scare himself into doing things. He tends to hear threats even when none are intended and to perceive demands on him in others' choices for themselves. He may therefore be motivated to assume positions of leadership whereby he can make the rules and set the expectations, or he may appear harshly critical of the decisions and behaviors of those around him. While his criticisms may appear superior and arrogant to his peers (and very naive to grown-ups), the young Scorpio can turn around and in the same breath be intensely compassionate if he feels the situation warrants it.

It is during this time that the young Scorpio may begin to say the opposite of what he means, but it is also during this period that he learns to figure out what he wants and needs through the process of elimination. He is experimenting with power during this period, learning to be strong without bullying, to negotiate without feeling weak. He is reveling in his sharp mind and memory, and exploring nonlinear ways of thinking.

*Needs*
Approval, support, encouragement.
Moral explanations.
Limits, boundaries.
Help in learning negotiating skills.

*Fears*
Surprises.
Lack of control.
Humiliation.
Losing.
Teasing.
Threats and accusations, being blamed.

## 12 YEARS–18 YEARS

The teenage Scorpio is introspective, moody, intense and shrewd. He may seem preoccupied with his body, scared of or fascinated by its responses, and he seems to endlessly test his own limits, capacities and endurance. If he feels contemptuous of his body, his testing may become self-punishment, or he may permit others to be mean to him. Concerned parents need to set firm and nonnegotiable limits in the area of physical testing. The young Scorpio, nevertheless, values self-control and self-discipline whether or not he exhibits these behaviors himself, and he may go from extremes of self-abuse to self-indulgence. Adolescent Scorpios tend to do things the hard way and to push themselves and others to their very limits.

The teenage Scorpio is at once fascinated and repelled by his sexuality and seeks ways to hide, exploit or control his needs and responses. He may experiment with flirtatious and seductive behaviors or become quite ascetic. His need for privacy during these years does not mean he's doing anything wrong; he needs a great deal of personal and real space to explore all of his options.

Continuing the patterns established earlier, the adolescent Scorpio remains private, serious, intense and secretive. He tends to take things personally, to react rather than initiate activity, and still remains afraid of being blamed. He acts fearless and often seeks the excitement of situations that are challenging and at least emotionally dangerous. He expects as much (or as little) of others as he does of himself and can be extremely sarcastic, disgusted and critical when others fail to live up to his standards. He eagerly seeks people who are as strong and as smart as he is but may become frightened, competitive or withdrawn when he finds them or despairing when he doesn't. The young Scorpio would like to be sought with equal fervor but often makes that task singularly difficult or unrewarding for the seeker. However, when the teenage Scorpio does find someone he believes is worthy of his attentions, he can be attentive, charming, loyal and romantic. He may also be jealous, possessive and obsessed. While he usually refuses to bribe people's friendship with gifts and favors (and may rebel against such a suggestion), he is generous and giving with those he loves.

The adolescent Scorpio may believe that emotions not stated dramatically will not be taken seriously. Or he may wait until a feeling or need reaches critical proportions before he pays attention to it. Teenage Scorpios often start out understating their needs and feelings, followed by dramatic exaggeration of those same feelings. Concerned adults need to remember that even though the feelings look dramatic and grandiose, they are real and need to be addressed.

The teenage Scorpio is often quite competitive and loves conquest. The chase is frequently the most exciting part to a Scorpio, who may lose interest once a trophy is won. He tends to believe the grass is greener wherever he isn't and occasionally resents others' good fortune, though he is usually too mannerly to say so. He may rebel against the family's rules and standards, or he may comply with a vengeance to what is expected of him. His rebellion is often subtle and private and may not manifest itself until he is in his late thirties or early forties.

The young Scorpio continues to love secrets and may be secretive even when everyone agrees there's nothing to hide—or he may appear blunt and tactless, "spilling" everything in the name of unvarnished truth, though in reality he remains quite careful about what he reveals.

The adolescent Scorpio is particularly adept at arts that require manual dexterity, such as pottery or sculpture. He usually excels in science and is generally at ease with things that require mechanical ability. He is a responsible, conscientious, persistent worker who usually does slightly more or less than he says he'll do. Ever aware of his environment, the young Scorpio can always report on what is going on and usually has suggestions for improving the situation. Parents welcome Scorpio's deep intelligence and fervor and often come to count on the shy, dry humor that comes unexpectedly through those usually solemn eyes.

*Needs*

Privacy.

Clear limits.

Information about sex.

Persistent, consistent adults.

Negotiating skills.

Competitive outlets.

Permission to be scared.

*Hates*

Waste.

Being unappreciated.

Being blamed.

Punishment.

Approval from someone he doesn't respect.

Hypocrisy.

Being laughed at, exposed, ridiculed.

Obligation.

Being called compulsive, rigid.

Being told, "You made your bed, lie in it."

Being told, "Shame on you."

Being asked, "What's the matter with you?"

# SAGITTARIUS CHILDREN

**(NOVEMBER 22–DECEMBER 21)**

## GENERAL CHARACTERISTICS

*(Note: While many of the characteristics described below will be accurate for most Sagittarians, other, sometimes contradictory, traits may also be evident in an individual child.)*

Parents will immediately adore their newborn Sagittarius, who is alert, cheerful and amiable. Squirmy and restless, baby Sagittarius seems to be either sleeping or in constant motion; placid is not a word used to describe the Sagittarius tot! Little Sagittarians are full of seemingly endless energy and curiosity. Their eyes are alert and twinkle with perpetual delight. They are often found brushing their hair away from their foreheads in order to give those bright eyes a clearer perspective. From infancy on, little Sagittarius is on a quest to understand things, to gather information, to uncover truth and define independence. Of all the zodiac signs, Sagittarius is one of the hardest to reduce to any single concept or theme. One continuing motif is Sagittarius's complexity, busyness and restlessness; and this theme is evident in the Sagittarius child from the time she can focus her curious stare on the world around her and begin to grasp for anything within reach.

Interested and interesting, little Sagittarians pursue information as if it were a life force. They need to understand and know reasons for the most minute bit of data. At best, they retain half of what they've learned, but they carefully sort and note the connections and overall patterns within their environment. Since their information is so broad and comprehensive, little Sagittarians may lack the focusing skills necessary to utilize all that they know; but they are excellent resource people, able to juggle extraordinary amounts of data. Sagittarians tend to gulp information in large chunks. They seek patterns and assign meaning to things that may appear ordinary to others. They are the opposite of literal and instead look for the metaphoric, symbolic, mythical and ironic aspects of information. Sagittarians are therefore remarkable storytellers, mythmakers and fablemakers. A fable is, after all, only an ordinary story to which someone has attached meaning; and little Sagittarius has a great skill for attaching meaning to all the information she puts together. For example, a five-year-old Sagittarius from the Midwest was on his first vacation to the West Coast. As the family picnicked on the beach, little Sagittarius gathered all kinds of information on why he couldn't see to the other side, why the water was salty, where whales lived, etc. A little while later, walking along the surf's edge, little Sagittarius announced to an astonished parent, "Oh, I see, God made the ocean so people would ask questions."

Little Sagittarius is able to personalize and make relevant even the most abstract data. She will compulsively share her information—invited or not—even to her own detriment. She will teach all the other children how to subtract, even if she sacrifices her own grade "A" in the process. Her very literal definition of honesty may also be troublesome; she may bluntly tell her teacher she has bad breath just before she is to be graded.

Because they are comfortable with the symbolic and impatient with literal interpretations of events, young Sagittarians seek metaphors and think in parables and broad sweeps. Their imagination is superb, and they are usually intrigued by any sort of larger-than-life story, including fairy tales, heroic sagas and fantasies. Though their search for truth may leave them skeptical, they nevertheless love the tales of Paul Bunyan, Wonder Woman and other omnipotent beings. They may also be fascinated by stories of how Grandpa came to this country, though they'll listen with their usual delight mixed with skepticism. They do not like being laughed at, talked down to or gossiped about for seeing the world in mythic terms.

Young Sagittarians see beyond the obvious, are visionary and future oriented. They are attracted more to potential than to what exists now, seeing the sparkling jewel within the rough rock found on the beach or the potential in a little friend who appears withdrawn. In many respects, Sagittarians' lives are a search for something to believe in, an absolute truth or perfection of some sort. They have an innate sense of principle and may argue and hassle for pure enjoyment. Thoughtful and philosophical, little Sagittarians seek an ethic or morality by which to live. They are therefore often extremely interested in other cultures and religions. They will carefully examine these alternate ways of experiencing and seeing life and extract personal grains of truth for themselves. They frequently have a facility for other languages, including mathematics and computer programming, and exhibit more than technical competence in these areas. Their proficiency is based on comprehension of other viewpoints and their ability to translate a broad understanding of human experience into concepts meaningful in their own culture. Adult Sagittarians make excellent and sensitive diplomats, missionaries, foreign businessmen or resettlement workers with immigrants. Journeying often takes on literal form in Sagittarius's love of travel or may be abstracted into love of scholarship and commitment to a lifetime of learning.

All this may sound quite puzzling and futuristic to the parent who peers over the rim of this book into the face of a two-year-old Sagittarius, but it is important for people around the developing Sagittarius to have some idea of the broader scope in which she thinks and lives. There is little parents need do to foster these traits in their Sagittarius child—they are inborn—but they need to be sensitive to this mythical, questing aspect and allow their child room for seeing the world in her own way. And for reward, parents and other trusted adults are allowed glimpses into the Sagittarius's mythical ways of seeing and interpreting the world.

The spirited little Sagittarius is restless both intellectually and physically. She detests and fears boredom and will do almost anything to avoid it. This drive to avoid boredom makes life with a young Sagittarius quite interesting and sometimes hard to follow. In their initial enthusiasm, Sagittarian children may seem almost fanatic in embracing a new concept or activity. Especially when enthusiastic, Sagittarius can be very verbal, charming and persuasive. If she discovers an exciting new club, the Sagittarian child may convince most of her friends to join it with her—and then move on to something else, leaving bewildered friends behind.

Superstition may figure strongly in Sagittarian thinking; since, in her commitment to find meaning, she may attach significance to trivial events. For example, "It rained; I wasn't meant to go to the movies." Some of this superstition is based on Sagittarius's feeling that she is truly at the center of the universe. Sagittarians tend to believe the environment exists for their pleasure. Sagittarius is a fire sign, and all fire signs deal with the relationship of the self to the world. In this light, the Sagittarius child may assume an importance or power that is unrealistic and grandiose, and may believe she has control, or that others have control, over aspects of life that are essentially neutral. Little Sagittarius may believe that if the car broke down on the day she didn't want to go to the dentist, it was she who caused the car to malfunction. This magical thinking can lead to expectations of superhuman feats on the part of the young Sagittarius herself or of others. She may develop strange rituals or superstitious behavior to try to control neutral life events. A teenage Sagittarius who had neglected to study for a math test slept with the book under her pillow, hoping to absorb magically the needed information before school the next day. The young Sagittarius needs to be taught to consider that most events in life just are, they don't *mean* anything and that the relationship between cause and effect is not magical.

The Sagittarius child is optimistic and idealistic. She expects to find the best in people and situations and often does. She seems lucky and opportunistic. She is resourceful, able to make the best of difficult situations and often resolutely overlooks unexpected or unfortunate occurrences that don't fit into her optimism. While this is an admirable trait, it may further confuse the Sagittarian belief in the magic of events. For example, a Sagittarian child may give her seat in the bus to an old woman, confident that someone will give their seat to her grandmother. Sagittarius is also adaptable and forgiving, able to flow with circumstances and extract exciting information from her experiences. Getting caught in a snowstorm becomes a way to learn additional survival skills and have an exciting social experience. In fact, if a person or situation does not contain the potential for new information, the little Sagittarius is likely to abandon it for something new.

The Sagittarian child seeks the challenge of learning from differences. She doesn't want to know how we're alike; she wants to know how we're different and how we connect. She is interested in tangents. Adult Sagittarians often become remarkable anthropologists, teachers, journalists and students of comparative cultures or religions. Adult Sagittarians can also appear superficial or disloyal, since as soon as they have extracted what they deem important from a given experience, situation or person, they are ready to move on. Young Sagittarians need to explore many areas of interest before they identify one or two that deserve additional attention. They need to take other people's feelings into account and learn to satisfy their search for new experiences without abandoning longtime friends.

Sagittarian belief in the "positive" may be so unshakable that they refuse to see negative aspects of reality. They may respond to stress in ways that look inappropriate because they don't want to believe it's really happening. A little Sagittarius who loves puppies was so surprised by a snarling dog that she moved toward it, disbelieving it would hurt her. She encountered the dog and reacted the same way several times before she was willing to admit that not all puppies are nice. Onlookers may be astonished that these children seem not to learn from experience and repeat errors in judgment time and again. A more accurate appraisal would be to look for ways the little Sagittarius is refusing to acknowledge negative situations.

Sagittarian children may therefore repeatedly climb the same symbolic mountain. While the courage and stamina this takes is obvious, the truly amazing fact is how often they ultimately succeed. Not believing in the impossible, Sagittarians often achieve what others only dream about. Life to the little Sagittarius is simply a series of exciting challenges, and she is undaunted by failure. She seems to have contempt for fear and is as likely to seek out a situation that scares her as to avoid it. Sometimes, however, Sagittarian children seem merely to be tilting at windmills and may misdirect a great deal of energy before they finally give up. Eventually, just like the rest of us, Sagittarians have to deal with disappointment.

There's something to be said for pessimism: it prepares us for life's harder moments. Sometimes Sagittarius, with its emphasis on optimism, is ill-prepared to deal with disappointment or defeat. The danger is that the Sagittarian child will apply her magical thinking to disappointment as surely as she applied it to her luck. She may switch from believing life wants her to have something (so, of course, I *will* have it) to believing life doesn't want her to have something (so, of course, I *can't* have it). The trouble with magical thinking is that it can as easily lead to cynicism and defeatism as to anything else. The disappointed young Sagittarius needs to be reminded that consequences are not magical. If she tries out for the school choir but can't carry a tune, being turned down has to do with the lack of a needed skill and is not a preordained rejection of herself as a person.

If thwarted over long periods of time, the idealism of the little Sagittarius can lead to chronic disappointment, cynicism and rationalization about why she can't get what she wants. Parents with a pessimistic or defeatist Sagittarius in the family need to look for ways to help her rediscover her quest. It is the sense of a quest that brings joy to the Sagittarius's spirit. She needs it, and she may need help reconnecting herself to her quest if she has just come through a period of unavoidable hardship. Parents also need to check out the ways a Sagittarian child may be explaining hardship to herself and make sure she hasn't decided life is magically against her. The return of the Sagittarian's buoyancy is well worth this family effort.

Sagittarian children are models of fairness and are finely tuned to situations that appear unequal. The little Sagittarius on the playground is the first to shout, "unfair!" She sincerely believes in equality of opportunity and will expend great amounts of energy and advice to assure equitable treatment and distribution. This trait is obvious in the ways in which little Sagittarians deal with peers. They will make sure everyone has a chance to play with the new toy or that all the candies are counted out and distributed evenly. Other children often seek out a Sagittarius child to handle matters of equality or distribution because they sense this innate fairness.

Sagittarius children may have trouble confusing their "fairness above all" philosophy with the assumption that everyone's needs are identical to their own. They may offer a bicycle ride to a friend in distress who would rather be offered a hug. In spite of the Sagittarian concern for difference, they often have trouble seeing how others are different. They assume others respond just as they respond. They need to be taught to ask about other people's wants, needs and what their behavior means.

This confusion stems from the manner in which Sagittarius interprets the golden rule. Along with hearing: "Do unto others as you would have them do unto you," the little Sagittarius may hear: "Do unto others and they will do the same unto you." So if little Sagittarius likes someone and shows it, she may assume the other person will automatically like her in response. Or if she secretly mistrusts someone, she may assume they will know and mistrust her in return. Little Sagittarius needs to learn that she hasn't that kind of control over other people. People will make up their own minds about liking her or trusting her, sometimes regardless of what she does.

Proof and trust are both Sagittarian issues. A Sagittarius is likely to seek proof that she is trusted and feel deeply hurt if she is not. She may, for example, expect to be the only one to whom an important secret is told. Sagittarius takes her trustworthiness for granted and can be indignant when others don't do likewise. However, trust is so important to her that she's willing to try and prove her worth to people and can sometimes get herself into trouble this way. She may lend a friend all her allowance to prove she trusts him, assuming she and the friend have similar concepts of fairness. Sometimes she ends up looking more foolish than trustworthy.

The Sagittarian child's humor is broad, often gentle and slightly ironic. She can be very funny and appreciative of other people's wit. She is a cheerful, entertaining companion who can extract humor from the most tense situation. Sagittarius is the Joker. The dramatic and witty little Sagittarius is also an excellent mimic who needs to be reminded occasionally that she doesn't need to be perpetually onstage. Little Sagittarius may hide her own emotions under this veneer of cheerfulness and good humor, tending to joke away or ignore difficult or painful feelings. She may believe that people like her only when she is entertaining or charming.

Young Sagittarius can laugh while her heart is breaking, and it is therefore difficult for others to ascertain exactly what she is feeling. It may be equally difficult for the Sagittarian child to tell others what she's feeling underneath the humor. As a result, the real needs and feelings of little Sagittarius may not be recognized by herself or others, and she has a hard time seeing how her humor prevents deeper communication. A Sagittarian adolescent who's just had an awful time at her first school dance may come home and relate the experience with such wit that the family ends up laughing instead of consoling her. She may feel repeatedly let down or disappointed, believing people don't take her seriously or are unwilling to listen to her real feelings. She may end up feeling depleted, unreplenished about her own giving and left out, unable to elicit the sympathetic responses she wants. Like the typical lines of a stand-up comedian, there's pain in what she's saying, but the way she's saying it is so funny that everyone laughs instead of cries.

Another thing that contributes to this situation is the Sagittarius's essentially loner stance. Her freedom is ultimately more important than relationships, and she is reluctant to help others if she believes that obligates her to do so all the time. A young Sagittarius may hesitate to help with the dishes if she figures she'll have to do them every night, or she may do a spectacularly sloppy job when she does get stuck with the chore. In her determination to remain free, Sagittarius may push people away or keep them at a distance. A young Sagittarius child will literally push people, things, toys out of her way. She knows exactly when she's had enough snuggling and wants to be set down to go about her business. She will respond with great defiance or deviousness to smothering love from any source. At an older age, she may consciously use humor to attract attention and affection without having to risk too much intimacy. When Sagittarius is center stage, she feels more in control of how close other people get.

Nevertheless, there is still an element of ambivalence here, especially in Sagittarius children who need love and recognition for the quieter, more vulnerable parts of themselves. No matter how funny the story, sometimes parents need to refrain from laughing and acknowledge the feelings underneath the anecdote. "Oh, that sounds painful. . . ." "How did you feel when that happened?" "You know, if it makes you feel like crying inside, you can just go ahead and cry instead of laughing. . . ." These and other appropriate comments that elicit understated feelings will teach the little Sagittarius to value herself more fully.

The Sagittarius child may also have difficulty relating to other people's emotions, though she can be warmly, if somewhat impersonally, supportive. She may be uncomfortable around a weeping friend, able to offer proper words of sympathy, but feeling inadequate or helpless inside. It is hard for the Sagittarius child to understand how others deal with sad, angry or hurt feelings without benefit of humor and a sense of life's irony.

Fervent, enthusiastic and spontaneous, little Sagittarians have a tendency to overextend themselves and then feel overwhelmed and immobilized. This time management issue is different for Sagittarius than for some of the other sun signs. Sagittarians have a hard time understanding *how* to make time to accommodate everything they want to do. Sagittarian children generally need to do several things at once, and while this adds excitement to their lives, it may appear chaotic to those watching. Little Sagittarius may procrastinate or have difficulty either starting or finishing things. She expects herself to accomplish any number of things and, also, to do them well. Sometimes the hesitancy to finish projects stems from her fear of being imperfect. Sagittarians may be impatient with themselves (and others) and expect to become instant experts in whatever they try. They do not necessarily see a correlation between practice and expertise, and expect magic or miracles to make them proficient in whatever they attempt. They are quickly bored with any long and arduous task and want to move on to something easier, more exciting, more quickly gratifying. Sagittarians may do just enough to get by or become rushed and careless in their efforts to finish anything boring. But if they decide a task needs to be perfected, they will do it over and over until they are satisfied; their sense of questing can work either way in these matters. Homework may be quickly dismissed or agonizingly pondered over. Despite their own impatience, Sagittarians are generous and kind and seldom begrudge the honors and achievements of others.

Little Sagittarians need a great deal of independence both physically and psychically. Especially as small children, their natural need for security may conflict with their Sagittarian need for freedom. They may careen back and forth between daring and conservative behavior. They may, for example, be outgoing and gregarious at home and extremely shy with strangers. As they come to trust in the security offered them, Sagittarius's friendliness and sociability become a more permanent and substantial part of their adolescent and adult repertoire. One of the ways in which Sagittarians typically show their need for independence is through a sense of restlessness. They tend to look half packed, ready to go, on the move. This restlessness is often best released in outdoor activities, and the Sagittarius child tends to be athletic, physical and deeply concerned with nature and animals. She gravitates toward individual traveling sports such as backpacking, bicycle trips, skiing and the like. Young Sagittarians love speed, and their need for fastness and challenge is best channeled into racing and other legal pursuits.

Truth is important to little Sagittarius, who may become instantly bitter or cynical if she discovers she's been lied to. Generally, young Sagittarius is talkative and honest to the point of bluntness or tactlessness; though, having learned the hard way, as adults they make fine diplomats and lawyers. Do not ask a Sagittarius child for an opinion unless you are prepared to hear the unvarnished truth. This Sagittarian directness does not, however, extend into knowing how to ask for what she wants and needs. When making personal requests, the Sagittarius child often gives information without asking that anything be done for her about that information. For example, a Sagittarius thinks that saying "My back hurts" is a request for a back rub. Of course, this is not likely to communicate fully, and the Sagittarius child needs to be taught to ask, "Will you give me a back rub?"

When a Sagittarian has difficulty asking forthrightly for what she wants, and consequently doesn't get it, she may blame herself and decide that she expects too much. Once again, the Sagittarian mode of thinking doesn't automatically connect cause and effect. She doesn't see how there can be misunderstanding or misstatement; and she will therefore jump to a mistaken conclusion. In a similar vein, when a Sagittarian wants something, she frequently makes and extracts promises rather than commitments. Since to her a promise is a sacred word, she doesn't understand that other people seldom take promises as seriously as commitments or honor them as carefully. Parents need to expend extra effort teaching a small Sagittarius how to ask for things and carefully explaining the reasons for both granting and denying requests. And since independence is an issue (Can I ask for things and still have my freedom?), parents need to take care to give the little Sagittarius precisely what she asks for; too much of even a good thing may leave the child feeling overwhelmed, restricted and afraid to ask again.

Sagittarian children are permission givers and will generally support any endeavor that does not seem to impinge on people's territory or freedom. They want to save the whales, end hunger, do something about the injustice they see around them. School-age and adolescent Sagittarians are often young crusaders in a variety of causes. While they need to be warned not to overextend their energies, the causes with which they involve themselves are usually safe ones, often spiritual and supportive of people's integrity.

Sagittarian children have a natural gift for play and often teach other people how to enjoy themselves. They are fun to play with and shop with as they enthusiastically encourage others to treat themselves with kindness, respect and a little healthy indulgence. People are attracted to the Sagittarius's playfulness and bright energy but may become frightened or judgmental if they think the child is losing control. Little Sagittarius's giggling may appear all but out of hand, and adults nearby may find themselves nervous or uncomfortable. The young Sagittarius needs to learn that she can discipline herself and still have fun. She can be taught to watch her behavior, to reassure herself and others that she will not fall off the chair, spill the milk or scare the cat—all in the name of her high good time.

Sagittarians believe life consists of natural abundance. Little Sagittarians are generous and giving and want to share their sense of bounty with those around them. This is one of the most important ways in which they show affection. They are forgiving in nature and will rationalize and make excuses for behavior that doesn't fit with their ideals. Honorable and trusting in the natural goodness of people, Sagittarians are more likely to remove themselves from conflict than to fight. They are not cowards, however, for they have a courage born of their faith in innate human goodness, and their experience often affirms this expectation.

No matter what happens to them, little Sagittarians believe things will be all right and that they will be all right. Their resilience is often an important contribution to family life, and both their questing and their playfulness are a delight to observe and participate in. Being around a little Sagittarius challenges the cynicism in other zodiac signs and helps all of us hope, "Maybe they're right, maybe everything will be just fine." It is the parents' task not to misuse this buoyancy but to give their Sagittarian child solid, secure experiences on which to base her optimism and hope, and then to let her fly . . .

NEEDS (Sagittarius's emotional emphasis)

Freedom and space.
Playtime.
Honest and realistic responses.
Wide ranges of information and experiences.
Challenges.

Permission to know, explore, discover and understand.
Laughter.
Creative outlets for fantasies.
Friends.
Fairness and justice.
Permission to not always be cheerful.
Permission to have and show emotions, especially fear.
Permission to tell the truth.
To know someone, to connect with them intimately.
Support for and recognition of the breadth of their information.
To learn about sympathy.
To learn how others see the world differently from the way they
  do.
Realistic understanding of their own power.
To learn to take things seriously.
To learn to defend themselves in a variety of ways.
To be trusted.
To learn self-discipline.
Not to be overprotected or overnurtured.
Not to be "cut down to size."
Not to have their enthusiasm dampened.

## COMMON ASSUMPTIONS (How Sagittarius views the world around her)

Opportunity knocks only once.
Bigger is better.
All the world loves a clown.
Forget your troubles, c'mon be happy.

## SENSITIVITIES (Potential sources of misunderstanding)

*Freedom:* Little Sagittarius is very sensitive to any restrictions to her freedom. Rather than rebel, she is likely to appear to comply and then proceed to do exactly as she'd intended.
*Truth and Honesty:* Most young Sagittarians are sensitive to hypocrisy and would rather hear any truth than any lie. Once having reached a conclusion, however, their opinions are quite difficult to

change, and they may exaggerate or distort the reality to emphasize their point on a matter of principle.

*Information:* The more they know, the safer young Sagittarians feel. They do not ask questions merely to irritate the adults around them; they really do want all that information!

*"Negative" Emotions:* Little Sagittarians prefer not to encounter or deal with sadness, anger or fear and may make jokes or giggle under stress. They need to be taught, by example and loving words, how to express the full range of their emotions and thereby get their needs met in appropriate ways.

*Control:* While Sagittarian children seldom "go out of control," they may frequently appear to be just on the edge. Adult temptation is to admonish the little Sagittarius to control herself. Teaching young Sagittarians breathing and centering techniques will go a long way toward reassuring both the adult and the child.

*Pacing Oneself:* Little Sagittarians seem to operate on bursts of energy and to be happiest when doing several things at once. With support, as they grow older they may become aware of the advantages of steady energy flow; if not, they nevertheless seem to accomplish their goals.

*Procrastination and Distraction:* The world is so interesting to young Sagittarius that she may have difficulty concentrating on any single task for long periods. She may therefore need rest or alternative activities between, or even during, strenuous mental activities. Procrastination is most likely to occur when little Sagittarius believes she must perform a task perfectly, when she doesn't think she'll be able to take a break or when she finds the activity distasteful. Some children eat the icky food first or do the worst chore right away; not Sagittarius, who deals with distasteful things only as a last resort. Reassurances ahead of time and contingency plans will reassure restless Sagittarian children.

## RELATIONSHIPS

Young Sagittarians are usually friendly and outgoing after they recover from their initial shyness. They are entertaining, often very funny and can be counted on to be cheerful, or at least pleasant. Sagittarian children like being around people and are especially attracted to those different from themselves. They also need ample time alone and will arrange their time so they get it.

*Mom:* Sagittarian children are very idealistic about mothers and the concept of motherhood and family. They expect their mothers to be artistic, romantic, visionary, accepting and understanding. They may idealize or sentimentalize their mothers and either elevate her to a pedestal or become bitter and cynical when she proves to be only human.

In response to such projected idealism from her child, mothers of Sagittarians often fall into the trap of striving to be perfect and become demanding and critical of their children, who in turn must strive to be perfect, too. Both mother and Sagittarian child may prefer their fantasies of the relationship to the reality of it. As Sagittarian children become confident that their charm and visionary nature is accepted in the family, and as mothers learn to relax and play with their Sagittarian sprite, pressure on both sides to be perfect may subside.

In her efforts to be flawless, a Sagittarian's mother may act evasive or become emotionally unavailable. Attention to specific, present needs will keep little Sagittarius grounded and ensure a more rewarding relationship for all concerned. Moms of Sagittarians often give generously to other people or the world at large but may overlook the needs of their own offspring or feel martyred and unappreciated in the home. Especially since little Sagittarians have an innate sense of fairness, such mothers need to remember that charity begins at home.

*Dad:* Sagittarian children expect fathers to be efficient, effective, thorough, responsible, organized, technical and concerned with health. Sagittarian children are afraid that fathers will be critical, perfectionistic and compulsive.

Fathers who want a close and comfortable relationship with their little Sagittarius would benefit from learning the developmental stages of childhood and clearly expecting only what is appropriate for any given age. Kindness and humor mean more to a little Sagittarius than all the chastisement in the world. Once this bond is established, fathers will not need to discipline their Sagittarian child heavily, only humor and teach her. A young Sagittarius wants to argue, debate and have intellectual conversations with her father. She will be deeply disappointed if he is too busy working or not interested in having this kind of relationship with her. A Sagittarian's dad needs to listen broadly, to interact and encourage his child's leaps and aspirations.

*Siblings:* Sagittarian children think of siblings as equals and friends. They may perceive siblings as less impassioned with ideas and more involved in interpersonal relationships. Siblings around a Sagittarian will often share traits of curiosity and restlessness. The fact that siblings usually have more longtime friends seldom bothers a little Sagittarius; she simply joins the group.

*Friends:* Young Sagittarius is generally surrounded by interesting and unusual people. She is witty, casual, social and undemanding. She may receive more commitment from others that she is willing to give in exchange. Her attachments are often ritualized and predictable and are primary vehicles for further learning. When she believes she has learned all she can from a friend, young Sagittarius may feel compelled to move on unless she can find other reasons to maintain the relationship. She is also likely to spend more time with acquaintances than with friends. Acquaintances often have more interesting and newer information, and she may feel the need to prove her affection and trust to acquaintances while taking her friends for granted. Sagittarian children are comfortable with extended periods between visits.


## MIND/INFORMATION/SCHOOL

Learning is young Sagittarius's reason for being and is a lifetime pursuit. The Sagittarian child thinks fast but may lack concentration. While she doesn't mind repetition and welcomes paraphrase and examples, little Sagittarius dreads being bored and will daydream or become very restless if caught in a boring situation. She may have difficulty memorizing or understanding complex topics that are not presented in a comprehensive manner. She can take in an entire room at a glance but may later be unable to describe the pattern of the rug. Disparate information may suddenly "gel" for her, leading to spontaneous insights and conclusions that, though accurate, cannot be explained or justified in a rational or logical way.

Unless special care is taken to challenge the young Sagittarius, she may find school boring, irrelevant, redundant or incomprehensible. She learns fast, however, and is quite willing to apply herself in areas that interest her. She especially likes stories, experiments, activities and field trips. She least enjoys having to sit still and absorb information passively.

*Higher Education:* Sagittarians usually pursue some sort of further education throughout most of their lives and will often teach themselves when not involved in formal classes. When she does pursue a degree, Sagittarius is likely to perceive formal education as a chance to explore a variety of ideas. She especially likes to include travel as part of her learning experience.

## RESPONSIBILITY/WORK/REWARDS

*Responsibility and Work:* The Sagittarian child takes responsibility quite seriously when it finally catches up to her. Expecting perfection from herself, she may avoid finishing a project or may be deliberately careless or late in order to reduce her anxiety or to ensure that she won't be asked again. Her room may never be quite entirely painted or the dishes may not be completely clean.

Careful and thorough when properly motivated, little Sagittarians often work just enough to assure themselves of adequate playtime. Their energy comes in enormous bursts at often inconvenient times. They are best at endeavors that require analysis and synthesis of information, and, in this area, they are quite comfortable with detail and ritual. Figuring out travel routes or comparing different belief systems are exciting and satisfying activities. They need to believe their work is improving the world and will often engage in activities that help others or make the world a more beautiful place. Endless and repetitive chores are among young Sagittarius's least favorites.

*Rewards:* Sagittarian children don't usually care about *things* and seldom seek or appreciate material rewards for their efforts. Instead, they want to be liked, respected and trusted; and they enjoy the security, status, increased authority and additional time earned from a job accomplished well. They do appreciate cash if the money they've earned allows them to purchase a longed-for treat.

## HOME

Young Sagittarians are adaptable and flexible and can make a home anywhere. Having established roots, however, they need their space to be "just right" and can be quite picky and critical if their environment does not meet their standards or preconceived ideals. In spite of their genuine attachment to a place, Sagittarian children are ready to move at a moment's notice and will happily begin settling in somewhere else. They may remain sentimental about previous places despite their excitement for the new.

Little Sagittarius's living space is a curious mixture of old and new, of artifacts and nature objects, along with the newest gadgets. They often utilize their ceilings in unusual ways. A small Sagittarius's space is at once functional and unobtrusive. Little Sagittarius prefer collapsible and lightweight furniture that can be moved or rearranged quickly and easily. Often they include exercise or athletic apparatus in their decor, and they are frequently attracted to items relating to horses, travel or other cultures. Sagittarians prefer turquoise, indigo, purples and the colors of autumn: oranges, yellow-oranges, rusts and shades of ivory.

Since Sagittarian wanderlust hits relatively early, these youths are likely to leave home as soon as possible, regardless of the comfort of their environment. At least initially, though, they tend not to wander very far.

## HEALTH

The young Sagittarian dislikes pain and is likely to expend more energy, time and money preventing physical distress than curing it. Illness may be a way for the Sagittarian child to relieve or release boredom, to get away from unpleasant circumstances, to distract attention from family problems, or gain relaxation time. When sick, little Sagittarian likes physical comfort, peace, quiet, plenty of food and to be left undisturbed. Several pillows and quilts are also appreciated.

Traditionally, the sign of Sagittarius rules the thighs and liver. Little Sagittarians experiencing health problems are likely to feel uncomfortable in these areas. The illness itself is likely to occur in the form of minor accidents, sleep or respiratory disturbances, or problems of excess: exhaustion, burn-out, overindulgence, overweight, hypertension, etc.

# CHILDHOOD AGES

*(Note: The fears detailed in this section are never to be used as punishment. They are presented as avenues for reassurance and caring.)*

## BIRTH–6 MONTHS

The Sagittarius infant is usually engaging and good-natured, with remarkable powers of concentration for her age. She is curious and interested in her environment. She is a fine and charming traveling companion.

> *Needs*
> Stimulation.
> Physical activity.
> Quick attention to physical needs.
> Quiet, private time.
> A lot of sleep.

> *Fears*
> Being helpless.
> Restriction.
> Being overwhelmed.

## 6 MONTHS–18 MONTHS

Baby Sagittarius is mostly curious and restless, learning to get around early and getting into everything. Her attention span is shorter now as her mobility increases. However, she is fascinated by fire and needs to be carefully supervised around flame. At this age little Sagittarius loves to travel and learn. She enjoys stories and varied physical activities. Her charm within the family is a delight, but the Sagittarian shyness with strangers may begin to show. Parents are sometimes tempted to try to keep their baby at this charming stage. Sagittarius will experience any such attempt as a lack of faith in her, and it will undermine her confidence in herself.

*Needs*
>Beginning distinction between reality and fantasy.
>Laughter.
>Freedom of movement.
>Supervision.
>Permission to explore.

*Fears*
>Restriction.
>Lack of information.

## 18 MONTHS–3 YEARS

The Sagittarius toddler is outgoing, cheerful, independent, playful, reckless, brave, cordial, curious, restless and always in motion. She is full of questions and generalizations. She needs to know *why* and especially wants to know about religion and God. Her idealism and perfectionism begin now, and she may feel herself overextended, bored or overwhelmed and passive in the face of her own and others' expectations. She may appear rebellious or apparently compliant and willing to try anything. She is creative and has a rich fantasy life. She is probably messy.

*Toilet Training:* Progress in Sagittarius's toilet training is usually erratic, with numerous "accidents." Sagittarius doesn't respond to motivation outside herself in this area and is easily frightened, which can make training even more difficult. She does want to please, however, and will eventually train herself on her own schedule. (The same pattern applies to thumb-sucking.)

*Needs*
>Short answers.
>Brief periods of stimulation followed by calm.
>Quiet times.
>Help and support with projects.
>Continued help distinguishing between reality and fantasy.
>To be taken interesting places.
>Grounding, centering, help feeling secure.
>A stable and constant environment or home base.

Boundaries and rules.
Information, explanations, reasons.
Gentle humor from and with others.
Sleep.

*Fears*
Getting lost.
Restriction.
Force.

## 3 YEARS–6 YEARS

The preschool Sagittarius is friendly, flamboyant, changeable, passionate and reckless. She is alternately confident and scared. Sagittarius is full of energy. Her attention span is short, and she continues to be extremely restless and curious, eagerly anticipating school. Sagittarius would be quite happy in a structured preschool with many learning tasks and short time spans for activities. This is a time when Sagittarius may have noticeable difficulty identifying what is real and what is her imagination. She may distort or exaggerate details (for example: "It was the *biggest* dog in the whole world!") or overgeneralize (for example: "I *never, ever* get to play outside after dinner and *all* the other kids do."). What may appear to be lying is often a symptom of Sagittarian confusion about reality or misunderstanding that she and other people see things differently. She daydreams a lot, and her active imagination often contributes to stories of her daily activities. The Sagittarius child needs help sorting reality from fantasy, assurance that reality is good enough without being exaggerated and acceptance of her visionary ways of seeing. She does not need punishment. She may have imaginary playmates and tends to animate toys and objects to play roles in her fantasy life. If parents are not scrupulously honest about what is and is not real during this period, it will only compound the problem. It is at this point that Sagittarius learns the golden rule.

*Needs*
Honesty.
Continued distinction between reality and fantasy.
Restraint.

Categories.
Honest feedback.
Information.
Understanding.
Explanations, not lectures.
Enough of what she needs, not having to stop before she's
ready.

*Fears*

Punishment for "lying."
Lack of boundaries, rules, structure.
Overprotection.
Deprivation.
Not being allowed to grow up.

## 6 YEARS–12 YEARS

Sagittarius will be either very interested in and/or bored at school.
She is now learning at a very fast rate and may be impatient with
those around her. She is enthusiastic about new information, inclusive, easily convinced and stubbornly determined to convert others
to the joy of learning. Sagittarius is often certain she has the right,
and only, answers and is willing to argue and debate endlessly to
prove her point. Headstrong and restless, she seeks shortcuts for
nearly everything and may appear careless, haphazard or confused
in this process. She is interested in things only briefly and may not
be very responsible, but she is deeply hurt or offended when she is
not trusted. By this time, Sagittarius is weighing the abstract against
the literal and has begun her spiritual search for answers.

School-age Sagittarians are spontaneous and may neglect to think
before acting. They may seem blunt, tactless or forgetful. Sometimes they appear to agree to other people's demands but afterward
simply go their own way. Their independence can cause conflicts in
relationships. They expect others to understand and abide by their
strong and fairly rigid sense of fairness. They want proof and
reasons for virtually everything. Their creativity takes the form of
generating ideas and arguments as well as interest in more traditional arts. Sagittarians of this age are often fascinated by horses.

*Needs*
Help starting and finishing things.
Reasons and explanations.
Fairness.
Freedom.
A variety of experiences.
Permission to explore, learn, theorize.
Support.
Religious information.
To be taught to think things through.
Endless teaching and listening.
Transportation.
Understanding.
To learn patience.

*Fears*
Restriction.
Boredom.
Force.
Overprotection.
Unrealistic expectations from others.
Inequality.
Being overwhelmed.

## 12 YEARS–18 YEARS

Adolescent Sagittarians are extremely independent, restless and possibly rebellious. They tend to be grandiose and expansive and are therefore potentially overextended in what they do or think they can accomplish in a given time. Sagittariaus still tends to presume, make assumptions, exaggerate and overgeneralize. She continues to be exuberant, sensitive and friendly but shy in new situations. She is curious, enthusiastic, dramatic and is reluctant to commit herself to a single exclusive relationship. She continues to seek answers and to pursue her big dream. She may explore traveling, dance and sports. She seems always to be in motion and may have trouble managing time or slowing down long enough to sleep. No matter what happens to her during this time, she will feel hopeful and idealistic about herself and what life intends to offer her.

Teenage Sagittarians are often practical jokers. They are optimistic and fun to be around. They generate ideas at an amazing rate and are extremely creative. Sagittarius has many varied friendships, and she may break away from family expectations concerning the choice of appropriate companions. In her search for variety and challenge, she may also disagree with her family's commonly held assumptions and religion. She will most likely define her own approach to, and choice of, suitable work and education.

Sagittarius may ignore the physical changes of adolescence and be uncomfortable with, or easily offended by, her own and others' emerging sexuality. She is curious about this phenomenon intellectually, however, and may experiment with levels of intimacy more from a need to know and understand than from physical desire.

*Needs*
> Freedom.
> Both trust and accountability.
> Rest and relaxation time.
> Humor.
> Support for changing goals.
> Constancy.
> Something to believe in: a personal ethic.
> Information.
> Challenge.
> Excitement.

*Hates*
> Being told to slow down.
> Having to keep promises.
> Having information challenged.
> Not being trusted.
> Having to be somewhere at a particular time.
> Being called superficial, dishonest, intolerant, dumb or average.
> Injustice.
> People who can't support what they say.
> Hypocrisy.

# CAPRICORN CHILDREN

## DECEMBER 22–JANUARY 19

### GENERAL CHARACTERISTICS

*(Note: While many characteristics described below will be accurate for most Capricorns, other, sometimes contradictory, traits may also be evident in an individual child.)*

When parents first gaze at their newborn Capricorn, they are intrigued by his large, serious eyes that seem to understand and accept all that is happening around him. He may act as though he's not quite sure he belongs here, as though he is waiting for some signal that he's welcome. Though tiny Capricorn seems to have been born old and full of wisdom and often looks like a little old man (or woman) at birth, he becomes rounder, more beautiful and babylike as the first days go by. Capricorns develop into cuddly and undemanding babies whose rare smiles are worth waiting for.

Little Capricorns often become solemn, cautious, formal and reserved children. They take others seriously and are seldom unkind or cruel, listening raptly and laughing with—but not at—other people. Capricorns are strong, ethical and compassionate, and they often favor and protect the underdog on the playground or at home. They empathize with and worry about those less fortunate than themselves. There is a lot of the "little grown-up" in them.

With additional development, the young Capricorn takes responsibility seriously and seems to worry for everyone. If the family must be somewhere on time, it is the Capricorn child who watches the clock. He is a hard worker with a great deal of self-discipline and follow-through. He is extremely trustworthy and will make great efforts to live up to his commitments and maintain his reputation. Because of this focus on responsibility, play may be difficult for this intense child, who is self-conscious, goal oriented and likely to feel

**223**

guilty at any hint of relaxation. The Capricorn child seems always to be *doing* something. He is full of projects and, even during the toddler years, this orientation toward projects will fill his play time. Other children may be content simply to mess around with the crayons, but little Capricorn may decide to illustrate his own storybook or draw a series of pictures for grandma. One of the biggest lessons in a young Capricorn's life is to learn that not everything needs to be done well. Without this lesson, little Capricorn is likely to expend the same care arranging the food on his plate as preparing his homework.

Introspective and emotionally sensitive, the Capricorn child takes great care to hide his vulnerability and is often considered the hardest child in the zodiac to get to know. A precocious maturity often obscures the essential childness of little Capricorn, and parents may be tempted to heap responsibilities upon this competent and self-assured little person.

Small Capricorn often seems more comfortable relating to the adult world than to the frivolities of other children. He may identify himself as "one of the grown-ups" in a family and not make a clear distinction between himself and people much older, and he might refer to his siblings as "the children." He is often remarkably well behaved and courteous for his age, at least when he wants to be. One mother of a Capricorn child reported, "From the time Amy was three, I could take her into restaurants and she'd sit patiently waiting for supper, conversing in a high, chirping voice about her day, just a little grown-up. When we had company, she'd join in adult conversation and seemed so at home we were sort of flattered and amused. I always said she was three going on thirty."

If the Capricorn child believes, as he often does, that he is responsible for running the whole show, then any error becomes a matter of exaggerated importance. As the young Capricorn attempts to live up to his or others' expectations of maturity, he may exhibit behaviors that look bossy, condescending, rigid or fearful of failure. Even if he wants to, no child is capable of assuming such heavy responsibility. Parents are sometimes intimidated by this show of competence in their Capricorn child, but they need to remain in authority, no matter how capably the child seems to be handling himself. If parents withdraw their authority, the child's sense of being in charge is intensified along with his anxiety that he has to do everything right. A power struggle is then created within the family between "the grown-up" and the real grown-ups. Starting with Capricorn's infancy, the kindest gift parents can give him is the sense that they are in control, that he will be allowed to test his limits, but that the larger issues of running the family and providing for his needs are securely in the hands of adults. A child who seems to compete with his parents' ability to organize things properly needs reassurance that the parents have managed in this style for many years and will continue to do so during Capricorn's childhood. There is more than one right way to do something, and there are many ways to make things work within the family.

Sometimes little Capricorn may appear to bully the people around him. If he believes people are taking too long to make up their minds or if he believes an answer is obvious, he may simply go ahead, assuming others will agree with his action. For example, young Capricorn may order hot fudge sundaes for the entire family if they are taking to long to make up their minds and be astonished to discover that they wanted something else. It may simply not occur to him to ask for input or feedback. Riding in a car with the family, young Capricorn may suddenly command, "Turn right!" and the driver may turn without thinking, only to find out that Capricorn wanted a better view of the sunset and took charge automatically.

Some Capricorn children, especially those whose parents have not stayed clearly in a position of protection and authority, can become overwhelmed by their innate sense of responsibility. They will tend to look immobilized, depressed, antisocial or self-destructive. A Capricorn child who switches from competent, confident behavior to lethargy and depression is signaling his distress at overwhelming responsibility. Parents who respond by reestablishing their competence in little Capricorn's eyes will find that he quickly returns to his usual busy interests.

Sometimes it is hard for little Capricorn to admit he'd like help lessening the inner pressure of his responsibleness. He may seek help and simultaneously resent the help that's offered. An eight-year-old Capricorn may be frightened at being left alone at home and, at the same time, resent having a baby-sitter. Reassurances that the older person is there to protect him, and does not represent a rebuke to his responsibility, will make it easier for the young Capricorn to accept the situation.

The Capricorn child is very task oriented and values excellence, technical expertise and a job well done. While he firmly believes in doing tasks well, he also values expedience and efficiency. He will often do only the exact amount expected of him. If little Capricorn is asked to wash dishes, he may do an impeccable job but neglect to rinse out the sink afterward: he wasn't asked to. Ambitious, logical and assertive, the Capricorn child may see needing help as a sign of weakness. Though he can be generous in support of others and enjoys being needed, he becomes quite angry at himself for showing similar needs. Young Capricorn can appear quite self-sufficient and may seem resistant to offered assistance.

Little Capricorn will accept help when he feels desperate or if he allows himself to be convinced it's not a sign of weakness. Occasionally the Capricorn child may feel punished for acting "too competent." Parents who assume their young Capricorn can handle anything are probably right, but he may suffer in silence and loneliness if he believes he is not worthy of help or that other people don't want to help him.

One way parents can support this self-reliant child without interfering in his concept of himself as independent and competent is through loving touch. A brief hug as he bends over the latest project, an affectionate kiss in passing and other signs of consistent affection and recognition let little Capricorn know of his value while he goes about his busyness. This is a child who is prone to grow up believing he has to "do it alone," and the consistency of loving physical contact from those who love him provides comfort and reassurance beyond an outsider's understanding.

Little Capricorn fears being mediocre or ordinary and will pursue excellence just because he wants to or for attention and a sense of control. If he is superb, there is no standard against which the Capricorn child feels he can be judged. He becomes his own standard and is comfortable. He does not particularly care whether others are judged by his standards and is sometimes uncomfortable at public recognition of his excellence if it means isolation from other children or having to bear their resentment. Little Capricorn is also anxious about not being able to maintain his standard once he has established it, and he may drive himself compulsively to remain up to par. He tends to confuse who he is with how he's doing. The Capricorn child with the neatest room in the apartment won't fear unfavorable comparison, but he needs reassurance that the cleanliness of his room, or whatever, does not in the family's eyes reflect on his personal goodness or value.

The wall of self-sufficiency with which the Capricorn child surrounds himself can sometimes leave others searching for a way in and wondering what they have to offer him. As early as age two, parents of small Capricorn will hear, "I can do it myself!" Allowing the child to do what he can and taking over before he feels failure is a kind and gentle approach to parenting this feisty toddler. To use his determination to the advantage of the child, parents can permit him to help with adult tasks that were perhaps uninteresting to other children. This will help to establish rapport between parent and child, teach realistic expectations, give him necessary instructions and safety precautions, and provide him with quick assistance if needed. A three-year-old Capricorn may indeed know how to scramble his own eggs in the morning, but it will be much better for him to do it within a sense of observant, loving protection, standing at the stove on a chair, inside the shelter and guidance of a parent's arms.

Though the Capricorn child often believes he has to do things alone, he also enjoys being able to say "I'm too little" if he believes it won't reduce his stature in other people's eyes. Persistence and gentle persuasion on the part of parents offering help will be well worth the effort. The young Capricorn will let down his guard a bit, remember and appreciate the kindness.

Even in the gentlest and most supportive family environment, a young Capricorn is likely to experience times of feeling lonely, different or separate from others. Because of these experiences, he may react with gratitude and surprise at acts of kindness or persistence in getting to know him. Parents cannot reason their little Capricorns out of these moods, but through hugs and reassurance they can provide support that they love him just for being a part of their lives.

The Capricorn child is often more aware of sadness and tragedy than children of other signs. While most infants may feel temporarily sad if a favorite toy is removed, they soon have trouble remembering their grief. The young Capricorn does not. He may learn early about grief, either through experiencing it or by figuring it out: if happiness exists, so must sadness exist. Capricorn may feel inexplicably sad sometimes, and he is certainly sensitive to the grief and pain of others. This sensitivity to grief is not the same as depression. Capricorn experiences a yearning or longing for happier times, a sort of remembrance of things past, and may privately commit himself to regaining or inventing happy times for himself and those around him. His definition of happiness, which includes safety and security, may appear boring to more adventuresome souls, but his contributions to family stability and good times will be appreciated nonetheless. When parents can alleviate this sadness, they certainly need to do so, but often merely acknowledging the feeling and offering comfort will reassure this child in a solemn mood.

Frequently the Capricorn child has an early and intense relationship with an older person, often a grandparent. Wanting to belong, yet remaining aloof, the young Capricorn often seeks respect instead of popularity and finds that adults have a much clearer idea of respect than other children. This child's fears of being rejected are usually quite strong. Once someone seems to like him, he may test their affection and look prickly or disdaining of the newly offered friendship. As soon as this testing period is over, little Capricorn returns to his usual courteous self. In most cases he is slow to open up and trust, though he may appear very cordial, socially skilled and accepting. When Capricorn does love, it is with fierce loyalty, passion and surprise. The young Capricorn is a gentle and kind soul and is eminently lovable, though after his early years it can take time for people to feel totally comfortable around him.

The Capricorn child needs a great deal of stability in his life and will create it himself if others do not provide it. He does not like inconsistency or surprise changes in routine. He likes to have his clothes laid out for the next morning, to know he's going to preschool as usual, and when he comes home that Sesame Street will be on, and then he'll have supper and a game to play before bed. He wants to know where others are going and when they'll be back. Little Capricorn may have difficulty relinquishing responsibility or trusting others to be responsible. He often "checks up" on siblings, playmates, even parents to make sure that the job is being done as well as *he* would do it or to be certain that while he relaxes he is still being adequately cared for.

Allotting time seems to be the exception in Capricorn's organizational skills. He seldom has enough time. List making is helpful, even for the smallest Capricorn, to set priorities for his activities and tasks and to experience the satisfaction of crossing items off the list. One family with a four-year-old Capricorn child lists his activities in different colored markers and puts the list on the refrigerator door on Saturday mornings, along with the rest of the family's list of weekend duties. Little Capricorn has memorized even the parts he can't read by color, and makes quite a show for himself of crossing off the items one by one.

A Capricorn child does not feel comfortable in a new situation until he has learned the rules and regulations. This doesn't mean he intends to follow all the rules, but he feels terrible if he unintentionally disobeys. Capricorn wants the option of obeying or not, and to have this option, he has to know where the limits are. If he chooses to disobey and gets caught, he will usually endure the consequences stoicallly. He is exceedingly fair, believes in justice and accepts having this standard applied to himself and his behavior. A young Capricorn who decides to raid the cookie jar has already considered the consequences, will answer truthfully and solemnly if caught and will give little protest to fair discipline, unless he's again testing his parents' authority.

Capricorn is just as adept at determining what his role is as he is at determining what the rules are. Once given instructions, he will follow the role pattern as conscientiously as he follows rules. Even his rebellious behavior is often a predefined role. For example, an adolescent Capricorn who is generally the responsible child in the family may go through some rebellion at this age, but he makes sure it doesn't interfere with tasks in the family that give him self-esteem.

Some Capricorn children push at people and at institutions until the limits are revealed or reached. Others assume they understand the rules and voluntarily restrict their behavior without checking things out. For example, the first Capricorn would get into everything at Grandma's house until Grandma explains what is on-limits and what is off-limits. The second Capricorn child would sit quietly on the couch assuming Grandma didn't want him to touch her curio shelf or rearrange the silk flowers, when asking may have given him permission to play with the flowers. Or he might decide he can't try out for a certain sport because there are no other boys his size playing on the field.

So we find two types of Capricorn children. While boundaries are important to them both, one will embrace rules wholeheartedly, the other will systematically test and rebel. The rebellious child will figure out how to get the cookies, regardless of the consequences, or in order to discover the consequences himself and experience them firsthand. The more docile child will not only not touch the cookies but may refuse them even when they're offered by a responsible adult.

Consequences in general are a Capricorn concern. No child knows more about cause and effect than a Capricorn, and he is therefore excellent at planning strategy. Parents who are not consistent in doling out consequences for childish misbehavior or who do not think in terms of cause and effect in their parenting style may clash with Capricorn's little legal mind. The Capricorn child usually loves to be right and is not likely to offer information unless he is relatively certain it's accurate. This means he is usually correct and truthful when he speaks—perhaps not always an endearing quality to parents who aren't expecting wisdom from the mouths of babes.

Because he considers many options before taking action, and since he has this intense awareness of cause and effect, the Capricorn child is often as aware of potential negative outcomes as of positive ones. He has already thought about what could go wrong as well as what could go right. He may therefore appear pessimistic, seeming not to expect much from the world. This apparent pessimism is often an indirect bid for reassurance and support; the little Capricorn wants to hear from someone he likes and respects that everything will be okay.

The Capricorn child learns quickly from experience and uses his remembrance of the past as a framework of safety on which to build new experiences. A young Capricorn who was allowed to stay up late last night may expect the same privilege tonight. A young Capricorn who fell off the swing yesterday may be reluctant to return to the playground and may need coaxing and reassurance more than children of other sun signs. He also has a deep respect for the past and will sentimentally cling to mementos, even of bad times. He enjoys stories of his own past and of others' pasts and will try to figure out how the past influences the present and future. "Is it because I was bad yesterday that you won't let me do this today?" While this behavior may appear conservative, once little Capricorn has his answers, he is ready to move on without even a glance over his shoulder. "No? Oh good, then may I please, please, please do this today?"

Young Capricorn is often a pack rat, collecting skills, people and objects in case he may some day need them. He believes it is sensible to be polite to a neighbor who may one day pay him to cut the grass, it is worthwhile to save old scraps of cloth in the event he ever decides to make a quilt or it may be useful to learn Japanese in case he ever wants to visit Japan. Resourceful, creative and somewhat opportunistic, the Capricorn child amazingly often gets the opportunity to use his "junk."

Ritual is important to little Capricorn, especially in times of stress. The Capricorn child becomes extremely upset when routine is altered without explanation or warning. He likes things and people to be predictable, even predictably erratic, and may become frightened and/or angry at the unexpected. To avoid this discomfort, young Capricorn sometimes plans seemingly endless contingencies and needs to know what everyone else is doing or plans to do. A preschool Capricorn may want Mom to explain exactly where the rest of the family is, what they are doing and when they'll be back. Then he'll want to know if he still gets dinner on time, whether or not Daddy is home from work.

In spite of the apparent practicality of the Capricorn child, underneath it all he is an idealist who may hide disappointment in himself or others with criticism and self-righteousness. A school-age Capricorn who has just been told he can't go to the movies with Mom because she was unexpectedly called back to work may exclaim, "If she'd finished her work when she was supposed to, we could've gone!" Rather than responding angrily, parents need to tell little Capricorn that it's okay simply to feel disappointed and not criticize.

Capricorn consciences develop amazingly early but may be confused with their sense of responsibility. In order to reduce the amount of inevitable guilt young Capricorn feels, wise parents will not permit their Capricorn child to punish himself and will be extremely gentle with their own judgments of this child's behavior. Little Capricorn's striving for excellence and perfection and the pain of falling short of his internal goal is more punishment than an outsider would inflict. Teaching the Capricorn child to extend to himself the gentleness he lavishes on others is a necessary task for parents of these children. Compassionate concern from parents is often permission enough for little Capricorn to be kind to himself. Young Capricorn can be fiercely protective and nurturing, and his compassion and appreciation extend to all living things and all things beautiful. His rejection of ugliness and cruelty usually carries with it a commitment to improve things.

Since he is solid, grounded and reliable, the Capricorn child often acts as a haven for more needy children or when kids' feelings get hurt. But there is a tendency for these same children to feel restricted by little Capricorn's solicitude once the crisis is passed or feelings have mended. The young Capricorn needs to learn he cannot base friendships on others needing him but needs instead to discover interdependence and a willingness to share his own vulnerability.

This same confusion extends once again into the realm of the young Capricorn's responsibility. A playmate who seeks little Capricorn's advice on pounding a nail may quickly tire of being told how to build the entire ship. The Capricorn child is often invited to join group projects since he is certain to get the job done, but others may feel reproached by his intense and insistent behavior. Since his feelings are easily hurt, it may be necessary for parents to repeatedly discuss this phenomenon with their Capricorn child and offer alternative behaviors. He needs to be reminded to let other people take charge sometimes and to determine beforehand what small portion of a task he wants to claim as his own. The Capricorn teenager does not need to take responsibility for the entire stage set of the school play; he can choose to paint only two trees and leave when that is accomplished. He does, however, need to let others know his intentions and be reassured by a teacher or parent that he won't be blamed for others' mistakes or lack of a finished product.

Little Capricorn sees the world through almost adult eyes and needs both time and permission just to play and relax. While he is seldom bored when alone and is quite able to amuse himself, he prefers the company of a few congenial friends and offers commitment, gentleness, productivity, grounding, practicality and a very dry sense of humor in exchange for affection, attention and reassurance. Parents can count on their little Capricorn to do what he says he will do and, with his willingness to help and his need to contribute, he is a wonderful and reliable member of the family.

# NEEDS (Capricorn's emotional emphasis)

Unconditional love with visible, consistent standards of behavior.

Reassurance that "being here" is good enough.

Protection, limits, consistent and obvious rules.

Privacy.

Reasonable, light-handed discipline.

Predictability and stability in the environment; preparation for and explanation of changes.

Permission to play, have feelings, state needs.

Visible manifestations of their efforts (products).

Forgiveness and help forgiving themselves.

Permission to act like children, to be "little" longer.

Permission to set priorities; everything doesn't have to be excellent.

Reassurance that parents and adults are not intimidated by them.

Permission to experiment and make mistakes.

Never to be threatened with abandonment, rejection or humiliation.

Never to be cruelly teased, scared or threatened.

Not to be forced into behaving in certain ways.

# COMMON ASSUMPTIONS (How Capricorn views the world around him)

If you want something done right, do it yourself.

All things worth doing should be done well.

Don't trust anyone too much.

# SENSITIVITIES (Potential sources of misunderstanding)

*Guilt and Responsibility:* The young Capricorn is likely to feel guilty and at least partially responsible when things do not proceed as planned. In order to avoid guilt, he may appear quite defensive, acting belligerent, apologizing frequently or offering excuses or rationalizations for unexpected outcomes. He hates being wrong or having his performance found wanting, and if his best seems inadequate, he may become frightened. The Capricorn child needs to be taught to determine realistically when he is responsible and when he is not and to forgive himself even when he is at fault. Loving example set by parents is the easiest way to do this.

*Fear and Distrust:* Sensitive to others, aware of imperfections and seeking perfection, little Capricorn may find fallible humans difficult to trust. He may, however, be outraged if he is not trusted himself and will sincerely attempt to fulfill other people's expectations of trustworthy behavior. Since he is afraid of being disappointed, he may test other people to be certain they mean what they say.

The Capricorn child is reluctant to acknowledge fear in all but the most blatant of physical circumstances. This stoicism means he seldom gets the reassurance he needs. From the beginning, the young Capricorn needs permission to be scared and to distrust. Parents who respond to little Capricorn's fears with warm reassurance and information are setting the stage for a healthy adult.

*Rules, Boundaries and Limits:* While the young Capricorn does not mind definition of goals by others, he is efficient and practical and does not like being told *how* to achieve that goal; he's usually figured out a better way. If the goal itself seems unreasonable to the Capricorn child, he may challenge that as well. The young Capricorn is usually best left unsupervised until he asks for help—or, in the case of the toddler Capricorn, until he quite obviously needs assistance. On the other hand, the young Capricorn is quite comfortable giving advice and telling others how to do things, occasionally eliciting rebellion from his "subordinates" or younger siblings.

Though the young Capricorn needs to know the rules in any situation, he is likely to test the firmness of others' boundaries and limits. He is more likely than children of other sun signs to make his own rules, goals and limits clear, even in games. This may be unsettling to parents who have experience only with more compliant children, but it offers careful parents the opportunity to make a partnership of raising the Capricorn child.


## RELATIONSHIPS

Throughout childhood, Capricorn children are sensitive to other people's expectations and rules and generally try to be considerate and helpful, except toward their own family in adolescence as they break free of their definition as a "child." Shy and introspective, they may have difficulty with ordinary small talk, preferring instead to work quietly beside someone or ponder the secrets of the universe.

*Mom:* Capricorn children expect mothers to be fair, honest, enthusiastic, emotional (usually angry), abrupt, playful, competent, and strong-willed.

Moms who have less confidence in themselves than their Capricorn children have in them may be pleasantly surprised to find themselves living up to their child's ideals or to find their behavior interpreted in a very positive way by this idealistic child. Little Capricorn may see playfulness or enthusiasm in their mom when no one else does, and as a result, moms especially like having little Capricorns around. Capricorn children can be counted on to appreciate Mom's humor.

*Dad:* Young Capricorns expect fathers to be fair, mediating, artistic, just, intelligent, appropriate, logical, socially adept and committed to their marriages. Capricorns usually do not avoid heated discussions with their dads.

A dad who feels he has difficulty meeting these expectations may find dramatic positive response from the Capricorn child simply by listening carefully and entering into serious discussions with him. The young Capricorn sincerely wants to believe in his dad's wisdom and justice and will give Dad every clue and opportunity about how to meet that expectation. Little Capricorn dislikes being lectured to, however, and needs to feel that Dad also values his opinions and ideas.

*Siblings:* Young Capricorns perceive their siblings as dreamy, incompetent, inferior, emotional, artistic, intuitive, unrealistic, accepting, compassionate, sensitive, disappointing and vulnerable. Capricorn children will therefore usually protect and parent their siblings. Regardless of birth order, Capricorns generally act like oldest children.

*Friends:* Capricorn children expect friends to be intense, loyal, equal, moral, ethical, analytical and introspective, and will return these behaviors. Mutual confidentiality is important. While basically a loner, the Capricorn child functions most comfortably with a best friend and may feel hurt and possessive if he feels left out of group activities that include his pal.

MIND/INFORMATION/SCHOOL

Young Capricorns are curious and eager to learn. However, they are surprisingly gullible and need time to figure out what's true and what's not true.

Early teasing or dishonesty by adults tends to result in strong skepticism and mistrust later on. Capricorn children have many interests and are especially likely to remember information that can be put to practical use or used to judge someone else's competence. They may not remember the capitals of all the states for very long, but they will certainly be able to list the names of all their neighborhood streets—in order. There is both pleasure and security for a little Capricorn in learning, though he may ultimately neglect to use this information on his own behalf. He may know all the basic food groups but refuse to use that data himself, even though he closely monitors the food eaten by those he loves. Capricorn children love lists and categories.

Intuitive and insightful, young Capricorns often have flashes of knowledge with no apparent source and may have difficulty defending their conclusions. Needing reasons, they are not fond of rote learning, but they excel at guessing others' expectations and therefore often anticipate test contents and provide correct answers. The ever expedient Capricorn child is perfectly capable of learning answers for a test today and forgetting the very same information tomorrow. Data relating to what's already known is more likely to be retained. Capricorn children seek connections and meaning in information and love correlations. As a result, young Capricorns often find meaning in chaos and can distinguish the difference between the important and the superficial. Irony, patterns and relationships form the basis for the Capricorn humor.

Given adequate time, Capricorn children are patient, compulsive, thorough, accurate and competent with information, but there may be strange lapses. Their need to be right and perfect is such that, caught in a difficult situation, they may bluff or give up. They tend to dare themselves into higher intellectual achievements, beginning to learn new skills by tackling the most difficult project or proceeding to a more challenging task before mastering the last one. They may learn to sew by starting with a tailored suit, or proceed to long division before they have quite mastered multiplication, believing if they accomplish the more difficult task, the lesser task will appear easy and fall into place. Their grit and determination—and faith—usually pull them through, but they seem to live on the edge of absolute chaos. Their penchant for the expedient may also keep them feeling just one step ahead of disaster or discovery. As adept as they are, Capricorn children somehow seem to lack final confidence in their skills; they are as aware of what they don't know as of what they have mastered.

Concentration is generally easy for Capricorn students, who are sometimes impatient with other students' slowness or distraction. Early difficulties with one of the senses, usually sight, hearing or speech, frequently lead to an ability to focus intensely and overcompensate even when the difficulty is overcome. Teachers usually like Capricorn's seriousness, dedication and dependability.

*Higher Education:* Though Capricorns seek to make themselves more useful, salable, authoritative and valid through advanced education, they would rather learn techniques of analysis and synthesis than memorize collections of facts. They may seek training in the arts and other abstract areas before embarking on an entirely different and more concrete career. Once they have switched to a career orientation, they will be quite careful in their choice of education, preferring practical, technical on-the-job training. Capricorns are late bloomers, often identifying careers and acquiring relevant education after the age of twenty-eight.


## RESPONSIBILITY/WORK/REWARDS

*Responsibility and Work:* Responsibility is the name of the game for Capricorn children. They often prefer working with a partner in order to dilute the pressure but may have difficulty delegating responsibility and trusting the other person to live up to Capricorn's standards. Young Capricorns are usually fully accountable and resort to blaming or lying only when absolutely cornered. They are likely to finish activities stoically left by the less conscientious and believe, again, that if a job is worth doing, it is worth doing right. If no one has put away the garden tools by nightfall, for example, the young Capricorn will do it or remind those who forgot; if the little Capricorn himself has forgotten and his oversight is discovered, he may deny it was his responsibility or say he thought another person had done it.

Work in the form of chores, roles or duties is extremely important to the young Capricorn's self-esteem, and he may identify himself by what he does. When asked who he is, after giving his name he may add, "I'm a paper boy," or "I'm the one who shovels your snow," instead of, for example, "I'm Joe's brother," or simply, "I'm me!" Generally an advocate of the work ethic, Capricorn children believe the things they value can be earned and expend a lot of energy doing just that. They are often little entrepreneurs and can usually find a way to earn money or affection quickly. They are serious workers who prefer leadership or partnership positions but will be conscientious and highly organized even in a subordinate role. The young Capricorn usually does a good job regardless of others' response but truly enjoys praise. He is not gracious about accepting criticism and will usually avoid negative feedback by doing work that's beyond reproach. Self-motivated and disciplined, Capricorn children may ultimately find that their work interferes with their play or make their play into work. Sometimes they allow themselves to play only if there's a useful, productive or educational benefit.

*Rewards:* The most valuable rewards for a Capricorn child after a job well done are his internal feelings of freedom, release of pressure and pleasure in achievement. Praise from a person the child likes and respects is also important, as is acceptance and, perhaps, fondness from friends. Capricorns also like money.


## HOME

Capricorn children need lots of space, privacy and storage. Their environment is usually practical, efficient, tasteful and both formal and casual, but it may not be very comfortable. It is full of souvenirs, old things, mementos, collections, objects of nature and, often, books.

Young Capricorns like rooms that can be alternately very light and very dark. They usually like pure sombre colors—deep blues, greens and purples, with light-colored walls. Furniture is usually low and functional, and bare wood is often preferred. Capricorn children love helping with the decoration of their rooms, and once the room is finished, they are likely to resist any further change. Capricorns do not like other people sharing or tampering with their space. This is one child who does best in his own room or needs to define a space of his own in a shared room.

Pleasant as their childhood environment may be, teenage Capricorns are often eager to leave home and find spaces entirely their own.

## HEALTH

Capricorn children usually avoid pain as much as possible. Though they are curious about health issues and collect information regarding them, they may not use what they've learned. Young Capricorns may use illness as a way to allow themselves much-needed rest, to release pressure from their internal expectations or get some time alone. Illness may also be used to divert parents' attention from more threatening problems or to avoid their own problems. When ill, little Capricorns usually like cleanliness, games and reading material and little social contact or fuss. They are particularly sensitive to cold temperatures, even though many prefer the cold to being overheated (one Capricorn friend wears sandals until the snow falls and then deeply lined boots).

Traditionally, Capricorn rules knees, teeth, bones, skin, joints and the sense of hearing. Little Capricorns experiencing health problems are likely to feel uncomfortable in these areas. The illness itself is likely to occur in the form of bruises, colds, hives, itching, stiffening, tension, chills or difficulty teething.

## CHILDHOOD AGES

*(Note: The fears detailed in this section are* never *to be used as punishment. They are presented as avenues for reassurance and caring.)*

Unlike children of some of the other sun signs, Capricorns are usually fairly consistent in their needs and behavior until they reach adolescence.

### BIRTH–6 MONTHS

The Capricorn infant is cuddly, shy, cautious and possibly fearful. His birth may have been difficult, unexpected or problematic. He may appear old and wise and "mature" beyond his age in serious-ness and intensity. He becomes stiff and rigid if he senses anything wrong in his environment but is affectionate and responsive when he feels safe.

### Needs

Cuddling.
Reassurance that parents won't leave him.
Reassurance that parents will protect him.
Reassurance that parents will meet his needs.
Reassurance that he isn't a burden to them.

### Fears

His own helplessness, leading to frustration, anger or terror.
Not being babied enough.
Neglect.

## 6 MONTHS–18 MONTHS

The baby Capricorn is bright, curious and loves to *do* things especially in imitation of grown-ups. He plays peekaboo and finger games, wants to feed himself and to handle his own toys and clothes. He has an intense love of and interest in nature, wants to be outdoors and often enjoys climbing as soon as he is mobile enough to chin himself up on furniture, steps, etc.

### Needs

Permission to learn, play and explore.
Attention and to be taken seriously.
Labels, names, identification, categories.
Reassurance.
Something to show for his efforts (product).

### Fears

Surprises.
Being thrown into the air and dropped.
Doing things too well and losing support.
Being on his own too soon.

18 MONTHS–3 YEARS

The Capricorn toddler continues to be curious, with more attention to information about work, people, old things and the past. He loves explanations, memories, reminiscences and his favorite blanket or toy. He is an astute and serious observer, who, though usually obedient, can also be rebellious, controlling and resistant. He can construct elaborate stories and rationales for his behavior. Though by age three Capricorn has a fair amount of control over his emotions, he is nevertheless still extremely sensitive and prone to feelings of guilt and shame. His anger may continue to flare up unexpectedly. He is beginning to set his own limits and make his own rules and tends to be too stern with himself.

*Toilet Training:* Capricorns take this task seriously and usually welcome the evidence of increased self-sufficiency and maturity. They are quick to learn, will respond to reason and are especially receptive to the idea that everyone else is doing this or has had to do it, too.

> *Needs*
> Explanations, reasons.
> Firm rules.
> Forgiveness, kindness.
> Permission to play, make mistakes, have feelings.
> Permission to continue to explore.
> Not to be allowed—or asked— to punish himself.

> *Fears*
> Being alone or isolated.
> Too much responsibility.
> Having to earn love.
> Being ridiculed for being competent.

3 YEARS–6 YEARS

At this age, Capricorns tend to test their newly learned "adult" skills, becoming alternately very bossy, superior, parental, critical and judgmental and, then, little, helpless and frustrated. Their seriousness and intensity really begin to show. Their increased sense of responsibility and competence may make it tempting and convenient for parents who feel harassed and overwhelmed to turn over adult responsibilities to this capable child. The little Capricorn is full of "oughts" and "shoulds" at this age. He may appear angry, rebellious, bullying and dissatisfied as he tests rules and pushes those around him to find out their limits. Capricorns are often frightened during this time and tend to deal with fear by scaring others. ("Watch out!") They are in special need of consistency now but are likely to challenge that constancy over and over to prove to themselves they can really count on it. On the other hand, in a good mood, these young Capricorns are considerate, sweet, loving, sensitive, concerned and caring. They continue to enjoy emulating the good adult behavior they witness. They remain interested, curious and watchful if these behaviors have been encouraged; if not, they may seem depressed and lethargic.

*Needs*
Information.
Honesty.
To excel and sometimes to win.
To continue to be able to be little, to get help, protection and care.
To know the rules, boundaries, responsibilities and limits.
To know the limits of their own power; not to feel all powerful, in control or fearsome.
To feel useful without being overwhelmed; they need specific, easy chores.

*Fears*
Lack of help.
Having to ask for help.
Abandonment.
Punishment for having feelings of being powerful.


6 YEARS–12 YEARS

Capricorns of this age are very independent, practical, realistic and stoic. They continue to appear mature and capable, and often become rather rigid, judgmental, moralistic, stiff, and rule oriented during this time. They may feel lonely and distant from other children. They remain serious, cautious, sensitive, bossy and worried. They are extremely aware of others' feelings and may become conscience-ridden and guilty if they believe they have hurt people. Capricorns may appear quite conservative now, doing things the safe way, as they have "always" been done or the way "everyone else" does them. They become very achievement conscious. Reminiscent of ages eighteen months to three years, there is once again testing and pushing for limits, hassling with time and authority figures, arguing and general discontent. They are no longer babies and will not allow themselves to ask for babyish support or reassurance, but they are also not yet adults. They feel caught in limbo, out of place, not sure how to just *be* a child. Capricorns may feel very intimidated during this period and suffer trying to maintain equality with peers.

*Needs*
Protection.
Structure, predictability.
Experience.
Respect.
To be taken seriously.
Permission to plan for contingencies.
Encouragement to have friends.

*Fears*
Humiliation.
Ultimatums, threats.
Abandonment.
Changes, surprises, altered rules.
Being ordinary or mediocre.
Having to be perfect.
That no one cares.
That he has intimidated the adults around him.

## 12 YEARS–18 YEARS

As he approaches maturity, the Capricorn is still serious, excellent, responsible, stoic, productive, practical and conservative. He is conscious of rules, security and goals. He continues to be aware of consequences, a much desired trait in adolescents. Concerned, conscientious, thorough, reliable workers, Capricorns of this age may be ambitious and often begin working at paid jobs to achieve financial independence as soon as possible. Frequently they attain positions of responsibility that are unusual for their years. They may, however, be self-critical and perfection oriented, concentrating on where they have failed instead of what they have achieved. Deep and sensitive, the teenage Capricorn is still well-defended and private, and in his dissatisfaction and loneliness may have periods of depression, looking moody, suspicious and volatile. He *chooses* to feel alone at this time. Regardless of the number of friends he has, he sees himself as a misfit. During this time of usual peer pressure, the Capricorn sets high standards for everyone, including himself, and may therefore experience a state of chronic disappointment. He seems to do things the hard way, rebelling against tradition and routine. He tests limits. He insists on making his own decisions, which are often conservative in unexpected ways. He seems compelled to ignore family traditions and to break out of family roles and away from family rules.

The adolescent Capricorn may nevertheless be a pleasure to have around. By this age he has developed a very dry sense of humor and delight. He often laughs at the ridiculous or the unexpected but seldom at himself. He is considerate, thoughtful and has a great willingness to listen, give aid and advice. He is committed to getting things done and can be relied upon to keep his word and help when the going gets tough.

Capricorns may be frightened of their bodily changes, though they welcome these changes as physical evidence of maturity. They may ignore or hide the changes or dismiss them. They are leery of their own fairly intense sexual urges and fear that people may be attracted only to their appearance.

*Needs*

Sexual information, including, but not restricted to, the technical.

Respect, privacy and support for their decisions.

Reiteration of their own value and self-esteem.

Responsibility.

Trust.

Positions of authority.
Excellence, beauty.
Reasons, meaning.
Consistency.
The safety of a nondemanding relationship.

*Hates*

Wasted time.
Doing a bad job, failing.
Being caught unaware, being surprised.
Criticism.
Being labeled by adults.
Being called rigid or paranoid.
Being told: "You have no sense of humor"; "You should
    know better"; "Because I said so"; "You're too young
    . . ."; "It's just a phase."

# AQUARIUS CHILDREN

## JANUARY 20–FEBRUARY 18

### GENERAL CHARACTERISTICS

*(Note: While many characteristics described below will be accurate for most Aquarians, other, sometimes contradictory, traits may also be evident in an individual child.)*

Parents of a newborn Aquarius will instantly notice her remarkable curiosity, twinkly eyes and strong sense of herself. Impatient baby Aquarius seems born wanting to get the show on the road. She is sure of her limitations and needs plenty of permission and protection to test herself to those limits. Even at the infant level, she will let her parents know when she wants something, when she's had enough and what she wants next.

Young Aquarians are afraid of being abandoned but welcome being left alone, which they regard as acknowledgment of their self-sufficiency. Little Aquarians (in fact, grown-up Aquarians, too) especially enjoy parallel activities in which two or more people in physical proximity are each involved in doing their own thing. Two toddlers in the same room, each playing with her own set of blocks, is heaven to the Aquarius babe.

Little Aquarians are fiercely independent and need to be able to do things their way. They tend to dislike admitting dependence or need for help. Aquarians may go to great lengths to assure themselves that they are self-reliant, even if it means losing something in the long run. For example, an Aquarius child who is too little to complete a hobby kit herself would rather discard the project and pretend not to care than let someone help her. She is likely to perceive dependence as a sign of weakness and feel defiant or contemptuous of herself in times of need. This harsh standard is reserved for herself alone. She is often compassionate with others in similar situations and willing to help someone else complete his projects while resolutely refusing help for herself.

It is essential to teach little Aquarius to extend the same compassion to herself that she extends to others. This is best done through verbal communication, with parents using reason and calling on the Aquarian sense of equality and fairness. For example, "If it's okay for Jimmy to get help with his homework, it's okay for you. It's only fair and doesn't mean you aren't independent." More will be said throughout this chapter on the importance of verbal communication with the Aquarian child and the pitfalls of such communication for parents.

Once out of babyhood, it may be difficult for little Aquarius to ask for what she needs; and when she does, her own anger at her perceived dependence may show in how she requests assistance. Parents need to pay more attention to the actual request than to the anger, give little Aquarius what she's requested and reassure their spiky child that her needs are reasonable and acceptable. While little Aquarius is likely to accept quietly substitutions for what she wants, the reason for the substitutions needs to be explained to her or it may lead to later difficulty identifying her needs or expecting to have needs met.

A conflicting theme in the Aquarian's life is the need to fit in and the need to feel individual, independent and unique. Aquarian children have an innate understanding of larger systems and need to know how they fit into them, how others fit in and how the system fits together with other systems. This is the basis for calling Aquarius the humanitarian sign. To some, the word *family* may mean those seated around the supper table, but to the Aquarian child, it is a multigenerational, extended concept of related people. And this child will feel driven to figure out how she fits into this larger unit and how she can maintain her individuality within it.

By early childhood, the needs of small Aquarians for social interaction are as strong as their desire for independence. They often balance these conflicting needs by becoming involved in group endeavors. Group activities that permit plenty of freedom within a predetermined structure and allow little Aquarius to come and go as she pleases will be great favorites. Activities that require more commitment may appear restrictive and threaten the young Aquarius's sense of independence and need to do things her own way, on her own time.

Aquarius children guard their identities fiercely. No amount of parental cajoling will convince them to engage in activities that they believe threaten their identity, and power struggles between parent and child over such activities may lead to communication break-downs and alienation. An Aquarius child cannot be talked or badgered into something in which she does not believe. If she is forced to comply with a parent's wishes (i.e., "Dammit, I was a Scout, so you're going to be a Scout!"), her resentment and loss of trust in that parent is likely to be long-standing.

Simultaneously, the Aquarian child wants to fit in socially and enjoys activities in groups that do not threaten her. To deal with her need for individuality, she may seek to be the exception to the overall rule. For example, little Aquarius may want to wear jeans like everyone else but desire a different color. Balancing her individuality with her response to peer pressure is an overriding theme in an Aquarius childhood. When being both exceptional and accepted, perhaps the only sixth grader in purple jeans, Aquarius feels personally valued and at peace with herself. Rather than try to change this child's mind, parents can help teach her options that assure her individuality and acceptance within her chosen peer groups.

The Aquarius child is fascinated by the unusual and idiosyncratic and repelled by the ordinary. Tolerant of other people's eccentricities and behavior, she is sensitive to categorical differences and skeptical of what categories mean. Groups at school defined by intelligence, social standing, race, or any other way that one group is determined superior to another, will mean little to her. Adults sometimes perceive the young Aquarius's interest in the unusual as a rejection of traditional ways. In reality, her interest includes both. While Aquarius is irresistibly drawn toward the new, she is inclusive and will not reject the old.

Parents need not fear their child's widespread tolerance and interest in different people, for Aquarius has well-defined personal limits and will not be overly influenced by dangerous, bizarre or destructive behavior or personalities. If parents become concerned that their Aquarius child will do anything the crowd does, they need only remember how hard it was to convince her to do something they wanted her to when she didn't believe in it. How the Aquarius child manages to proclaim her individuality in the midst of the social group need not be extravagant or frightening, only symbolic to her.

One first grade Aquarian persuaded her mother to let her get her ears pierced, thereby assuring her difference from most of the other girls.

This intensely felt need to be special tends to separate, or isolate, little Aquarius from her peers. She may go through stages where she hangs on to differences that have proven unproductive just to ensure her individuality, followed by stages when she relinquishes all individuality in order to fit socially. Parents can offer support and options and provide limits to her behavior, but the Aquarius child will need to work out this theme for herself. She is dealing with a dilemma: how to be different and still relate to everyone else.

One frequent solution to this dilemma for the Aquarius child is to gather other people around her who feel as different as she does. Aquarius often fears competition, and if her friendship group consists of other self-identified little eccentrics, the possibility for competition is lessened. Another, though less rewarding, solution is self-effacement and false modesty. An Aquarius would rather be viewed as negatively different than as similar to everyone else. She is more likely to feel unappreciated than to feel undifferentiated.

Aquarius is an air sign; air is the element of cooperation and equality. Aquarian children cooperate beautifully, espousing team spirit. Sometimes they find themselves in leadership positions almost by accident because of their fairness and commitment to a group or cause. They believe in equal opportunity and often champion those less fortunate. Aquarians truly believe they are their brother's keepers. Because they have excellent organizational skills and are willing to take the risks associated with increased responsibility, as leaders, young Aquarians exhibit surprising maturity. An Aquarian youth who noticed that a number of students could not afford a particular school trip quietly organized a fund drive to raise scholarship money. Aquarian children often search for a cause into which to throw themselves.

Adult or other authoritative recognition of leadership skills may leave the young Aquarius feeling uncomfortably singled out for attention. Aquarius enjoys the recognition and responsibility but may fear it will jeopardize her peer relationships and identity within the group. The young Aquarius is therefore likely to refuse or ignore extra recognition of her efforts. She is only doing what she expects of herself and may abandon these efforts if she begins to feel that the recognition is setting her apart from her friends. One very artistic teenage Aquarius who played the piano beautifully suddenly stopped when she felt that the enthusiasm of her teacher and parents would isolate her at school. She then took up writing poetry, an art form her parents did not understand or interfere with.

This pattern of doing and undoing can leave little Aquarius worn out and feeling unappreciated or deserted. She needs quiet recognition, to know she is valued without being made an example to others. Parents can teach little Aquarius to slow down and take pleasure in her achievements and then move on without guilt.

Aquarius often feels herslf to be a lonely, "different" child. As an adult, when she has the maturity and comprehension to deal with this conflict on a more intellectual level, some of her sense of estrangement will ease. Meanwhile, childhood for these children is not the golden age of their lives.

The common factor in the dynamics of the Aquarian childhood is the need to make her own way. To a large extent, parents *cannot* lead the Aquarian child. She is motivated by her own internal need to balance her sense of shared humanity with her individuality. *Why* this is an issue may be incomprehensible to parents with very different astrological and personality backgrounds. Nevertheless, with or without familial support, little Aquarius will work to resolve this issue: she must. And loving parents need to let her resolve it without undue interference or demand for conformity. Such detachment is sometimes hard. Parents can best be involved in this process by talking with their Aquarian as an equal, relating to her as a fellow human being who may be smaller and younger but is no less thoughtful than they. Parents need to be curious about why the Aquarian child does what she does and help her think things through instead of trying to guide her. Parents who are willing to let the child lead them in this manner can help her choose safe options and make self-loving decisions. The trust and loyalty they will receive in exchange is well worth the effort.

Friends become very important to the young Aquarius, and she will often value them as family. Friends, especially a small company of other "different" children, seem to help relieve her sense of isolation. Throughout childhood, Aquarius believes that friendship and social activity will dispel the pain of her differentness, and if socializing fails, she may feel extremely isolated and alone. Little Aquarius needs to feel liked, valued and, above all, included. In such transitions as the loss of a close friend, the ending of a social experience, changing schools or play groups, Aquarius will need extra support and verbal encouragement from her parents.

Little Aquarius tends to spread her social needs across as many friends as possible, believing that several relationships are safer than one important person and that her needs are less likely to overwhelm several friends. In this way, no one person gets to know all of her and little Aquarius may feel both relieved and wistful at other people's ability to share intimately. She may use crisis, her own or others', to get close to people, until she learns more rewarding and permanent ways to reach out. Little Aquarians therefore do well in group settings where they can distribute their needs and maintain a few closer relationships. Their search for connection and intimacy often leads to productive and rewarding group activities and, frequently, to a deep attachment to a much older person, usually a grandparent.

For parents, the most frustrating aspect of the Aquarian's dilemma may be the sense of detachment they experience from their child. Of course this detachment will be magnified or lessened by other parts of her personality, but sometimes it's hard for those who love an Aquarian to know quite how to find their way in. Aquarius may never feel really "grounded," either to herself or to others. She may come across as flighty, constantly a little spaced out, as though she's not quite present. An Aquarius can be told three times in a row to set the table or clean her room and simply not hear the request. She may walk, or later drive, right past her destination while busy with her own thoughts.

The best way to connect with an Aquarian child and help her focus her attention is through verbal communication. Aquarius loves ideas, loves to think about things, loves to talk and be listened to and talked to in return. However, the most important warning to parents is not to talk at, or lecture, Aquarian children. Aquarians are deeply resentful of being held captive audience, of being treated unfairly, of not being given the chance to speak their own views and of having to comply with parental demands with which they do not agree. Of course verbal communication needs to be tailored to the age of the child, but even preverbal Aquarian children will respond to voice tones and verbal requests from their parents, and they will want to be as articulate as their development allows.

Respectful verbal communication is one of the ways by which Aquarians establish their equality and feel that their individuality is being taken seriously. However, even in the most respectful and communicative families, little Aquarius is going to need to resist and rebel against authority. It is part of her childhood task, and parents need to expect this and to make adjustments to allow time and energy for this contest of wills.

Little Aquarians do not like to see themselves as dependent or helpless or in any way less than parents and other grown-ups. From a very young age, their sense of equality may overlook their size, skills and development. This firm belief that they can do anything anyone else can do leaves the Aquarian child in an awkward and painful position. She may finally believe that no one else can, or will, protect and care for her; and if she can't do something herself, no one can do it for her. This may seem a rather presumptuous position to the parent of a five-year-old, but it doesn't feel presumptuous to the five-year-old. Parents need to be firm in their love and protection for little Aquarius. They need to set limits and offer reassurances in the face of endless testing that differences in skill level are not a measure of basic self-worth or equality, and that others can help. She doesn't have to do it alone.

The young Aquarius's need to test and rebel is so strong that harried parents may perceive it as an almost automatic response and be tempted to manipulate their child into certain behaviors. The Aquarian toddler may appear especially troublesome. Weary parents need to resist the temptation to trick their rebellious little Aquarius into compliance. Forbidding this willful little child to eat her carrots, on the—probably correct—assumption that she will rebel and do so, may result in the carrots getting eaten, but this only sidesteps the issue. It can teach Aquarius that rebellion is rewarded and set up very roundabout communication patterns between parent and child that will be harder and harder to unravel as the child becomes more articulate. Parents who maintain clear and firm limits, without tricks, will find that the little Aquarius's rebellions are really shorthand methods for discovering her impact on the world. If her defiance is met with understanding and firm control, instead of matching stubbornness, young Aquarius will soon be on her way to some new interest.

Part of the Aquarian child's sense of uniqueness includes a desire to be unpredictable. She hates to hear anyone say, "I knew that's what you'd do," and may do the opposite of what's expected just to maintain her sense of autonomy. If an Aquarius child wants to go for a walk and her mother wants her to go for a walk, too, it's going to be very hard for the child to take that walk unless the parent says, "I'd like to take a walk with you. Is it all right if I come along?" Parents need to offer firm but minimal guidance and rules for the young Aquarius to follow and then let her find her own way without forcing her to react to external pressure. It is important that young Aquarians be taught to make decisions based on what they want, rather than a need to prove their difference from others. So it is wise for parents to ask the little Aquarius instead of telling her. Parents, too, might learn something about equality and closeness.

In many ways, raising an Aquarius child invites parents to take a more "hands-off" approach than would be advisable with different sun signs. This will work well in situations where parents have thought out the limits to which they are willing to let their little Aquarian go at any age and what they need to do to protect her in her explorations.

The Aquarian child will have the most trouble dealing with secret rules: those unspoken assumptions that exist in every family to some degree or another. She will do most of her testing and rebelling around these secrets. With her innate understanding of systems, she will want to test her perceptions, challenge inconsistencies and uncover dishonesty. Her motto in the family might well be: liars beware! It is not an appropriate childhood task to have to reveal the family's concept of itself. Parents wishing to relieve their child of this burden would do well to look at their family system and assumptions, especially if their Aquarian child is challenging them to do so.

Aquarius is unquestionably the most humanitarian sign. She often shows her love through involvement with causes, concepts, religious or spiritual beliefs and may appear rather aloof or impersonal when searching for ways out of uncomfortable personal situations. For example, if a young friend has a bad experience with a babysitter, young Aquarius may be appropriately sympathetic for a few minutes and then start a Children's Rights Group to prevent similar occurrences for other children. Little Aquarians may want to save the whales, march against nuclear war, write the president or perform other acts that surprise parents as being beyond their years and comprehension. Aquarians tend to nurture by solving problems, and their intent may be misunderstood by friends who are simply seeking a sympathetic ear or shoulder to cry on, not a social cause started in their honor.

Aquarius children are generally fast and reckless, both physically and mentally. Often they love surprises, and their humor reflects their delight in the unexpected. An underlying cautious streak leads them to resent surprises that frighten them, but little Aquarians are enthusiastic risk takers when they feel they have enough control over the situation to make it safe. A young Aquarius may eagerly anticipate her first ride on a roller coaster but become hostile and resistent if she's forced or tricked into riding on one before she's ready. Having taken a risk, little Aquarius may be in no hurry to repeat it. She's simply done with it and ready for something new. Impatient, small Aquarius may also sometimes push herself to do something that scares her, just to get it over with. However, if someone else pushes her, they are likely to encounter the legendary Aquarian stubbornness. Once cornered, little Aquarius will not budge until she's absolutely ready.

The young Aquarius is thoughtful, intellectual, logical and appears very, very rational. She is often intellectually advanced for her age. Teachers may want her to skip grades in school, but as this may disrupt her sense of peer group, it is not recommended without consideration and consultation with the child herself. Aquarius likes to be reasonable. She usually dislikes displays of emotion or sentimentality and believes anything can be figured out if given enough time and information. Other people may perceive Aquarian behavior as cool and be tempted to push her for some kind of emotional reaction. The Aquarian child does have feelings; she just doesn't display them as quickly or as publicly as others might like.

More than anything, Aquarian children hate to be lectured. Parents seeking an emotional reaction from a stubbornly silent Aquarian child would do well to avoid verbally accosting her. An angry parent shouting, "How could you do such a thing?" will not find this confrontation has the desired effect, nor will a parent's asking, "Didn't you love Grandma? Why aren't you crying like the rest of us?" produce signs of sadness. While the requested feelings may eventually be forthcoming, little Aquarius will be reacting to pressure rather than expressing the emotions she has inside. Young Aquarians may decide that for others any answer is better than silence or truth and resent this intrusion on her autonomy long after everyone else has forgotten the incident.

Although she usually needs time to think about things, final answers often occur to little Aquarius in an intuitive flash with no apparent source or rationale. Forcing an issue with logical or emotional demands is counterproductive with little Aquarius and may elicit only rebellion. Basically, the Aquarian personality is committed enough to ideals like truth, honesty, equality, so that she will solve problems; though she may refuse to solve them someone else's way when she's backed into a corner. The young Aquarius is curious and quick, and once a decision is thoughtfully reached, she may be highly opinionated. She has an orderly, scientific, theoretical mind and is adept with the technical.

Aquarius is intrigued by any sort of system, be it bureaucratic, political, familial or electrical. She searches for abstract connections within and between related systems. She loves planning strategy and talking about large generalities. Aquarians dislike chatter and would rather say only what's important and meaningful to them. They have little patience with the past and are true students of the present and the future. They may be fascinated by communication systems, especially television, as well as with the technical gadgetry of the media itself. Aquarian children love gadgets of all kinds and will tend to collect them and put them to creative uses.

Though impatient with repetition, little Aquarius likes duplication, usually owns two of everything and gravitates toward arts that permit replication: photography, poetry, print making, etc. Aquarius is a highly creative and original sign. Part of the fun of sharing life with an Aquarius child is being invited to see the world through her unique eyes. Small Aquarius can always think of new ways to do old things and is especially adept at manipulating anything new in the culture. Sometimes adults may perceive this curiosity as defiance, but it is not. Small Aquarians would rather try a new method and risk failure than utilize a tried-and-true formula. Aquarian children seldom read recipes, and when they do, generally feel compelled to change something. Aquarian concoctions have revolutionized many fields and little Aquarian minds are rarely unwilling to try something new. They will usually rise to almost any challenge or dare. Small Aquarians sometimes brag that they'll try anything once, and more cautious parents may need to spend time teaching the Aquarian child how to assess risk and how to protect herself.

Aquarian children love excitement and will sometimes invite change just for the sake of change or to challenge comfortable patterns with something new. Tense and expectant, Aquarian children often seem as though they are just waiting for something to happen. They prefer any change in the status quo to feeling bored. They do not know how to relax. Keeping Aquarius interested and involved is a challenge all its own for parents of these little dynamos. Little Aquarians need a steady flow of new information and challenge to feel most alive, and they will generate their own if the environment itself is not stimulating. However, once their curiosity and interest has been engaged, they are not capricious and will stick to a task to which they have committed themselves. Erratic behavior and sudden switches in interest are Aquarian signals of boredom and should not be confused with rebellion.

Life is fresh and exciting with an Aquarian child. Parents who were inclined to sit comfortably and let life flow by will be challenged and revitalized by little Aquarian's energy and curiosity. Her delight with newness will keep them advised of the most up-to-date trends and discoveries. Her sense of fairness will assure that they get their share of what's valuable to her. Parents may occasionally be nonplussed by her unexpected maturity and wisdom in solving problems and organizing family matters. And since she loves surprises herself, young Aquarius is certain to keep other family members delighted and astonished with her unpredictable and original behavior, outlook and insights.

NEEDS (Aquarius's emotional emphasis)

> Freedom.
> Assurances of uniqueness and commonality.
> Minimal guidance and rules.
> To learn to extend her understanding of others to herself.
> Reassurance that needs and emotions are not signs of weakness.
> Permission and encouragement to enjoy the rewards of her efforts.

Friends, appreciation, acknowledgment.
Control over touching, affection.
Clearly set limits, light-handed control.
A cause to believe in.
Brief explanation.
To learn to personalize problems and situations, develop empathy.
Not to be cornered, forced into rebellion.
Not to be talked at or lectured to.
Few substitutions.
Not to be forced or pressured into expressing herself.
Not to be manipulated with her rebelliousness.

COMMON ASSUMPTIONS (How Aquarius views the world around her)

I don't need protection; I'll beat the system.
I don't need anyone else.
No one else ever felt this way, or everyone else feels this way.
I must not put all my eggs in one basket.
One for all and all for one.

SENSITIVITIES (Potential sources of misunderstanding)

*Independence/Dependence:* Since young Aquarius has such a difficult time feeling dependent, she may entirely deny she has any needs that require the cooperation of another person. The Aquarian child may decide that the expression of needs and feelings reveals a weakness of character and become very insecure about her perceived fundamental unworthiness. Or she may become very angry with herself for having needs and let the anger effectively drive away those very people who are willing to help her. Little Aquarius needs reassurance that no one does everything alone: no man is an island. Her comprehension of systems can teach her how we are all interdependent and, especially, that all of us have needs and feelings that are worthy of attention.

*Rebellion:* Young Aquarius's way of testing limits is not sneaky or manipulative. Through open rebellion, she will test what happens in order to discover how much she can depend on her parents' protection, strength and consistency. This defiance is often more annoying to parents than it is dangerous for the child. Parents need to exercise thoughtful self-control to avoid meeting the child's rebellion with their own counterdefiance. When parents respond to rebellion with power plays, it confirms little Aquarius's belief that no one can protect her. Extreme reactions to Aquarius's rebellion may lead to a more compliant child but also a very angry one. Parents who are firm and consistent and retain their sense of humor have the best chance of maintaining little Aquarius's trust and affection.

*Freedom:* Aquarian children generally abhor restraint of any sort, and they especially fear boring situations. They need both physical and intellectual challenge and prefer not to be accountable to anyone. Family rules that allow leeway for personal options are most likely to be followed, and exposure to a variety of different lifestyles, interests, and problem-solving models will satisfy the Aquarian child's curiosity and need to explore.

*Friends:* Though the Aquarian child is often basically a loner, she seeks a variety of friends to meet a variety of needs. Friendships are as important to her as blood relationships, and she will go to great lengths to make a family of her friends and friends of her family. Young Aquarius's attraction to the different or unique assures an odd assortment of friends in her life and at least modest popularity. Though little Aquarius is attracted to people's eccentricities, she seldom wants to be just like them.

*Causes:* Often young Aquarians search for a cause into which they can throw themselves. They want something larger than life, something big enough to contain all of their energies and idealism. If Aquarius combines this search with rebellion, or if her values are different from those of her family, young Aquarius may find herself feeling unsupported, alienated from family members and others who are important to her. Parents who teach their values lovingly and firmly have little to be concerned about as the small Aquarian briefly dons different hats and experiments with alternate ways of being. If little Aquarius is not met with overt antagonism and forced to defend her stance, her restlessness assures that she will not usually stay long with any unsupported cause. However, the Aquarian quest for personal identity and uniqueness is relentless, and the possibility exists that she will ultimately develop values different from those of her family and, with integrity, pursue them regardless of family opinion. One five-year-old Aquarian in a family of meat eaters spontaneously decided he was a vegetarian, and no amount of argument could persuade him otherwise. Today, fifteen years later, he continues to eat no meat.

*Truth:* Young Aquarians cannot tolerate being cornered and forced to talk, express emotions or give explanations. If parents demand these things, small Aquarius will become adept at guessing the words parents want to hear, offering any words she thinks will end what she perceives as verbal battering. Parents who really want to know what's going on in the Aquarian child's mind will allow time for little Aquarius to think about things and figure them out. Parents need to respect their child's privacy, even if they never hear the entire explanation or process.

*Equality:* In order to maintain equality with her peers, young Aquarius may refuse the rewards and responsibilities of her efforts. Similarly, she may reject other people's authority due to her belief that "If we're all equal, no one has the right to tell me what to do." Aquarius may literally confuse equality with sameness. Reassurances that each person is skilled, but in different ways, may alleviate some of this confusion, reduce her defensiveness and encourage her cooperation.

## RELATIONSHIPS

Little Aquarians' lives are all about relationships, building social and group skills. Interaction is essential to them; they need external feedback in order to define themselves. Talking is also essential for the Aquarian child: conversation, arguing, debate, banter, etc. If intense interaction is not forthcoming, little Aquarius may use anger or crisis in order to engage another person. She also demands, and gives, absolute equality and respect in her relationships and is sometimes painfully aware that no one is better or worse than anyone else.

*Mom:* Little Aquarians expect Mom to be available, steadfast, nurturing, generous and practical. Friends of the Aquarian child usually idolize her mother.

Moms who have difficulty living up to these expectations may be tempted to substitute food or gifts for emotional interaction. Time and attention are more valuable gifts for the young Aquarius, who resents being "bought off" even if she benefits from it. Mom's willingness to express herself and to debate values with young Aquarius is the proof the child seeks of love and commitment. Mothers of little Aquarians may also perceive the child's search for autonomy as personal rejection or criticism and may react by overprotection or withdrawal of emotional support. Aquarian children need unconditional love and support as they experiment and seek their own style—even if it differs from family expectations.

*Dad:* Young Aquarius often either idealizes her father or doesn't expect much from him, or both. She may see Dad as controlling, manipulative, rigid, secretive or competitive, even if she benefits from his interest in her or from his aloofness. Dad may seem overpowering to her, and as an adolescent she may be intimidated by her own sexuality when she's around him. A father's presence, expectations, or behavior may overwhelm little Aquarius, and she may feel that he is competing with her in some way or somehow blaming her for things beyond her control. The words to note here are "he may *seem*." Little Aquarius has a hard time separating Dad from her image of him.

Dads who want to diffuse the threat little Aquarius feels will remember to treat their child as an equal person, worthy of interest and respect. He will share his feelings, information and humor with her and refrain from placing undue demands on her behavior or intruding on her privacy. On the other hand, he will also remember that she is a child, and worthy of all the nurturing and protection he can muster. Dads of small Aquarians will find that loving support and acceptance add greatly to the child's trust. Little Aquarians who can have a good intellectual argument with their dads, and sometimes win, are deeply satisfied.

*Siblings:* Young Aquarians tend either to treat siblings as friends or to have little connection with them at all. While the Aquarian child perceives herself as generous, rational and logical, she is likely to see her siblings as emotional, headstrong, impulsive, self-centered and single minded. There may be intellectual competition and fierce debate among siblings, though restless little Aquarius is usually unable to maintain hostility for long and may capitulate quickly on behalf of equality.

*Friends:* The young Aquarius is fiercely loyal, tolerant and generous with friends. She is attracted to those who are equally intelligent and share her values. She especially seeks those who are interesting and different. Unfortunately for bewildered little Aquarius, those very characteristics that attract her often mean that friends are on the move and may pass in and out of her life just as she's becoming comfortable with them. In her needs to control safety and trust in situations, she may find herself leaving people who are important to her before they leave her. Sometimes her appraisal of situations is in error, and she may lose close friends unnecessarily. Little Aquarius expects humor, loyalty, honesty, fairness and friendliness from peers and will return the same. She may be disappointed and amazed when others fail to live up to her standards or to appreciate or even notice her devotion.

MIND/INFORMATION/SCHOOL

The young Aquarius has a fast, original, incisive mind that is capable of great intuitive flashes of insight. She loves systems and patterns and willingly organizes both people and information. She loves to theorize, abstract and explain. She thinks in chains: with thoughts leading to thoughts leading to more thoughts. It's sometimes hard for her to turn off her mind enough to sleep. She has a great curiosity and will aggressively seek information and patterns, becoming quite excited about new data. She always knows exactly what everyone in her environment is doing.

The Aquarian mind is rational, logical and often scientific. She believes anything can be figured out or explained rationally. She enjoys learning but may become defensive if someone begins to explain things she thinks she already knows. She has little time for small talk or idle chatter and tends to include emotional expression in the latter category.

Though she generally likes preschool, the young Aquarius is restless and may find regular school boring. She may resent having to slow down to meet the needs of slower students in the class. She learns best through association, connecting disparate bits of information, and needs to understand current information before she moves on. Her need for understanding may annoy teachers who prefer rote memorization or who meet only the needs of the majority of the class. Little Aquarius often has a photographic sort of memory for what interests her. Though in other areas she may lack detail, her memory can often accurately and completely reproduce the input from one sense: pictures, dialogue, tunes, etc. The Aquarius child collects books and is usually an excellent reader who doesn't like reading as much as she likes talking, conversing, discussing or learning by actually doing something. She loves experiments and discovery through experience.

*Higher Education:* Aquarians generally consider higher education for its social benefits first, then in terms of information learned. They are often gifted in the arts, though they may choose something else for a career; Aquarians become nervous about being paid to do what they love and having their artistic achievements judged. Thus they are likely to pursue investigative or organizational careers or those in the legal professions, the media or computer science. They love psychology and may choose to earn a living figuring people out. They are likely to pursue further education to please someone else rather than for themselves.

## RESPONSIBILITY/WORK/REWARDS

*Responsibility and Work:* Young Aquarians like being responsible for the large picture—for groups of people, organizing things, etc.—but they are less enthusiastic about details. They love orchestrating the annual United Fund Drive but resent writing up the report afterward. Similarly, they are ambivalent about being "the best" or "the only" at anything and will generally gladly share both responsibility and accountability.

Once they have been delegated responsibility, however, young Aquarians take their task seriously and may be compulsively thorough. They tend to keep score and often expect to be paid, or repaid, for their efforts, emotionally or materially. They believe they have a cosmic obligation to utilize their talents and may have difficulty saying no, becoming resentful when they feel put upon or overworked.

Little Aquarius sees work as simply an extension of responsibility. When she believes her work is worthwhile and important (feeding the dog is worthwhile, washing the dishes is not), she will extend great amounts of effort to do an excellent job. She is very intense while concentrating on a task, and while she doesn't like being disturbed, she does enjoy having someone nearby. The young

Aquarius may become quite competitive as she performs her work and often seeks to be the best in order to avoid comparison or criticism. Like Capricorn, little Aquarius wants to be the standard by which everyone else is judged; unlike Capricorn, if she reaches that goal, she may become uncomfortable at the apparent lack of equality.

*Rewards:* The Aquarian child definitely needs rewards for her efforts. If only a nod of approval or a token of appreciation, she needs to have her work noted. Fulfilling her own idealistic standards often leads to self-satisfaction for the young Aquarius, and she likes to hear that others think better of her as well. She keeps a mental tally of her achievements and successes and will often seek rewards in the form of help or special dispensation she feels she's "earned." While young Aquarius likes cash and gifts, these are better saved for odd and capricious moments and not used as direct rewards, which she may angrily perceive as bribes.

## HOME

Though little Aquarians see their space as a refuge from the world, their friends are welcome and encouraged to visit. Little Aquarius prefers people to come to her rather than going to them. While she needs an area of her own, she is not bothered by having others nearby. She likes her space to be comfortable, livable, full and easy to care for. Little Aquarius's taste, which may be quite expensive, are often reflected in her surroundings, which will be, if possible, tasteful, plush, textured and probably monochrome, confined to variations of a single (usually light) color. Older Aquarians may pass through a period of liking things shiny, smooth and uncluttered, and becoming entranced with things like chrome and glass, but they generally quickly revert to their previous preferences. Often a young Aquarian's space is filled with gadgets, electronic gizmos, and a variety of media hardware.

## HEALTH

When little Aquarius gets sick, she wants, expects, and needs lots of babying, nurturing, tender loving care and food. Illness may be the only way the Aquarian child knows how to allow herself to be dependent or get exclusive attention. She may also become ill because she was careless ("It won't happen to me."); as the result of experimentation ("How long can I go without eating?"); or simply as a change of pace, especially when she needs to slow down. While she likes attention, she may use illness as a time for privacy and resent unnecessary intrusion.

The Aquarian child is interested in health from an abstract standpoint. She knows about the systems of the body, nutrition, preventive care, and epidemics. When ill, she wants to know why; and as she matures, she also wants to know treatment options and to have a voice in those decisions.

Traditionally, Aquarius rules shins, nerves, all the systems, and unusual manifestations beyond the "average" (i.e., large hands, very blue eyes, tiny ears). Little Aquarians experiencing health problems are likely to feel tense and nervous, and may exhibit these feelings through trembling, tics, headaches, spasms, hiccoughs, or minor accidents caused by carelessness. They may have allergies caused by systemic reactions to a variety of external stimuli.

## CHILDHOOD AGES

*(Note: The fears detailed in this section are never to be used as punishment. They are presented as avenues for reassurance and caring.)*

### BIRTH–6 MONTHS

The Aquarius infant is sparkly and engaging. She is alert and quick to respond to people, objects and activities in her environment. Since her attention span is especially short, she is easily distracted. She loves surprises, unexpected (and safe) occurrences and things that glitter. She likes gentle physical games and contact but becomes irritable, uncomfortable and tense with any sort of physical restriction.

> *Needs*
> Minimal physical restraint (including clothing).
> To be talked to, played with, laughed with.

A great deal of sensory stimulation.

Interaction with a variety of people and, if possible, other infants.

Sensitivity from adults about how and when she's had enough petting.

To be left alone when she wants to be, with reassurances that someone is nearby.

To be rocked, especially by a grandmother.

*Fears*
Restriction.
Abandonment.

6 MONTHS–18 MONTHS

Baby Aquarius is intensely interested in her surroundings. Curious and restless, she seems constantly on the move and often earns the fond nickname "Crash." Little Aquarius seems fearless and relentless in her investigation of her environment and needs careful but unobtrusive supervision until she is old enough to assess realistically danger by herself. Even at this age, she is fascinated by television, computers and electricity. Baby Aquarius may be precocious, learning to walk or talk earlier than expected; she is certainly stubborn. Since Aquarian rebellion begins toward the end of this period, parents may become particularly exasperated by their one-year-old Aquarian, only to be recaptivated by the child's continual love of change and surprise and her natural buoyancy. Baby Aquarius may seem to test endlessly, asking for something and then rejecting it or wanting it only briefly.

*Needs*
Space.
Beginning control over her environment.
Quiet time.
Few, but firm and loving limits.
Reassurance that someone is always nearby.
Stimulation.
Unobtrusive supervision, especially around electrical or electronic gadgets.

*Fears*
Restriction.
Being ignored or abandoned.

## 18 MONTHS–3 YEARS

The Aquarius toddler continues to be curious, alert and seemingly "into everything." She needs to know how things fit together and loves arranging things, nesting toys, simple puzzles and the like. Even more, she is intrigued by the media: television, tape recorders and small computers will fascinate even this tiny Aquarian. She is social and interested in people, especially other toddlers. She loves tricks and magic.

In the toddler, Aquarian rebellion is in full swing. She may seem defiant, stubborn, perverse and changeable. She loves excitement and challenge and will create her own if she is feeling ignored or neglected. She is beginning to develop the famed Aquarian logic and may seem argumentative or very literal. Her behavior may appear erratic and unpredictable, and she may appear tense or high-strung to those nearby.

*Toilet Training:* Training the little Aquarius may be an arduous task. To begin with, she does not like undue attention paid to her body, and she is almost certain to rebel against any type of physical or emotional force or pressure. Young Aquarius needs to be told what is expected of her and then allowed to figure out, with loving support, her own way to do it. She is more likely to cooperate with Mom than with Dad in this area.

*Needs*
Short explanations.
Few, but firm and loving limits.
Challenges and a variety of experiences.
Permission to continue to explore.
Permission to have "baby" needs, too.
Permission to become increasingly independent.

*Fears*
Restriction.
Being dependent.

Lack of information.
Lack of limits.
Being ignored, overlooked, forgotten.

### 3 YEARS–6 YEARS

The preschool Aquarius discovers friends. Since being with peers assumes a vast importance, little Aquarians are especially happy in suitable preschool programs. Close supervision is often necessary, however, in group situations. She is restless, reckless and curious, and always seems to be exploring, experimenting or testing. Without fully developed motor control, she may inadvertently hurt herself or someone else. Though she is quite competitive at this age, little Aquarius is likely to feel guilty winning and resentful losing.

Little Aquarius continues to be rebellious, volatile and erratic, and is busy discovering and testing limits and roles. Her "logic" is beginning to develop at this age, and preschool Aquarius may debate, hassle, argue, and "reason" with anyone nearby. This is the beginning of the adult Aquarian's considerable verbal skills. If unnecessarily restricted or shamed, little Aquarius may become agitated or she may become detached and identify primarily with inanimate objects, especially computers.

*Needs*
Peer group.
Information.
Choices and options.
Short explanations.
Quiet time.
Personal attention.
To feel special and included.
Understanding and compassion.
Few, but firm and loving restrictions.

*Fears*
Exclusion, being left out.
Restraint.
Comparison to others.
Retaliation.

Isolation.
Labels.
Being slowed down.

## 6 YEARS–12 YEARS

The school-age Aquarius is extremely attuned to her peer group, whether in rebellion to or compliance with their standards. Fairness is extremely important to this young Aquarian, and team spirit seems all-consuming, whether the child is on the team or not. The school-age Aquarius is cooperative and charming when she wants to be and is quickly developing her social, verbal and leadership skills. She is simultaneously very individualistic and independent, with a rigid (but probably unique) sense of right and wrong. She is keenly aware of what "everybody else" is doing at all times and of current fads and activities.

While she is inclusive and social, she may nonetheless feel lonely and isolated, not really part of something, regardless of the reality of the situation. She may feel either superior or shy. She may react impersonally, relating more to groups than to particular individuals, or she may pretend she doesn't care. She may break or seek exceptions to rules to test their firmness, and she may debate apparently insignificant points. She is impatient with herself and others. She fears entrapment, though she may frequently feel stuck. Her behavior may appear erratic in her attempts to create movement or excitement in her life.

*Needs*

Brief explanations.
Respect for her privacy and individuality.
Quiet time.
To be taught social skills.
Political explanations.
Structure.
Social activities.
Intellectual stimulation.
Verbal exchange.
To be listened to.
To disagree, to be different.

*Fears*
Entrapment.
Being too different or too ordinary.
Being unheard, ignored or unappreciated.
Having to be exceptional.
Force.
Being pressured for response.

## 12 YEARS–18 YEARS

The adolescent Aquarius is very similar to the school-age Aquarius, only more so. She is more apt to represent the extremes of her previous behavior. Either she may act very different from or very much like her peer group; she may be either very social or become quite withdrawn. She remains rebellious and contrary and is very alert to current peer norms and behavior, either adopting or openly defying them. Independent and experimental, or depending heavily on peer values, the teenage Aquarius can be expected to reflect positively or negatively exactly what's occurring around her. She usually rejects parental or traditional values and eagerly searches for a new role model, an exception. She may then bitterly reject these models when she discovers they are mere humans, or she may idealize their foibles. She is disdainful of financial success, admiring instead such qualities as honesty, loyalty and integrity.

The adolescent Aquarius remains idealistic and humanitarian and is a willing and diligent worker for those causes in which she believes. She is bright, quick and original, with innovative solutions to problems and a readiness to take risks to improve things. She thrives on options and choices. She does not like to be held accountable for her behavior and decisions. Because she fears restraint or attempted restraint from authority figures, she often acts quickly before others have a chance to interfere. She may be highly opinionated and believe only she has the right answers, especially if she believes everyone is alike, that is, like her. She may sometimes appear cold or unsympathetic. On the surface she approaches emotional difficulties with facts and logic, while beneath this cool exterior lies a deep compassion she fears will incapacitate her to ineffective emotional dependence.

The teenage Aquarius is usually rather put off by her own body changes, regarding them as inconvenient at best, embarrassing at worst. She is, however, quite curious about this phenomenon when viewing bodies as a system to be understood. When not acting nonchalant, she may watch herself and others with minute attention, offering knowledgeable analysis of the development she sees. She prefers friends and buddies to lovers, though she may use sexual behavior (or lack of it) as a way to be "in" or different, or as a means to get close to people.

*Needs*
Firm limits.
Equality.
Respect.
Independence, freedom, privacy.
To know firm consequences.
Verbal interchange.
Information in general.
Information about love as well as sex.
Peer groups, social activities.
A cause.
Permission to find her own way and values.

*Hates*
The illogical, inconsistencies.
Rote memorization, arbitrary information or reasons.
Being bored, ordinary.
Being second-guessed ("I knew you'd do that . . .").
Being cornered.
Being forced to explain her behavior.
Arbitrary restrictions and limitations.
Prejudice, stereotypes.
Not knowing what's going on.
Being left out.
Being called irrational or subjective.
Being told, "I don't care what everyone else is doing . . ."
Being told, "You made your bed; lie in it."
Being told, "That's how it's always been done . . ."

# PISCES CHILDREN

**FEBRUARY 19–MARCH 20**

## GENERAL CHARACTERISTICS

*(Note: While many characteristics described below will be accurate for most Pisces, other, sometimes contradictory, traits may also be evident in an individual child.)*

Parents will be immediately drawn to the vulnerability, helplessness and sweetness of newborn Pisces. The Pisces infant is soft and cuddly and willingly allows himself to be held and pampered. He is the "doll" many moms wish they had had and will elicit the most tender feelings from both parents. Pisces can appear more fragile than he really is, and parents may need to reassure themselves that this baby will indeed endure. There is a temptation, in response to Piscean vulnerability, for parents to want to be a more perfect mom or dad for this child and to fear their mistakes will be damaging. Pisces is not that fragile, and as he gets older his apparent fragility is less obvious. While baby Pisces may continue to act shy and withdrawn in new situations, he is adaptable and becomes curious and quite charming once he feels safe.

Pisces is the most elusive sign of the zodiac. It is a water sign, sign of the fish, associated with the ocean, with great depth and changeable surfaces. Pisces exhibits the widest range and least predictable patterns of behavior. Pisces people are intensely sensitive to the expectations of others; the Pisces child is likely to behave in ways that try to meet the expectations he believes others have of him. He may adopt a variety of roles and behaviors that often reflect parental expectations (and sometimes parental sun signs) rather than assert his own personality. As a result, it is most difficult to make blanket statements about the behavior of the young Pisces, and this chapter will deal primarily with motivation for Piscean development rather than definition of specific traits. Circles and mirrors are images associated with Pisces, and these images may be more helpful to parents raising a Pisces child than all these words will be.

The young Pisces often believes that who he is, all by himself, isn't quite enough. He may be acutely aware of his imperfections or feel that somehow he just doesn't fit in. He may have fantasies that he was perhaps born in the wrong place, wrong time, or into the wrong family. While many children at some time wonder if they are adopted, little Pisces wonders longer and harder than most. As a child he never feels at home in the world, and it may be hard for parents to know quite how to help.

The Pisces child who feels he doesn't fit anywhere becomes an adult who can fit in everywhere. He develops social skills, grace and often a nonverbally conveyed warmth. However, this growth is incomprehensible in the mind of a child, and it is small comfort to a little Pisces wondering why everyone else is having such a good time, what everyone thinks is so funny or what he's going to say when the next person asks him a question. He may appear fearful or shy to others or retreat into a fantasy world that is more interesting and less threatening and offers him at least the illusory courage to do what he needs to do. If little Pisces pretends, just for today, to be Luke Skywalker, he may enjoy conversations, parties and jokes. He will borrow the self-confidence he needs from his fantasy.

The Pisces child both fears and seeks a sort of psychic invisibility. If no one notices him, he remains relatively safe and can do what he wants without having to be accountable to anyone else. If no one notices him, he reasons, his imperfections won't be exposed and he won't be rejected. However, there is a price he pays for seeking safety in withdrawal. Every child needs feedback and interaction with those from whom he is learning and who are in charge of his care. Every child needs to feel special, loved, noticed, singled out for attention and nurturing. Eventually, even tiny Pisces needs approval and support and will become frightened at the withdrawal that only minutes earlier had made him feel safe. Parents with a Pisces in the house need to notice when he's back from his private spaces and see that he gets fairly immediate attention and support.

The little Pisces caught in this conflict between hiding and reveal-ing himself chooses one of two paths: he decides to let—in fact insists that—people see him as he really is or he decides to hide those parts of himself he thinks are most imperfect and asks that only his "good" parts be recognized. These decisions are not conscious, not like choosing between ice cream or cake. These are deep, oceanic decisions that occur beneath the surface of this malleable child.

The Pisces child who chooses full revealment is often crystal clear and in tune with his surroundings. He is confident, spontaneous and creative and has energy left over to share with others. He can relax his watchfulness and balance his adaptability to other people's needs. In a sense, he takes one horrendous risk, and the worst is over for him, at least until the next big scare comes along. The Pisces child who chooses only partial revealment must now decide which parts of himself to hide. All by himself, this youngster finds himself judge and jury of his tender self-image, sorting out pieces of himself he thinks will be unacceptable to those around him. It cannot be a pleasant process, and it is made more uncomfortable by the fact that most of it occurs beyond his awareness.

A young Pisces who is hiding substantial parts of himself has a hard time believing that the recognition and positive feedback he receives is really meant for him, for he is aware that there are parts of himself that do not show on the outside. Instead, he may believe he's fooling everyone, that if they *really* knew him they wouldn't like him so much. He may feel contempt for the adults whom he has apparently fooled and be skeptical of their ability to take care of him if they aren't smart enough to catch him hiding himself. Sometimes the young Pisces starts to undervalue the parts of himself he is showing, believing they are not as "real" as his "real" self in hiding.

Some Pisces children go into hiding by adopting a role that is foreign to their real selves. They think, "I'll be exactly what you want me to be (instead of myself) because you seem to like that better." Even a Pisces child's misbehavior can stem from an unconscious belief that a parent secretly wants him to behave in certain ways. The Pisces child is adept at picking up messages that are nonverbal, indirect and secret. Often his behavior is a reflection of the underlying expectations in the family. Remember the mirror image; Pisces mirrors the family's collective self. This mirror can reflect both positive and negative images. "You want a little ballerina, you get a little ballerina"; "You want a bully, you get a bully."

The Pisces child, who adopts an alien role or mirrors the family's needs instead of his own, walks a careful tightrope between exposure and safety. He doesn't want to be exposed as a fraud. At the same time, he yearns for the release of exposure and the end of the game. He has a deep longing for someone to see and accept him as he really is, and when he finds someone who he believes both sees and loves him, his loyalty and gratitude are immense. Astonished parents may protest that they *do* see and love their little Pisces just as he is. This declaration may be lost on little Pisces unless it is repeated and demonstrated over and over again. The "coming out" process is usually a long one for Pisces, and every child does it at his own speed.

Parents who succeed in convincing the young Pisces of their unconditional love may suddenly uncover a child who needs to confess all of his transgressions and who feels ashamed of his hiding. He may test them to see if the offer of love still holds true once his essential unworthiness and trickery are known. The Pisces child who feels visible and loved at the same time may also feel completely exposed and vulnerable. Though this is precisely the situation he's longed for, he will have conflicting feelings about it and may temporarily withdraw or lash out at those he loves. Parents need to provide lots of love, support and information during such transitions. This is a time Pisces needs "how-to" skills for defending himself, and he needs to be taught the difference between withholding parts of the self and hiding parts of the self. The young Pisces is most vulnerable when being observed, so he will accept information publicly, but most of the risks he takes and changes he makes will occur without witness.

Pisces may spend his entire childhood wrestling with his dilemma, but he is so adept at guessing other people's wishes and expectations that parents may never know what is going on inside him. He is indeed a remarkable child to have around. Most people enjoy having someone nearby who is adaptable, who agrees with them and who excels at doing just the things they like to do. The Pisces child's adaptability can invite people to project their secret longings and dreams onto him, and he may expend a great deal of energy trying to make these dreams come true. The most anguishing conflict for the young Pisces occurs when two people he loves have contradictory expectations of him. (How can he be Mommy's little pianist and Daddy's little football player?)

Parents with unfulfilled dreams (all parents, all people, have unfulfilled dreams) need to take responsibility for the choices they have made and make sure little Pisces has as much freedom as possible to make up his own mind and chart his own course.

The Pisces child may complain or brag that many people think they know him, but no one really knows him. He may have difficulty describing himself or establishing an identity. He may feel nothing he does makes a difference and be surprised to learn of the impact he has on other people and that they care. The young Pisces can appear cold, calculating and not empathic when he attempts to assess things "realistically" instead of following his usual intuitive thinking style.

Little Pisces may appear withdrawn or excessively dramatic as he experiments with differing ranges of feeling and behavior. He may exaggerate the importance of events others find insignificant and overlook events others find much more meaningful. He may need to dramatize events to feel their impact or believe his stories have to be bigger than life to have any impact at all. Life with little Pisces is often like living in a soap opera, where ordinary events take on special meaning. In fact, one five-year-old Pisces announced to her mother who'd just received a traffic ticket and was quite upset, "Don't worry, Mommy, it's only a movie." The young Pisces tends to be subjective, to take things personally and attempt to find personal significance and meaning in any event. He loves Hollywood.

The Pisces child often lives in a world filled with rich fantasy. He may have an imaginary playmate, and he frequently constructs elaborate stories to explain the activities around him. He's not just playing in the woods, he is hunting bear, and next door Billy is a helpful Indian chief, and his little sister is a princess and so on. The legendary creativity of the adult Pisces has its roots in childhood fantasy, but it is a difficult road for a child to follow. Mundane occurrences assume magical proportions and little Pisces often has a skewed understanding of cause and effect. He may really believe his mother got sick because he was mad at her. He may bargain with the universe, promising to be good if only "you'll make Mommy better." If Mom recovers, Pisces's sense of magical power is confirmed. If Mom doesn't recover, his guilt is confirmed. Parents need to keep teaching Pisces that he does not and cannot make things happen.

Pisces is a suggestible child who may entirely believe what others tell him. He needs to have jokes labeled as jokes and not have the family burst out laughing at his gullibility. A Pisces who is teased early in life may seem cynical later on and may have a hard time trusting others. The Pisces child is especially vulnerable to self-fulfilling prophesy, and parents need to exercise special caution not to tell him who they think he is. Even attributes intended as compliments may sound like demands to be lived up to in small Pisces's mind. "You're always late" will be lived up to for sure, and "What an honest child you are" may elicit a torrent of confession about all the times he was not. In adolescence this gullibility and taking on of attributes are still strong but less obvious. An adult who teasingly calls a Pisces "arrogant" will be believed and may unwittingly initiate a major change in the young Pisces's life.

All of these subterranean influences going on beneath the pleasant adaptability of the Pisces child's surface can lead to a rather persistent confusion about what is reality. If what he thinks is real conflicts too often with what the family thinks is real, he may begin to fear he's crazy. Families that include Pisces children need to be extremely careful about their use of the word *crazy* and to make sure they don't confuse difference with craziness. The Pisces child often believes that in any system one person *is* crazy, and may expend great effort to prove it isn't him.

Since the Pisces child is often extremely intuitive, he may be aware of what's going on before others, especially emotional nuances, and even before the person who has generated the feeling is aware of it. If little Pisces checks out his perception and is told he's wrong, he again may worry about being crazy. If a Pisces child asks, "Mommy, are you angry at Daddy?" Mom better take a few minutes to check out her real feelings before telling Pisces he's wrong. Concerned parents need to listen for the grain of truth in Pisces's questions and not categorically deny their child's perception.

The Pisces child needs to be told what's going on. Though he usually hates secrets, he may feel a thrill of excitement to be included in privileged information, and he may be terribly hurt if left out of secrets. His behavior often reveals the secret long before his mouth does, however, and he is seldom a good liar. The young Pisces may see only what he wants to see. He may see what he wishes were true instead of what is true. He clings to positive rather than negative fantasy and may stubbornly defend it even in the face of contradictory evidence. "No, you and Mommy are *not* getting a divorce, I don't care what you say!" Parents may find it hard to have a sense of sharing little Pisces's reality, of being able to see the world the way he does, especially when his idealization of things includes them. Ultimately this kind of optimism, which is based on denial, is a despairing stance: the youngster who cannot acknowledge flaws in the world can never rejoice in improvement.

This looks like the position of a romantic idealist. It often produces wonderful works of art, even from a small child, but leaves Pisces feeling powerless in the world. From this point of view, he can't see how anything he does can change things, or he may be afraid to spoil an already perfect world. A little blending of Aquarian idealism from the sign before him or Aries's concern with individual rights from the sign after him, helps Pisces reach a better balance in his world view. The problem is really Pisces's either/or vision of things. Small Pisces needs to be taught to assess where he can have an effect and where it's impossible for him to have an effect. The popular image of Pisces as a fish swimming simultaneously upstream and downstream reflects this conflict.

Small Pisces's magical thinking may show up in forms of denial. If he denies something exists or denies its importance, he believes he will not have to deal with the ramifications or feel responsible. For example, if Dad is upset because the car has a flat tire, little Pisces may believe he should comfort Dad in some way, but he may tune out the entire episode in order not to feel he has to get involved. Or small Pisces, terrified he will be blamed, criticized, held responsible, punished or rejected, may suddenly appear critical himself in defense: if only Dad had been more careful, the tire wouldn't be flat, etc. Small Pisces tends to appear either defensive or submissive when blame is floating around. He wants to deflect it all or take it all, but he doesn't know how to strike a balance.

Although Pisces may present a vulnerable exterior, secretly he may believe he's the strongest person around. The Pisces child would rather suffer himself than watch someone else in pain. If a friend's bicycle is broken, young Pisces will feel just terrible about it and volunteer not to ride his own bike in sympathy. Pisces is almost always the advocate of the underdog. He may confess to putting the tack on teacher's chair even if he didn't do it, just to spare the real culprit. And he will often take on collective guilt, feeling guilty even though he didn't do it. The young Pisces often thinks it's his duty to shoulder pain, and he may carry the pain of the world or the family on his little shoulders. He hates even the thought of hurting someone else's feelings.

The secret belief that he is stronger can lead to Pisces's putting other people's needs before his own. He may believe he has to wait until others are satisfied or happy before it's his turn, or he may sacrifice things he needs out of a sense that sacrifice in itself will help others. ("If I don't eat this candy bar, the starving children in Africa won't be quite so hungry.") The Pisces child who puts other people's needs first may appear compassionate, considerate and generous, but he is still trapped in his behavior, not getting what he needs for himself. He may later become bitter over these voluntary sacrifices, or he may attempt to get his needs met deviously—like getting sick or having accidents to get attention and have his needs moved to the front of the list.

While children of many other signs need encouragement to share, to be considerate and generous, the Pisces child does not need such behavior reinforced. In fact, he needs to be rewarded for selfishness: for the time he's willing to come first, to state what he wants, to ask directly for attention and nurturing. This may be a direct "about face" for parents with children of very different signs, and they may find themselves saying to Aries, "You have to share your toys with Pisces," and saying to Pisces, "You don't always have to share your toys with Aries."

Not all of Pisces's compassion and sensitivity to others stem from his innate confusion about his own selfhood or needs. He is genuinely compassionate and concerned. He is sincere and devoted to those he loves and willingly gives others the benefit of the doubt. There is a lot of healing in the Pisces child. He cries real tears. He doesn't laugh at jokes at the expense of the underdog and often doesn't even get the point of nasty remarks or ridicule. This sensitive child is tolerant, truly generous and quite willing to do his share to add to the beauty of the world and the well-being of its people. When his nurturing needs are met, little Pisces often gives freely with a great sense of abundance, enriching the lives of all around him.

Being willing to let himself get filled up with nurturing, however, may be difficult for little Pisces. He will have to struggle not to let other people's needs come first or not to refuse to take things that he thinks should be sacrificed for others. He may have trouble asking for things if he feels he hasn't been "perfect enough" to deserve them. Young Pisces tends to believe the grass is greener elsewhere, to want what he cannot have and not to take what is offered. He likes challenge and finds forbidden and unavailable things quite attractive. With people as well as with things and ideas, he is attracted to potential, and he may feel he has settled for less than what he started out to get.

One clue helpful to parents of a Pisces child in determining what he wants and needs is to look at what he's giving others. Pisces tends to believe others will behave toward him as he is behaving toward them. This is a variation of the belief "An eye for an eye," and it works in both positive and negative ways in the life of the young Pisces. Small Pisces often expects and elicits immediate reaction or retribution. Since he can misbehave in ways that are sneaky, he may believe that others are also sneaky; when he behaves well, he may see only good behavior. Parents need to help Pisces think about this expectation of equal exchange with the world, explain that others are not necessarily working with the same assumptions and teach him to ask directly for what he thinks he ought to be getting in exchange for current behavior.

Pisces children are often especially sensitive to their environments and are frequently the first to feel too cold, to be distracted by a jackhammer outside, or to pick up levels of tension in the people around them. They have difficulty screening out external (and internal) stimuli.

Constructive and creative ways to help young Pisces distance himself and cope with distractions, especially during times of stress, are often the most reassuring forms of parental attention. A special story, song, a box of crayons and paper are often just the avenues he needs to get through tough moments.

The young Pisces is visionary, prophetic and often quite intuitive. He seems to have a broader view of the world than most other children and is often very tolerant and accepting of other people's behavior and opinions. In many ways, young Pisces's life is a spiritual journey: Pisces is the pilgrim in search of perfection, truth, God. With this search comes commitment to making the world a better place. Older Pisces children begin to choose their ways of making this contribution, perhaps through art, including music, or human service work. The Pisces child often feels a strong sense of mission or purpose and an obligation to do what he can. A Pisces child caught up in a vision he feels is too overwhelming (and feeling he has to try and change the world can be pretty overwhelming to a six-year-old) may look lethargic and passive. A Pisces child whose visions are appropriate to his age and capabilities will look much more energetic and active. Pisces needs help establishing realistic goals and "how-to" information for turning his dreams into achievable tasks.

The Pisces child is truly a sensitive barometer of the emotional climate in a family. He may reflect happiness and compensate for distress. He can be counted on for sympathy and concern. He willingly shares his life and vision with supportive people. He is helpful, usually responsible and has a keen and wonderful sense of the ridiculous. Young Pisces is often sentimental and romantic, a view that softens even the hardest corners of life. Parents who treat their little Pisces with tenderness will find that he returns the favor tenfold. His gentleness and sweetness can add immeasurable richness to their lives, and when Pisces is grown and more comfortable with himself as an adult than he was as a child, his loyalty and contribution to a loving family may grow even deeper.

NEEDS (Pisces's emotional emphasis)

Acceptance just as he is.
Permission to defend himself and lessons how.
Permission to get angry.
Support for artistic skills and abilities.
Firm limits and boundaries.
Affectionate touch and words.
Reality checks.
To know the consequences; to be held accountable.
Not to be allowed to sacrifice unnecessarily or to put others'
    needs first.
Not to be allowed to feel he has to justify his existence.
Not to be rescued (to do for himself what he *can* do for himself).

An acceptable outlet for his fantasy and drama.
Ways to evaluate what is real and of relative importance.
To be taught to fight (only) his own battles.
Self-reliance.
Practicality.
Grounding.

## COMMON ASSUMPTIONS (How Pisces views the world around him)

An eye for an eye and a tooth for a tooth.
Turn the other cheek.
Forgive and forget.
If I ignore it, it will go away.
Discretion is the better part of valor.

## SENSITIVITIES (Potential sources of misunderstanding)

*Sacrifice:* Young Pisces often feels he must sacrifice or hide his needs so others can get their needs met. He may perceive his needs as inconvenient, inappropriate or burdensome, and since he believes he is stronger and can endure more emotional suffering, he may work to fulfill other people's needs first.

Sometimes little Pisces may sacrifice in order to keep relationships equal. If there are not enough candy bars to go around at Halloween, Pisces may graciously decline his. Especially if the Pisces child is born into comfortable circumstances, he may feel guilty about having "too much" and not utilize fully the opportunities available to him. For example, he may not take horseback riding lessons at the country club if he knows his best friend cannot afford them too, or he may not wear his designer clothes if he feels too conspicuously affluent.

Attentive parents will need to explain the purposes of sacrifice clearly to their Pisces child and give him permission to use all the opportunities available to him and to find balance through ways other than personal denial. This child is likely to misinterpret many of the messages carried by Christianity and to confuse them with his sacrificial impulses. He is afraid of being called selfish.

*Rationalization:* Once young Pisces has determined how he wants to see things, he may feel the need to explain himself. If he is old enough and has verbal skills, he can do it very well. But if he is young or sees himself as not very articulate, or if he is not really certain of his stance, this drive to explain can be frustrating. He may offer explanations that sound garbled or incomplete, or he may offer explanations that sound reasonable but ultimately give no information.

On a daily level, Pisces may become defensive or give responses that seem to miss the point. A Pisces child asked why he didn't tell Mom he used up the last of the milk may feel criticized and counterattack or lead Mom away from the issue ("Danny didn't tell you last week."). Sometimes he may apologize and still not answer the question. Even if he seems to answer the question ("I thought you knew."), he may not be describing the whole truth, which is he simply forgot. Parents noticing this behavior need to persist in getting a real answer and to assure the child that he will not be unjustly punished or blamed.

*Self-protection:* The Pisces child has a hard time learning to build realistic defenses. His feelings may be frequently hurt, and his only automatic defense is simply to escape: into his room, into the woods, into fantasy. He may go to great lengths to avoid conflict since he doesn't feel equipped to handle it, and he may perceive arguments as some sort of failure on his part.

The young Pisces needs permission to fight and then he needs to be taught how to fight for himself as well as for the rights of others. He may need support, guidance and skills for standing his ground when the going gets rough. Parents who can manage to keep teaching while angry can help Pisces by encouraging him to fight back with them in the inevitable disagreements that occur in any family. "Hey, just 'cause I'm mad at you doesn't mean I don't want to hear your side of it. Why did you leave the bike in the driveway? You can stand up to me. I'm not going to hurt you, I just want to solve the problem."

## RELATIONSHIPS

The Pisces child is usually a loyal and considerate companion. He often seeks the best in people and is delighted when people teach him something new. Although he may have many acquaintances, he is slow to open up to people who want more intimacy. When he does open himself, he seeks a spiritual union with someone and needs to believe they understand him at a very deep level. Though the young Pisces sometimes misinterprets others' intentions, he can be quite pragmatic about relationships and is a wonderful helper and problem solver for others.

*Mom:* Often young Pisces seeks out or is given the option of two mother figures. He values either or both of them for their logical minds and thinking capabilities. He may perceive Mom as charming, intellectual, witty, but possibly not emotionally available to him. He may worry at her carelessness or assume he cannot trust her ability to take adequate care of him.

Moms who want to improve their image with little Pisces will be careful to do exactly what they say they are going to do and to explain the reasons for any change of mind or course of action. Moms shouldn't promise Pisces things they can't deliver, even in an attempt to make him feel better in the moment. Moms who are available to discuss ideas such as God, religion and art, and who listen carefully and value Pisces's unusual input, will find this a good way to build intimacy with him.

*Dad:* Young Pisces sees his dad as jovial, permissive, indulgent and good-natured. He may especially enjoy talks of spirituality with Dad and get Dad to reveal aspects of his personality the rest of the family doesn't see. This can be a special bond between young Pisces and his father.

Pisces may resolutely perceive Father as good and Mother as bad, seeing Father as the adequate parent and Mother as the inadequate parent. Efforts must be made to contradict this assumption. Mom should get to be wonderful once in a while too, and Dad must not become so flattered he isn't willing to let Mom share the limelight in young Pisces's eyes. One way to balance this situation is for both parents to participate in teaching little Pisces to fight and stand up for himself.

*Siblings:* The Pisces child may see his siblings as less interesting or slower than he is or a potential burden to him in his search for truth and perfection. He may also feel inferior to his siblings. If he thinks he is sacrificing his needs in order to let them get their needs met, he may feel resentment toward them, or he may adopt an attitude of protective caring over them.

*Friends:* Young Pisces often chooses children with whom he feels safe and with those he knows will protect and care for him. Sometimes he may do the opposite and choose children who need his protection and caring, or he may do both simultaneously and have one group of friends he takes care of and another group who take care of him. He finds security in predictable relationships and is often attracted to people who are more ambitious than he is.

## MIND/INFORMATION/SCHOOL

The young Pisces usually has a quick and retentive mind. He grasps concepts quickly and maintains awareness of details. He needs to be able to relate all information to himself and will best understand things if they are presented in a large context and if he is permitted to actually *do* as he learns. All the arithmetic in the world may not make sense to little Pisces until he is sent to the store with six quarters, two dimes and eighteen pennies in his pocket; then he will learn to add and subtract in a hurry and coincidentally begin to display some of his shrewd financial skills as well.

The young Pisces's memory is primarily sensory, and he will remember and understand better if several of his senses are involved. He is highly imaginative and tends to generalize his information and to perceive things in terms of form, balance and rhythm. He is wonderfully artistic. Small Pisces has a great need to know and to understand and will expend whatever effort it takes for him to truly grasp what is important to him; adults need only to make the task easier.

The Pisces child is often extremely intuitive and may take in a great deal of information on a less than conscious level, picking up cues and data he is not even consciously aware of. Though the young Pisces has an orderly and categorical mind, he may have difficulty defending the information he has, and may as a result, distrust his intelligence or memory. It is at this point that he may believe others are smarter than he, especially if he believes they have the ability to recall and verbally defend specific facts. Little Pisces also tends to daydream and often to get "lost" in a world of his own or in the midst of something else. (This may also happen in the neighborhood, and he may lose things, articles of clothing, as well as bits of information.) These losses are often recoverable and are usually the result of lack of attention rather than defective mental ability.

The challenge for grown-ups trying to teach a small Pisces is to get and hold his attention. Once his attention is arrested, Pisces is an easy student to reach. Though he understands the value of learning, he may feel that school is tiresome and search for ways to avoid going.

*Higher Education:* Though further education for young Pisces is often delayed or interrupted, he usually does some additional learning simply for the love of new information. He continues to seek "the answer" all his life. Once committed to further schooling, he can be intense and competitive, though he may resent his need to attend a formal institution. He is usually drawn to areas of study that offer research opportunities and direct experience, or he may seek training in the arts or human services.

## RESPONSIBILITY/WORK/REWARDS

*Responsibility and Work:* The young Pisces is often quite casual about his tasks and responsibilities, and will frequently do just enough to get by. He is restless and, though serious in his approach, can be easily distracted. Little Pisces needs to be allowed to take frequent breaks and move around. He needs time for planning, dreaming and review. He tends to be unrealistic in managing time and may also need help setting appropriate goals and allocating enough time to finish. The young Pisces needs to believe that his share of the work is fair; if it's not, he may do it anyway, with resentment or carelessness, or not do it at all. If a Pisces child has stopped doing his chores or is suddenly sloppy and uncooperative, parents need to check out his sense of fair share.

The Pisces child who has been allowed to assume a great sense of responsibility may indeed work very hard but not know how or when to stop. If he's interested in a project, he may throw his entire being into it. If he's not interested or thinks he will fail, he may procrastinate until the task no longer needs doing or someone else has done it. While he is procrastinating, he is not just doing nothing: chances are little Pisces is learning something else far more important or interesting to him and is intently pursuing this new exploration. He has difficulty evaluating the results of his work realistically.

*Rewards:* Approval is a primary reward for little Pisces. He also responds well to recognition and loves having more free time or permission to be selfish as a result of a job well done. Often the delight of the people around him is ample reward, though, like other children, Pisces likes money, too. Rewards for young Pisces should be explicitly agreed on; spontaneous gifts should be given only *after* he's gotten the agreed-upon reward. For example, first give young Pisces the money he earned; don't give him a gift instead.

## HOME

The young Pisces may feel he fits in everywhere and nowhere; in any case, he can make himself at home virtually anywhere and tends to expand to fill whatever space he occupies. The Pisces child is adaptable and usually does not mind sharing space with another person. He enjoys having more than one place where he belongs. The area he lives in may serve a dual purpose, such as entertainment and study. He usually decorates in subdued tones of blue, blue-green or ivory. He likes shelves with cubbyholes. While it is not necessarily neat or convenient, little Pisces's space is usually loaded with interesting things and tools of communication. The young Pisces either holds on to everything interesting or is entirely disinterested in anything material. The Pisces child may have a strong allegiance to his neighborhood.

## HEALTH

The Pisces child often knows a great deal about health but may be careless about his own. He may fear being sick and avoid it or allow himself to get sick just to confront his fear of it. He loves the attention he receives when ill and may use a period of sickness to slow down, avoid something unpleasant, get attention or get some quiet time for himself. When he is sick, the young Pisces likes someone to take over for him and enjoys being the center of attention. Pisces especially responds to the healing and calming virtues of music.

The young Pisces is particularly sensitive to environmental influences and pressures. His illnesses usually reflect that vulnerability: allergies, colds, flu and other contagious diseases, food poisoning and nervous ailments that are clearly responses to stress (muscle spasms, diarrhea, etc.) He is equally susceptible to medication, however, and may respond to a far smaller dosage than other children.

Traditionally, Pisces rules the feet and some glands. The young Pisces experiencing health difficulties may also be anemic, depressed or have problems with his sinuses and back. The ailments of the Pisces child may be difficult to diagnose but will often respond well to unorthodox treatments, especially natural remedies.

## CHILDHOOD AGES

*(Note: The fears detailed in this section are* never *to be used as punishment. They are presented as avenues for reassurance and caring.)*

### BIRTH–6 MONTHS

Newborn Pisces is a charming, dreamy and adaptable baby. He knows he is helpless and snuggles against grown-up arms as if he belongs there, trusting the loving. He may not be quite sure he wants to be here yet and invites those around him with smiles and murmurs to make staying worth his while. Parents attempting to entice tiny Pisces to join the family usually delight both themselves and the baby by inventing words and touches and rituals that are deeply satisfying to everyone.

Baby Pisces's longing for attention and escape begin early, and even at this age, the infant may have periods when he seems to be in his own world. Parents may be surprised to find that the baby whose howls brought them running just moments before is now dozing contentedly. Adults need to trust that the baby's needs are real and not feel personally rejected if baby Pisces calms down just as they were warming up. Maintaining contact even when tiny Pisces doesn't seem to care is important for grown-ups and baby alike.

Pisces's sensitivity also begins early, and even the newborn Pisces is vulnerable to hidden messages and environmental disturbances. He is easily frightened and startles at unexpected stimuli. Parents will want to handle this child gently and, especially in the first few months, to protect him from unnecessary sensory discordance. Music and rocking (especially together) are comforting to the new Pisces child.

*Needs*
Physical and verbal affection.
Attention.
A sense of abundance: more than enough food, warmth, and touch always available.

*Fears*
Being ignored, forgotten, lost, abandoned.
Falling, being dropped.

## 6 MONTHS–18 MONTHS

Baby Pisces may be especially fearful around strangers and withdraw when approached by someone he does not know well. Like the young Taurus, little Pisces likes people to come to him, however, and he may wait patiently in the chair by the wall, sizing up the situation, until someone notices him. This tiny child is deeply in touch with nature and loves living things; this is a wonderful candidate for infant swimming lessons and music appreciation courses. His sensitivity and compassion are also beginning to blossom, sometimes in the form of a sort of melancholy sadness, but his social skills are developing well and he is learning how to be truly charming.

Sensitive baby Pisces continues to be aware of the levels of events around him. He is keenly tuned into the emotional climate and may already be restricting his own feelings and needs to accommodate those around him. Parents need to be especially aware and supportive of tiny Pisces's attempts to ask for things for himself, and they may need to remind themselves not to encourage "unselfishness" in a child of this age.

*Needs*
Attention and affection.
Exposure to the arts, especially music, and to nature.
Strong physical support and nurture.
Food, warmth and touch available constantly and consistently.

*Fears*
Being isolated, neglected, ignored, dropped.
Lack of escape.

## 18 MONTHS–3 YEARS

The Pisces toddler is very intuitive and is already establishing his rich fantasy life. He has already begun his love affair with music, and he may have an imaginary playmate who "tells" him what he knows intuitively or tries out behavior he is too shy or scared to attempt. He often lives in a world peopled with magical, mystical beings. He makes up reasons for everything and may offer the most plausible or unlikely explanations for events. He is highly imaginative, he believes in magic and miracles, and he has a strong sense of eternity and wonder. Since he is still quite sensitive to his environment, little Pisces may invent reasons for emotional realities as well as physical events, and parents need to pay extra attention to their tiny Pisces, who may be blaming himself for situations far beyond his control or understanding. He may become defensive or self-justifying if he feels responsible, and he may be reduced to tears if he takes things personally. Crayons, paints and musical instruments are wonderful outlets for Pisces at this age, and structured storytelling experiences are excellent outlets for fantasy.

This little Pisces is extremely gullible, suggestible and vulnerable to shame. People nearby need to be extra careful about what they put into tiny Pisces's head. He is beginning to be reactive, to consider others' needs before he chooses his behavior, and he may appear indecisive or irrationally opinionated. He is adaptable and changeable at this age but may, as a result, be very difficult to predict or rely on, and he may be very messy. The young Pisces is quite curious now, especially about religion, healing and the universe. Accurate information and feedback on all subjects are very important: this is the age at which he begins to develop his own reality.

*Toilet Training:* The Pisces toddler may have difficulty concentrating on the task at hand, and initial success may be purely accidental. Rewards and extensive praise for success and physical contact to ensure attention are two possible approaches for little Pisces. Pisces also needs permission *not* to become trained until he is ready. Since he may not be physically ready until relatively late, parents need to train tiny Pisces with gentleness, patience and compassion. When the time is right, chances are little Pisces will do it all himself, seemingly overnight. Later bed-wetting accidents, which are likely for small Pisces, should be ignored or handled impartially.

*Needs*

Thorough explanations; accurate clear information.
Limits, rules and boundaries.
Physical reassurance and support.
Not to be teased or shamed.
Strong reminders of consensual reality.
An outlet for his remarkable fantasy and imagination.
Periods of solitude.

*Fears*

Being a burden.
Being invisible, different, ignored.
Being overwhelmed; being unable to sort out stimuli.
Being humiliated, teased.
That he's fooled others with a role.
Being bored, trapped, limited.
Lack of safety, structure, limits.

## 3 YEARS–6 YEARS

The preschool Pisces is dreamy and rebellious. He seems constantly to be testing new behavior, copying, trying, rejecting. His behavior may appear erratic, and he often swings from one end of the spectrum to the other: sweet, considerate and responsible one time; restless, critical, listless the next. He still seeks his fantasy world and spends a considerable amount of time challenging and defining reality. One role he is testing is "helpless," and he may try to see how much he can get others to do for him. Another role is "responsible," where he tries to do for everyone else. In either case, he is likely to make incorrect assessments of his power and intelligence. Parents need to keep a close watch on the conclusions little Pisces is drawing from their reactions to his behavior.

The preschool Pisces needs to know what's going on. He is curious, bright and quick to make assumptions. He takes information literally and may have difficulty understanding abstract concepts, though he is fascinated by ultimate abstractions like God and death. Though things may appear very "either/or" to him at this age, Pisces still has difficulty making decisions if he believes his choices will displease someone.

If he equates criticism with punishment or rejection, little Pisces may begin rationalizing and making excuses to justify his behavior. He may appear super self-critical if he's trying to be perfect or act lethargic and listless if afraid a new attempt will lead to failure. Parents need to act decisively if he begins "confessing" his wrong doings at this age: little Pisces should not feel that need, and it means he is confusing his self-worth with perfection.

*Needs*
Reality checks.
Permission to change behavior.
Honest reactions and feedback.
Explanations and information.
To be included and told what is going on.
Compassion.
Permission to be compassionate and sensitive.

*Fears*
Loss of reality.
Lack of limits, boundaries, rules.
Being ignored or being left out or behind.
Denial of his reality.
Getting lost.
Being pushed, hurried.
Restricting labels.

6 YEARS–12 YEARS

The school-age Pisces is a romantic idealist. If he believes he can't make a difference, he may act tired and lethargic and simply appear to dream his way through school, sometimes taking refuge in solitary activity like art or reading. More likely, he believes he does make a difference, and he may push himself to excel, to be perfect; if he can't have perfection, he'll have nothing at all. He can be outraged when things aren't as he wants them to be ("but it shouldn't *be* that way!") or hide his disappointment under a make-believe indifference. Since secretly he may feel inferior or fraudulent, the young Pisces may push himself to make up for his perceived shortcomings, and though he is often successful, he may feel overwhelmed by his own and other people's standards.

Though he is compassionate and friendly and often well liked, the school-age Pisces may nevertheless feel as though he does not belong and think others possess some magical knowledge or skills he lacks. He may continue his elaborate internal fantasy life to reassure himself of safety and worth, and/or he may stoically bear up under what he feels are considerable pressures, becoming physically sick when they become unbearable. Pisces seems caught in dichotomies at this age: active/passive, leader/follower, emotional/intellectual, inferior/superior. Firm decision making is even more difficult than it has been. He may want someone to rescue him, to make things all right, for he believes he cannot do that himself. Loving parents will teach little Pisces to do it himself and will help him make decisions that do not feel overwhelming later on.

The school-age Pisces is still imaginative and creative, and he usually excels in one of the arts or athletics. He continues to be nurturing, helpful and understanding, and his curiosity continues to grow. He is acutely aware of the feelings of others now and may restrict his behavior drastically if he thinks his choices will hurt someone else, or feel agonizingly guilty if he thinks his behavior already has. He has difficulty excluding anything because he's afraid of hurt feelings; even taking one stuffed animal and leaving another is enough to make him feel funny in the stomach. Though his indecisiveness may irritate those around him as much as it does himself, he is generally a pleasure to have nearby, and he continues to enjoy physical closeness and emotional intimacy.

*Needs*
  Limits, structure.
  Reality checks.
  Ethical concepts.
  Realistic evaluation of responsibility.
  Help finishing things.
  Help beginning things.
  Physical contact.
  Honest information and expression of feelings.
  Periods of solitude.

*Fears*
Boredom, being trapped, limited, restricted.
Not being smart or perfect enough.
Being invisible, overlooked, ignored, left out.
Challenges to his reality; denial of his reality.
Making a fool of himself.
Being overwhelmed, swallowed up: losing his identity.

## 12 YEARS–18 YEARS

The adolescent Pisces integrates all of the behavior previously described and epitomizes the issues described at the beginning of this chapter. He is sensitive, moody, reflective, introspective, dreamy and idealistic, and is often searching for a cause—something to fight for, something worthy of his energies and ideals. He may become deeply involved in a spiritual exploration or throw himself even more deeply into the arts, athletics, school or helping other people. He is looking for something or someone to devote himself to, something or someone worthy of the sacrifice he feels he must make. The child not permitted this exploration overtly will do it anyway, covertly.

At this age, Pisces is still impressionable and gullible, believing many of the romantic myths that have been handed down about appropriate gender behavior and expectations of and from others and the world. Although he usually appears to be in control, he is often worried or frightened at the behaviors he believes are expected of him. He may be chronically disappointed or rebellious or construct a fantasy that includes the best of what he wants to see. While he may take periodic refuge in solitary or group activity, the best outlets for these energies continue to be theater and the arts or volunteer work in a human service agency.

Though he is intense and involved, teenage Pisces is likely to feel unauthentic and to believe no one really knows him. He may perceive himself as a sad clown or stoic martyr. He may have trouble identifying himself beyond his feelings of unfocused sadness. He may appear confused and uncertain, and if angry at himself or others for letting himself down, he may punish himself in subtle or obvious ways: by isolating himself, not allowing himself to accept rewards, refusing to acknowledge other people's affection and support. He may appear rebellious or responsible as he continues to try out different roles and feel phony regardless of outcomes. His achievements can feel hollow, and he may find himself wondering, "Is that all there is?" Parents need to remind the young Pisces to play, and even though he is an early adult, to continue offering him the protection and support necessary for him to let down his guard.

The teenage Pisces's behavior may be alternately dramatic or understated. He may believe he has to exaggerate emotional pain in order to have it noticed or taken seriously. He may believe the amount of pain he feels is a reflection of the intensity of the event. His behavior may look irrational or eccentric as he experiments with who he really is and learns how to make an effective impact on others. He may believe others should guess his needs and be able to make him feel better. If he believes he is being confined by a label, he may do precisely the opposite; he greatly fears being hemmed in or prematurely described by others without his permission. Encouraging him to "lighten up" and exposing him to structured moments of beauty and frivolity may lessen his sense of dread.

The adolescent Pisces is intensely aware of his body changes and may either hide or exaggerate them. Believing in Hollywood's example, he may experiment with extremely seductive behavior and other postures, but he seems really to want a spiritual rather than a sexual union. While he may pretend he subscribes to the sexual code of his peers, he is often quite shy and may report much more than he actually does. He is a sweet and thoughtful companion and, even with his family, is usually easy and delightful to have nearby.

### Needs

Discussion of ethical considerations, responsibilities, dreams.

Ways of coping with disappointment.

Ways to evaluate situations.

Spiritual support and guidance.

Emotional support.

A cause to believe in.

Privacy and periods of solitude.

Information.

Appropriate outlets for creativity and idealism.

Reality checks.

*Hates*
Hypocrisy.
Imperfection.
Cruelty.
Labels.
Rules.
Being called crazy.
Having his reality challenged.
Having to make decisions and choices.
Hurt feelings.
Having to live in *this* imperfect world.

# ASTROLOGICAL TABLE

The following table will help you determine the official sign your own child belongs to. From 1970 through 1987 the table gives the exact days on which the sun moves from one sign to the next.

|  | 1970 | 1971 | 1972 | 1973 | 1974 | 1975 |
|---|---|---|---|---|---|---|
| AQUARIUS | Jan 21 | Jan 21 | Jan 21 | Jan 21 | Jan 21 | Jan 21 |
|  | Feb 19 | Feb 19 | Feb 19 | Feb 18 | Feb 19 | Feb 19 |
| PISCES | Feb 20 | Feb 20 | Feb 20 | Feb 19 | Feb 20 | Feb 20 |
|  | Mar 21 | Mar 21 | Mar 20 | Mar 20 | Mar 21 | Mar 21 |
| ARIES | Mar 22 | Mar 22 | Mar 21 | Mar 21 | Mar 22 | Mar 22 |
|  | Apr 20 | Apr 20 | Apr 19 | Apr 20 | Apr 20 | Apr 20 |
| TAURUS | Apr 21 | Apr 21 | Apr 20 | Apr 21 | Apr 21 | Apr 21 |
|  | May 21 | May 21 | May 20 | May 21 | May 21 | May 21 |
| GEMINI | May 22 | May 22 | May 21 | May 22 | May 22 | May 22 |
|  | Jun 21 | Jun 22 | Jun 21 | Jun 21 | Jun 21 | Jun 22 |
| CANCER | Jun 22 | Jun 23 | Jun 22 | Jun 22 | Jun 22 | Jun 23 |
|  | Jul 23 | Jul 23 | Jul 22 | Jul 22 | Jul 23 | Jul 23 |
| LEO | Jul 24 | Jul 24 | Jul 23 | Jul 23 | Jul 24 | Jul 24 |
|  | Aug 23 | Aug 23 | Aug 23 | Aug 23 | Aug 23 | Aug 23 |
| VIRGO | Aug 24 | Aug 24 | Aug 24 | Aug 24 | Aug 24 | Aug 24 |
|  | Sep 23 | Sep 23 | Sep 22 | Sep 23 | Sep 23 | Sep 23 |
| LIBRA | Sep 24 | Sep 23 | Sep 23 | Sep 24 | Sep 24 | Sep 24 |
|  | Oct 23 | Oct 24 | Oct 23 | Oct 23 | Oct 23 | Oct 24 |
| SCORPIO | Oct 24 | Oct 25 | Oct 24 | Oct 24 | Oct 24 | Oct 24 |
|  | Nov 22 | Nov 22 | Nov 22 | Nov 22 | Nov 22 | Nov 22 |
| SAGITTARIUS | Nov 23 | Nov 23 | Nov 23 | Nov 23 | Nov 23 | Nov 23 |
|  | Dec 22 | Dec 22 | Dec 21 | Dec 22 | Dec 22 | Dec 22 |
| CAPRICORN | Dec 23 | Dec 23 | Dec 22 | Dec 23 | Dec 23 | Dec 23 |
|  | Jan 20 | Jan 20 | Jan 20 | Jan 20 | Jan 20 | Jan 20 |

|  | 1976 | 1977 | 1978 | 1979 | 1980 | 1981 |
|---|---|---|---|---|---|---|
| AQUARIUS | Jan 21 | Jan 21 | Jan 21 | Jan 21 | Jan 21 | Jan 21 |
|  | Feb 19 | Feb 18 | Feb 19 | Feb 19 | Feb 19 | Feb 18 |
| PISCES | Feb 20 | Feb 19 | Feb 20 | Feb 20 | Feb 20 | Feb 10 |
|  | Mar 20 | Mar 20 | Mar 20 | Mar 21 | Mar 20 | Mar 29 |
| ARIES | Mar 21 | Mar 21 | Mar 21 | Mar 22 | Mar 21 | Mar 21 |
|  | Apr 19 | Apr 20 | Apr 20 | Apr 20 | Apr 19 | Apr 20 |
| TAURUS | Apr 20 | Apr 21 | Apr 21 | Apr 21 | Apr 20 | Apr 21 |
|  | May 20 | May 21 | May 21 | May 21 | May 20 | May 21 |
| GEMINI | May 21 | May 22 | May 22 | May 22 | May 21 | May 22 |
|  | Jun 21 | Jun 21 | Jun 21 | Jun 21 | Jun 21 | Jun 21 |
| CANCER | Jun 22 | Jun 22 | Jun 22 | Jun 22 | Jun 22 | Jun 22 |
|  | Jul 22 | Jul 22 | Jul 23 | Jul 23 | Jul 22 | Jul 22 |
| LEO | Jul 23 | Jul 23 | Jul 24 | Jul 24 | Jul 23 | Jul 23 |
|  | Aug 23 | Aug 23 | Aug 23 | Aug 23 | Aug 22 | Aug 23 |
| VIRGO | Aug 24 | Aug 24 | Aug 24 | Aug 24 | Aug 23 | Aug 24 |
|  | Sep 22 | Sep 23 | Sep 22 | Sep 23 | Sep 22 | Sep 23 |
| LIBRA | Sep 23 | Sep 24 | Sep 23 | Sep 24 | Sep 23 | Sep 24 |
|  | Oct 23 | Oct 23 | Oct 23 | Oct 24 | Oct 23 | Oct 23 |
| SCORPIO | Oct 24 | Oct 24 | Oct 24 | Oct 25 | Oct 24 | Oct 24 |
|  | Nov 22 | Nov 22 | Nov 22 | Nov 22 | Nov 22 | Nov 22 |
| SAGITTARIUS | Nov 23 | Nov 23 | Nov 23 | Nov 23 | Nov 23 | Nov 23 |
|  | Dec 21 | Dec 21 | Dec 22 | Dec 22 | Dec 21 | Dec 21 |
| CAPRICORN | Dec 22 | Dec 22 | Dec 23 | Dec 23 | Dec 22 | Dec 22 |
|  | Jan 20 | Jan 20 | Jan 20 | Jan 20 | Jan 20 | Jan 20 |

|  | 1982 | 1983 | 1984 | 1985 | 1986 | 1987 |
|---|---|---|---|---|---|---|
| AQUARIUS | Jan 21 | Jan 21 | Jan 21 | Jan 21 | Jan 21 | Jan 21 |
|  | Feb 18 | Feb 19 | Feb 19 | Feb 18 | Feb 18 | Feb 19 |
| PISCES | Feb 19 | Feb 20 | Feb 20 | Feb 19 | Feb 19 | Feb 20 |
|  | Mar 20 | Mar 21 | Mar 20 | Mar 20 | Mar 20 | Mar 21 |
| ARIES | Mar 21 | Mar 22 | Mar 21 | Mar 21 | Mar 21 | Mar 22 |
|  | Apr 20 | Apr 20 | Apr 19 | Apr 20 | Apr 20 | Apr 20 |
| TAURUS | Apr 21 | Apr 21 | Apr 20 | Apr 21 | Apr 21 | Apr 21 |
|  | May 21 | May 21 | May 20 | May 21 | May 21 | May 21 |
| GEMINI | May 22 | May 22 | May 21 | May 22 | May 22 | May 22 |
|  | Jun 21 | Jun 21 | Jun 21 | Jun 21 | Jun 21 | Jun 21 |
| CANCER | Jun 22 | Jun 22 | Jun 22 | Jun 22 | Jun 22 | Jun 22 |
|  | Jul 23 | Jul 23 | Jul 22 | Jul 22 | Jul 23 | Jul 23 |
| LEO | Jul 24 | Jul 24 | Jul 23 | Jul 23 | Jul 24 | Jul 24 |
|  | Aug 23 | Aug 23 | Aug 22 | Aug 23 | Aug 23 | Aug 23 |
| VIRGO | Aug 24 | Aug 24 | Aug 23 | Aug 24 | Aug 24 | Aug 24 |
|  | Sep 23 | Sep 23 | Sep 22 | Sep 23 | Sep 23 | Sep 23 |
| LIBRA | Sep 24 | Sep 24 | Sep 23 | Sep 24 | Sep 24 | Sep 24 |
|  | Oct 23 | Oct 23 | Oct 23 | Oct 23 | Oct 23 | Oct 23 |
| SCORPIO | Oct 24 | Oct 24 | Oct 24 | Oct 24 | Oct 24 | Oct 24 |
|  | Nov 22 | Nov 22 | Nov 22 | Nov 22 | Nov 22 | Nov 22 |
| SAGITTARIUS | Nov 23 | Nov 23 | Nov 23 | Nov 23 | Nov 23 | Nov 23 |
|  | Dec 22 | Dec 22 | Dec 21 | Dec 21 | Dec 22 | Dec 22 |
| CAPRICORN | Dec 23 | Dec 23 | Dec 22 | Dec 22 | Dec 23 | Dec 23 |
|  | Jan 20 | Jan 20 | Jan 20 | Jan 20 | Jan 20 | Jan 20 |